Recentering globalization

Koichi Iwabuchi

Recentering globalization

Popular culture and Japanese transnationalism

Duke University Press   Durham and London

2002

© 2002 Duke University Press

All rights reserved

Printed in the United States

of America on acid-free paper ∞

Designed by C. H. Westmoreland

Typeset in Bembo with Stone

Sans display by Keystone

Typesetting, Inc.

Library of Congress Cataloging-

in-Publication Data appear on the

last printed page of this book.

Contents

Acknowledgments

This book is based on my Ph.D. dissertation submitted to University of Western Sydney Nepean in 1999, which was awarded the best Ph.D dissertation prize for that year by the Australian Association of Asian Studies. So many people supported me in various ways writing this book. I most thank Professor Ien Ang for her always rigorous and productive criticisms and suggestions on my earlier drafts and her warm encouragement. I also owe thanks to those who read and commented on my earlier draft such as Judith Snodgrass, Tessa Morris-Suzuki, Mandy Thomas, Shuhei Hosokawa, Anne Allison, James Lull, and Ulf Hannerz; and to those who helped me improve my English expression such as Eduardo Ugarte, Roberta James, Adrian Snodgrass, Sandra Wilson, David Wells, David Kelly, and Jennifer Prough. My thanks also go to those who assisted my field work in Japan, Taiwan, Hong Kong, and Singapore; to mention just a few, Hara Yumiko, Adachi Miki, Kimura Akiko, Honda Shirō, Yoshimi Shunya, Kosaku Yoshino, Georgette Wang, Lee Tain-Dow, Su Yu-Ling, Grace Wang, Tanaka Akira, Yao Souchou, and Cheng Shiowjiuan. I also wish to thank to all the people who spared their precious time for my interviews in Taipei, Hong Kong, Singapore, Kuala Lumpur, and Tokyo. My thanks are also extended to the staff of Duke University Press, especially to Ken Wissoker for his support for this project, and to Shelley Wunder Smith for her attentive editorial assistance to the last moment.

Nepean Postgraduate Research Award of the University of Western Sydney, Nepean financially supported my doctoral life. The field research was supported by a Toyota Foundation Grant 1996–1997. The School of Cultural Histories and Futures of University of Western Sydney Nepean also supported field research and the copyediting of the manuscript. In Singapore in January 1995, my research was conducted as a research associate of the Institute of Southeast Asian Studies. In Tokyo, the Institute of Socio-Information and Communication Studies of the University of Tokyo and

NHK Broadcasting Culture Research Institute generously allowed me to access their library resources.

Portions of chapters 2, 4, and 5 originally appeared as material in the following publications: "Uses of Japanese Popular Culture: Media Globalization and Postcolonial Desire for 'Asia,' " *Emergences: Journal of Media and Composite Cultures* 11, no. 2 (2001); "Becoming Culturally Proximate: A/ Scent of Japanese Idol Dramas in Tawain," B. Moeran, ed., *Asian Media Productions* (London: Curzon, 2001); "Nostalgia for a (Different) Asian Modernity: Media Consumption of 'Asia' in Japan" *positions: east asia cultures critique* 10, no. 3 (2002).

Finally, I would like to share the pleasure of this accomplishment with my wife and daughter, Michiyo and Lina, who have seen this project through to the completion, despite numerous frustrations. Their encouragement and distraction afforded me spiritual nourishment. I dedicate this volume to them as a token of affection and gratitude.

Note on Japanese Names

This book follows the Japanese convention that family names precede personal names. However, the names of the Japanese authors of English language works (except translations) follow the English convention of the personal name preceding the family name (e.g., Kosaku Yoshino). Macrons are put on long Japanese vowels except in the case of place names (e.g., Tokyo), words commonly used in English (e.g., Shinto), and author names which usually appear without a macron in their English language works (e.g., Shuhei Hosokawa).

Introduction:

The 1990s—Japan's return to Asia

in the age of globalization

Something unexpected has happened. Japan is beloved in Asia! To whit: "Export machine—While Asia's older generation is still haunted by Japan's wartime brutality, Hello Kitty culture is hot with the region's youth, who are happy to snap up all things Japanese" (Export machines 1999, 30–31); "Cute power! Asia is in love with Japan's pop culture . . . Everybody loves Japan! . . . Ask anybody in Asia: Western-style cool is out. Everything Japanese is in—and oh, so 'cute'!" (Cute power! 1999); "Asian youth says 'We love Japan'—Japanese popular culture such as fashion and TV dramas deeply penetrates Asia" (Daitōa atsuzoko kyōeiken 2001); "Pop passions—From animation to idols, Japanese youth culture building formidable army of devotees throughout the region (Asia)" (Pop passions 2001).

Animation, comics, characters, computer games, fashion, pop music, and TV dramas—a variety of Japanese popular culture has been so well received in East and Southeast Asia that the above-mentioned media coverage might not sound as remarkable as it actually is. This is not to say that the export of Japanese popular culture is a new phenomenon. The culture has long proliferated outside of Japan, and particularly in East and Southeast Asia, at least since the late 1970s. Japanese comics and animations, such as *Doraemon,*[1] a fantasy featuring a catlike robot who makes the wishes of children come true, have become part of everyday life for children in many parts of Asia. One is also reminded of the Japanese soap opera *Oshin,* which has been well received in more than fifty countries since it was first broadcast in 1983–84. While its distribution has been limited to mostly non-Western countries, this melodramatic life history of a Japanese woman who overcomes various sufferings in the early part of twentieth century has captured the popular imagination not just in Asia but also in Arab countries and in Latin

America. Recently, however, the spread of Japanese popular culture in East and Southeast Asia has advanced a stage further. The Japanese and other Asian media industries are systematically and collaboratively promoting a wider range of Japanese popular culture for the routine consumption of youth in various markets in East and Southeast Asia. Many youth feel a more intensive sympathy with the romance in Japanese TV dramas, or with the latest fashion, trendy popular music styles, or the gossip about Japanese idols than they do with the American counterparts that have long dominated the world youth culture. The presence of Japanese popular culture in many parts of East/Southeast Asia no longer seems to be something spectacular or anomalous but rather has become mundane in the globalizing (urban) landscape.

This study was motivated by the sense of surprise and curiosity aroused in me when I first heard and read, in the early 1990s, about the international circulation of Japanese audiovisual popular cultural forms and the successful entry of the Japanese media industries into the booming East and Southeast Asian markets. I was surprised, not least because Japanese cultural export to other Asian countries seemed to me a provocative and contentious issue in light of Japan's colonialist past and lingering economic exploitation in the region. An argument for the lack of Japanese cultural influence in Asia was, in my perception, more sustainable. This perception goes together with a more generalized assumption that Japanese culture would not be accepted or appealing outside the cultural context of Japan. As a Japanese, I had implicitly accepted the idea of Japan as a faceless economic superpower: Japan has money and technology but does not have a cultural influence on the world.

My apprehension about the inherent tension of this paradox conforms with a rather common discourse on Japan which suggests that such a lack of cultural power confers upon Japan a curious "quasi–Third World" status. Ōe Kenzaburō, a Nobel Prize–winning Japanese novelist, once lamented this Japanese image of a faceless economy: "You know why Honda is great. But we don't care about Honda. We care that our cultural life is unknown to you" (quoted in Bartu 1992, 189). Ōe (1995) expressed the discrepancy between economic power and cultural influence in terms of Japan's ambiguous (*aimaina*) identity in the world as it internalizes and articulates both first-worldliness and third-worldliness. No matter how strong its economy becomes, Japan is culturally and psychologically dominated by the West.

Edward Said (1994) makes a similar suggestion in *Culture and Imperialism* when he refers to Masao Miyoshi's (1991) remark concerning the impoverishment of Japanese contemporary culture. Said argues that "Miyoshi diagnosed a new problematic for culture as corollary to the country's staggering financial resources, an absolute disparity between the total novelty and global dominance in the economic sphere, and the impoverishing retreat and dependence on the West in cultural discourse" (400). For Said, Japan is "extraordinarily symptomatic" of a distorted modernity which urges us to consider "how we are going to keep up life itself when the quotidian demands of the present threaten to outstrip the human presence" (399). To be fair, Said's main concern in the book—the intertwined relationship between Western imperialism and culture—and his evaluation of Japanese modernity, which has been constructed under an unambiguous Western hegemony, are compelling indeed. Nevertheless, the total absence of a consideration of Japanese imperialism / colonialism in his analysis of imperialism and culture is striking to me. In Said's account, Japan is treated predominantly as a non-Western, quasi–Third World nation which has been a victim of Western (American) cultural domination. Japan's double status as an ex-imperial, lingering economic, and to a lesser extent, cultural power in Asia, on the one hand, and as a culturally subordinated non-Western nation, on the other, disappears behind a totalized notion of Western global cultural power. When I first encountered information about the spread of Japanese popular culture to other parts of Asia, I was made to realize that I also had embraced this assumption.

However, in the 1990s the development of media globalization has made the asymmetrical cultural relation between Japan and other Asian nations come into renewed focus. Along with the forces of media globalization, the strengthened economic power of Asian countries has led to the intensification of media and cultural flows in Asian markets, dramatically increasing the circulation of Japanese popular culture in the region and driving hitherto domestically oriented Japanese cultural formation to become more extroverted.

The development of communications technologies such as VCRs, cable TV, and satellite TV, and the concurrent emergence of global media corporations in the late twentieth century, have brought about an unprecedented abundance of audiovisual space all over the globe. While the financial crisis in Asia in the late 1990s has had a temporary negative effect, the booming Asian markets, where about three billion people live and where a high level of economic growth has been rapidly achieved, have become the hottest battlefield for transnational media corporations in the 1990s (e.g., Shoesmith 1994; Lee and Wang 1995; TV's new battles 1994). Best illustrated by the emergence of pan-Asian satellite broadcasting, such as STAR TV in 1991, the idea of the actual and simultaneous reach of the same media products and popular culture in many parts of Asia has been an irresistible one for transnational media industries. Fascinated with the size of the potential audience in the region, Western global players such as News Corp., CNN, BBC, MTV, ESPN, HBO, and Disney became allured by the idea of pan-Asian mega-broadcasting.

The emergence and proliferation of global media conglomerates prompted several Asian governments to react against the foreign (mostly American) invasion from the sky. For example, Malaysia, Singapore, and China have advocated for the protection of "Asian" values from decadent Western morality transmitted through the media. In those countries, the globalization of the media bears witness to the impossibility of rigidly guarding national boundaries against foreign (mostly Western) media invasion (concerning Asian governments' various responses to STAR TV, see Chan 1994).[2] The increasing transnational flow of media has also had repercussions on Japanese broadcasting policy and the media industries, but in a different way. To Japan, as the second largest TV market in the world, media globalization offers an opportunity to expand a hitherto largely domestic-oriented media production system to other Asian markets. Japanese mass media have often compared the impact of transnational satellite broadcasting to the mid–nineteenth century arrival of American Commodore Perry with his fleet of "black ships" which forced Japan to open up to the outside world after two centuries of seclusion (e.g., Kumamoto 1993a; Furuki and Higuchi 1996; Okamura 1996; Ryū 1996).[3] The implication is that Japan can no longer enjoy a self-contained domestic market, but rather is now under threat of being forced to open its doors to the world. However, unlike in the mid–nineteenth century, what is at stake this time seems less a foreign invasion of Japan than a Japanese advance into global media markets (e.g., Shimizu 1993; Shinohara 1994).[4]

In the early 1990s there had been some doubt about the competitiveness of Japanese TV programs, and there was concern about the relatively passive attitude of the Japanese TV industry toward entering Asian markets (e.g., Shima 1994; Nihon hatsu no bangumi Ajia kakeru? 1994). Yet, as indicated by the fact that STAR TV has constantly broadcast Japanese TV programs from the beginning along with the proliferation of media space in Asia has resulted in a dramatic increase in the demand for Japanese programs throughout the 1990s (e.g., Nihon no bangumi 1994; Ajia ga miteiru Nihon no terebi 1995; Sofuto kyūbo 1995; Tachanneru no nami 1996). The total export hours of Japanese TV programs has increased from 2,200 in 1971 to 4,585 in 1980 to 19,546 in 1992 (Kawatake 1994), and a passionate consumption of Japanese TV dramas and idols has been seen in many parts of East and Southeast Asia. In 1997 the Japanese Ministry of Posts and Telecommunication for the first time established a committee to report on the promotion of commercial exports of Japanese TV programs (Japanese Ministry 1997). The significant potential of Japanese TV exports to Asian markets has thus come to be widely recognized both within and outside Japan in the 1990s.

These developments in the export of Japanese audiovisual cultural products to East and Southeast Asia induced me to problematize widely held assumptions about the insignificance of Japanese contemporary culture in the world and to attend to the duality of Japanese cultural power relations. These questions appeared even more significant because the diffusion of Japanese media intersected with another significant historical shift that had emerged in 1990s Japan, which can be described as Japan's "return to Asia." Japan's "return to Asia" project, like Australia's "Asianization" project (see Ang and Stratton 1996), has been driven by the rising economic power of several modernized Asian countries, but its impact extends well into the cultural sphere. Japan began explicitly and positively reasserting its Asian identity in the early 1990s after a long retreat following the defeat of World War II. The cultural geography of "Asia" has recurred to the Japanese national imaginary as Japan faces the challenge of (re)constructing its national/cultural identity in the era of globalization. The expansionist nationalism that inspires Japan's desire for connecting (with) Asia resurfaced in the context in which widely proliferated Asian modernities, the restructuring of the post–Cold War geopolitics, the development of transnational media/cultural flows, as well as the spread of Japanese popular culture in the region, all joined together.

The purpose of this book is to examine the rise of Japanese cultural power in light of intra-Asian popular culture flows against the backdrop of the conjuncture of media globalization and Japan's "return to Asia" project. I do this through an analysis of Japanese discourses on Japan's export of popular culture to East and Southeast Asia and through empirical studies of the strategies used by Japanese media industries to enter Asian markets, as well as studies of the asymmetrical bilateral consumption of Japanese and other Asian popular culture. The analysis will show the various ways in which burgeoning popular culture flows have given new substance to the ambiguous imaginary space of "Asia," with which Japanese intellectuals, Japanese media industries, and Japanese individuals (as consumers) must come to terms (Mizukoshi 1998). A key concern of this book is how Japan has for the first time encountered other Asian nations as "modern" cultural neighbors. Across the Asian region, vast urban spaces have emerged in the last few decades. There, the experience of West-inflicted capitalist modernity has given birth to various modes of indigenized modernities, in such a way that they have become a source for the articulation of a new notion of Asian cultural commonality, difference, and asymmetry. I will elucidate how the transnational flow of popular culture has significantly rearticulated Japan's historically constituted relation with "Asia" in a time–space context in which cultural similarity, developmental temporality, and different modes of negotiating with Western cultural influences are disjunctively intermingled with each other.

The "Japan–Asia–the West" triad

The relative lacuna of discussion on Japanese transnational cultural power in Asia is not simply contingent, but implicated in the shift in Japanese cultural orientation after World War II. To put it bluntly, the idea of a Japan lacking in external cultural power has been collusive with a postwar strategy of constructing an exclusive and unique Japanese national identity. It is often argued that Japanese people themselves are reluctant to diffuse Japanese culture in the world. Hannerz (1989, 67–68), for example, argues that "the Japanese . . . find it a strange notion that anyone can 'become Japanese,' and they put Japanese culture on exhibit, in the framework of organized international contacts, as a way of displaying irreducible distinctiveness rather than in order to make it spread." Japan's obsession with the uniqueness of its own culture has been widely observed in the popularity of *Nihonjinron* discourses, which explain distinctive features of Japanese people and Japanese culture in essentialist terms (e.g., Dale 1986; Mouer and Sugimoto 1986; Befu 1987; Yoshino 1992). Those Japanese cultural practices and materials that have been internationally exhibited or represented in the global forum have been predominantly officially sanctioned items of "traditional" culture which have little to do with contemporary Japanese urban culture. "Traditional Japanese culture" is a culture to be displayed in order to demarcate Japan's unique, supposedly homogeneous national identity.

Many studies show that Japanese national/cultural identity has been constructed in an essentialist manner through the country's conscious self-Orientalizing discourse, a narrative that at once testifies to a firm incorporation into, and a subtle exploitation of, Western Orientalist discourse (see Sakai 1989; Iwabuchi 1994; Ivy 1995; Kondo 1997). Japan is represented and represents itself as culturally exclusive, homogeneous, and uniquely particularistic through the operation of a strategic binary opposition between two imaginary cultural entities, "Japan" and "the West." This is not to say that "Asia" has no cultural significance in the construction of Japanese national identity. Rather, Hannerz's astute observation about Japanese national identity illuminates a historical rupture brought about by Japan's defeat in World War II, which dramatically changed the Japanese cultural orientation from an extroverted to an introverted focus through the suppression of Japanese colonial connections with other Asian countries. In other words, the complicity between Western Orientalism and Japan's self-Orientalism effectively works only when Japanese cultural power in Asia is subsumed under Japan's cultural subordination to the West—that is, when Japan's peculiar position as the only modern, non-Western imperial/colonial power tends to be translated with a great skew toward Japan's relation with the West.

While Japan's construction of its national identity through an unambiguous comparison of itself with "the West" is a historically embedded project, Japan's modern national identity has, I would argue, always been imagined in an asymmetrical totalizing triad between "Asia," "the West," and "Japan." It is widely observed that Japan and Asia tend to be discussed and perceived within Japan as two separate geographies, whose inherent contradiction is unquestioned. Japan is unequivocally located in a geography called "Asia," but it no less unambiguously exists outside a cultural imaginary of "Asia" in Japanese mental maps (e.g., Ueda 1997, 34; Mizukoshi 1999, 181–82).[5] This duality points to the fact that "Asia" has overtly or covertly played a constitutive part in Japan's construction of national identity. While "the West" played the role of the modern Other to be emulated, "Asia" was cast as the image of Japan's past, a negative portrait which illustrates the extent to which Japan has been successfully modernized according to the Western standard (Tanaka 1993; Kang 1996). *"Datsua nyūō"* (Escape Asia, enter the West) is a well-known late-nineteenth-century Japanese slogan which first articulated Japan's will to become a modern imperial power, not to be colonized by the West through the effort of de-Asianization. "Datsua nyūō" signifies less an actual departure from an existing, coherent entity of Asia than a process of fabricating essentialized, imaginary geographies of "Asia," "the West" and "Japan" in the course of Japanese imperialist modernization. Takeuchi (1993, 96–100, 278–85) argues that there were two major approaches to Asia in prewar Japan. One was *datsua* (escape from Asia) and the other was *kō* (expressing Asian solidarity in resisting Western imperial domination). Takeuchi (1993, 103) points out that the Japanese invasion of Asia represented the ultimate synthesis of the two concepts, where the former absorbed and exploited the latter. In the process of Japanese imperial expansion, Japan was perceived to rise above other Asian countries and "Japan" and "Asia" became two separate entities in Japanese discourse. The binary opposition between "traditional," or "under-developed," Asia and the "developed" West has been necessary for Japan to be able to construct its national identity in a modern and West-dominated world order. Japan has constructed an oriental Orientalism against "inferior Asia" (Robertson 1998b, 97–101).

However, the Japanese discursive construction of "Asia" is marked by the impossibility of clear separation between Japan and Asia. As Stefan Tanaka (1993, 3) commented when discussing Japanese Orientalism in the early twentieth century, Japan's "Asia" poses an uneasy question of "how to become modern while simultaneously shedding the objectivistic category of Oriental and yet not lose an identity." While an essentialist pan-Asianism has existed alongside the wish for de-Asianization since the late nineteenth century in Japan,[6] the 1930s and 1940s, particularly, saw the passionate advocacy of pan-Asianist ideology by Japanese nationalistic thinkers. They understood the issue of "commonality and difference" in Japan's relationship to other Asian nations, I would suggest, mostly in terms such as "similar but superior," or "in but above Asia." As the only non-Western imperial and colonial power which invaded geographically contiguous Asian regions, Japan resorted to an ideology of pan-Asianism to camouflage its imperial ambitions. The idea of the Great East Asian Co-Prosperity Sphere,[7] promulgated in this period, was a claim for an Asian solidarity based in an inherent "Asian" bond that would be able to counter Western evil.

The advocacy of a cultural and racial commonality between Japan and other Asian nations naturally conferred upon Japan a mission to rid Asia of Western imperial domination and to itself civilize other Asians instead (Peattie 1984; Lebra 1975). Undoubtedly such a conception of its mission was highly motivated by Japanese anti-Western sentiment in response to the Western racist refusal to allow Japan to become a member of the imperial club (Dower 1986). The assertion of Japanese cultural commonality with other Asian countries was necessary for any confirmation of Japan's superior position in the region, a confirmation that would sustain Japan's bid for the same status as that of Western imperial powers. At the same time, Japan's mission *civilatrice* in the region paradoxically confirmed its subordination to the West, since the country's claim of superiority over other Asians was based upon its experience of a quick, successful Westernization (Duus 1995). Only submission to Western cultural power made it at all possible for Japan to differentiate itself from other "backward" Asians.[8] As I will discuss later, this issue of derived cultural superiority still lingers as a source of ambivalence which has long governed Japanese discourse on its relation with Asia.

Japan's defeat in World War II and the subsequent American occupation drastically changed, even curtailed, Japanese cultural orientation toward other Asian countries as a colonial power. The American vision of the Cold War has deeply influenced the restructuring as well as the intellectual analysis of postwar Japan (Harootunian 1993; Ishida 1995). Attention has focused on Japan's cultural relation with "the West," and especially the United States as Japan's most significant cultural Other, against which Japanese national identity has been constructed.

A glance at transformations in the meaning of the term *Japanization*, which articulates Japanese transnational cultural power, reveals the shift in Japanese cultural orientation. In prewar Japan, *Japanization* was articulated in the term *kōminka,* which means "the assimilation of ethnic others (such as Ainu, Okinawans, Taiwanese, and Koreans) into Japanese imperial citizenship under the Emperor's benevolence." *Japanization* also referred to the indigenization and domestication of foreign (Western) culture. The famous slogan *"wakon yōsai"* (Japanese spirit, Western technologies) exemplifies the latter usage. These two different meanings of *Japanization*—the assimilation of the colonized (Asians) into Japanese society, and the indigenization of Western culture—coexisted in prewar Japan (see Robertson 1998b, 89–138).[9] After the war, as I will discuss in chapter 2, the prewar meaning of "assimilation of Asian Others" was suppressed, and usage of the term *Japan-*

ization focused on the second meaning, "Japanese indigenization or domestication of Western (primarily American) cultural influences." Moreover, the meaning of the term, used to express the process of indigenizing foreign (i.e., Western) culture, changed from "imitation," which connoted Japan's inferior status, to "domestication" or "appropriation," which emphasized the active agency of the Japanese (see Tobin 1992b). To the extent that Japanese cultural capacity was at all conceptualized, it was as an introverted urge to counter external, dominant Western cultures.

Since what Harootunian (1993) calls "America's Japan" has long governed Japan's vision of itself, Japan's connections with "Asia" have been truncated in various ways. The most notorious is Japan's avoidance or refusal to take responsibility for its part in the war and its inability to offer an official apology and compensation for its victims. Japanese cultural introversion after the war was accompanied by Japan's project of forgetting its imperial history, of burying in oblivion the fact that Japan did try to force its colonial subjects to become Japanese as part of its assimilationist colonial policy.[10] As Gluck (1993) argues, Japan has long been imprisoned within a never-ending "postwar" which is mainly constructed by its relation to the United States. Thus, its war memory has been persistently imagined in terms of its own victimhood. Japan's conception of the "postwar," which negates continuity with the past, made it possible for Japan not to face seriously the aftermath of its own imperialist violence in the former colonies and occupied territories. Under the umbrella of American global power, Japanese interest in and connection with Asia in the postwar period has not just tended to eschew East Asia, which had previously been the main region for Japanese colonial expansion, but has also focused on the economic aspect. Here, the issue of Japan's war compensation for Asian countries was not dealt with as an opportunity for Japan's sincere expression of its war responsibility. Rather, it was subtly exploited as the first step for Japan's economic expansion in the region in the form of official economic aid (Ishida 1995). Accordingly, the sense of being the leader of Asia lingered in economic terms, as shown by the regional rise of the theory of the "flying geese pattern of economic development," in which Japan is assumed to play a leading role in that development (see Korhonen 1994).[11] This has been particularly so since the 1960s, when Japan was in the midst of high economic growth.

This is not to neglect the fact that the connection in fields other than the economy between Japan and other Asian nations has never been totally cut off after the war. Many people in Japan have been critical of the Japanese government's refusal to face seriously its war responsibility and the aftermath of its imperial and colonial rule in Asian regions. They have tried to make alliances with people in other parts of Asia to fight against any form of domination and repression. However, the prevailing attitude toward "Asia" taken in Japan has been rather economy-oriented and condescending. It was the rise of regional anti-Japanese sentiment in the early 1970s that forced the Japanese government to reconsider the significance of its cultural ties with other Asian countries and to develop the so-called "Fukuda Doctrine," a policy of cultural diplomacy for Southeast Asia. However, the purpose of promoting such a cultural-exchange policy was less to promote a grassroots dialogue by seriously engaging the issue of Japan's war responsibility than to further Japan's economic interest by smoothing the way for the expansion of Japanese corporations into Southeast Asia. There have also been transient "Asian booms" in popular culture and tourism in Japan, but the imaginary distance between "Japan" and "Asia" has been firmly maintained (Murai, Kido, and Koshido 1988, 12–29). "Asia," therefore, continued to signify lack and poverty, a posture that covertly sustained the complicit opposition-ing between Japanese self-Orientalization and Western Orientalization.

Japan's civilizational mission of reconciling the East and the West

Not until the 1990s did the rise of global Asian economic power push Japan to once again stress its "Asian" identity. Even Gluck (1997) remarks that Japan's postwar posture is finally ending, as she observes significant changes occurring in Japanese society. These changes resonate with those of world geopolitics in the early 1990s, and they are recumbent upon the end of the Cold War and the rise of Asian economic power. The loss of the unambiguous Cold War ideological enemy and the relative decline of Western, particularly American, hegemonic power gave rise to a reactionary thesis that would subsume the previous paradigm of the antagonistic East–West divide. By dividing the world into seven or eight clearly demarcated "civilizations," in terms of the largest organically integrated cultural entities,[12] conservative American thinker Samuel Huntington (1993) has infamously argued that civilizational differences will be the major cause of international conflicts in the post–Cold War era.

Huntington's argument has been countered by the discourse of "Asian values," which was advocated as key to understanding the recent economic success in the region. The rapid economic growth of several countries in Asia has, for the first time in history, turned negative connotations associated with the term *Asia* into positive ones. Accordingly, several leaders of Southeast Asian countries, such as Lee Kuan-Yew of Singapore and Mahathir Mohamad of Malaysia, main advocates of the Asian value thesis, have earnestly emphasized the limitations of the universality of the Western modernization model, with its associated social and cultural values, such as democracy and human rights (Zakaria 1994; Mahathir and Ishihara 1995). Although they are in sharp conflict with one another in terms of political interests, the relationship between these two discourses can be described as a collusive interplay, as they share much in their essentializing of the cultural/civilizational differences between West and East.[13]

In this context, the Japanese experience of modernization and its economic power are no longer perceived as scandalous or spectacular, since the ascent of Asian power is becoming more important to the West. While Japan has also said "no" to the United States in connection with specific trade disagreements, the most assertive Asianists have been the leaders of Southeast Asian countries, notably Singapore and Malaysia. Although Huntington recognizes the uniqueness of Japanese civilization, as the only case where a civilizational unit also corresponds to that of the nation-state, Japan is nevertheless losing its unique position vis-à-vis the West, as world attention has focused more on "Asian values" and on the increasing political assertiveness of other Asian countries, one result of their increasing economic power.[14]

Furthermore, in an atmosphere of increasing regionalism during this period—manifest in the emergence of the EU (European Union) and of NAFTA (the North American Free Trade Agreement)—Asian leaders have tried to promote equivalent vehicles for economic regionalization. The United States has warned Japan that it should attach more importance to APEC (the Asia Pacific Economic Cooperation Forum), which includes Western countries such as the United States, Australia, and New Zealand, than to the EAEC (East Asia Economic Caucus), which excludes these "white" economies (see Berger and Borer 1997). Japan, heeding the U.S. warning, refused to join the EAEC. Nonetheless, Japan could not neglect Asia as a vital market for its products, and a new Asianism emerged in Japan in the early 1990s. Although this trend was somewhat dampened by the Asian economic crisis of the late 1990s, the question of how to return to Asia has reemerged as an important economic as well as political issue for Japan.

The legacy of pan-Asianism, then, is still alive, as can be discerned in Japan's newly articulated interest in Asian identity in the 1990s. Economic motives for the return to Asia have often been disguised with nostalgic racial and/or cultural justifications. As the president of Fuji Xerox claimed: "Just as Gorbachev once declared that Russia's home was in Europe, so it is only natural for us to say that Japan's home is in Asia, not in the United States or Europe" (quoted in Saitō 1992, 17). Political ambition, deeply motivated by an anti-West sentiment, is once again expressed in terms of the inherent commonalities amongst Asian nations. Some even advocate an exclusivist and essentialist view of a new Asianism. Prominent Asianists such as Ogura Kazuo (1993), for example, champion pan-Asian solidarity and have pointed out the common cultures, traditions, values, and racial origins shared by Japan and Asia (see McCormack 1996). Ishihara Shintaro, in his book *The Voice of Asia,* coauthored with Malaysian prime minister Mahathir Mohamad,[15] strongly asserts the necessity of an Asian unity to counter perceived Western political and economic domination (Mahathir and Ishihara 1995, 205). He proudly evokes Japan's natural affinity with other Asian nations by declaring that Japan has never been a mono-racial nation but a hybrid nation of many Asian races. This is possibly a shamelessly strategic comment, as Ishihara is known to have made the exact opposite statement on an earlier occasion (Oguma 1995).

On the other hand, in reclaiming Japan's geopolitical significance in the clash of civilizations thesis, Japan has been able to reemphasize its longstanding mission of reconciling tensions between East and West in an emerging chaotic and antagonistic world order. The major tone of the discussion is that Japan should not identify itself with either side, West or East, but rather should attempt to play a mediating role between the two in an age of global interconnection which otherwise supposedly engenders a sense of uncertainty and antagonism to cultural difference in the world at large.[16] The point is clearly articulated by the well-known sociologist Imada Takatoshi (1994). Imada argues that what is required for the present chaotic world— where neither Western universal hegemony nor modern principles such as functionalism, rationalism, efficiency, and unity any longer produce centripetal forces—is the negotiation of difference without suppressing or negating it. It is a capacity for "editing" different cultures and civilizations that should characterize the new Japanese civilization in the 1990s and beyond. Although he concedes that Japan has not yet fulfilled its mission, Japan's long experience of editing Western and Eastern civilization would qualify it as a principal world editor.[17]

The imaginings of Japan's mission as a mediating leader is not necessarily motivated by reactive or chauvinistic sentiment. Nevertheless, we can still discern a strong impetus to keep the mutually exclusive trichotomy, mentioned above, intact. Many slogans emergent during early 1990s show this tendency. The most famous one is *"Datsuō nyūo"* (Escape the West, enter Asia), an inversion of "Datsua nyūō." Others, cautious of excluding the United States, advocate *"Nyūō nyūa"* (Enter the West and Asia), *"Datsua nyūyō"* (Escape Asia, enter the Pacific) or *"Han'ō nyūa"* (Enter Asia together with the West). An underlying common assumption of these slogans is that "Asia" and "the West" are imaginary entities, demarcated from each other, between which "Japan" is floating as a leader of the former. If, as Berry (1994, 82) argues, Singapore—and perhaps other Asian countries as well—is trying "to resolve its contradictions between localization and globalization by asserting a new coherent identity that is regional," Japan's strategy is not to identify with either of the clearly demarcated entities, "Asia" or "the West." More precisely, Japan resists subsuming itself under the category of "Asia" or "the West," and is still trying to find a unique place between them. Japan tries to distance itself from either side in order to retain its distinct identity. In this strategic project of reorienting its own position within a familiar Asianism narrative, Japan's homecoming has still less to do with its will to become an interlocutor among neighbors than with its narcissistic search for a Japanese national identity (Hein and Hammond 1995).

Return to modernized Asia

The Asia which Japan encounters in the 1990s, however, is no longer contained by the image of traditional, underdeveloped, backward neighbors to be civilized by Japan. In this regard, it is important to stress that what has substantiated the cultural geography of "Asia" in the 1990s is less some essential and distinct concept of "Asian values" than the advent of global capitalism in the region. As Dirlik (1994, 51–52) argues: "What makes something like the East Asian Confucian revival plausible is not its offer of alternative values to those of Euro-American origin, but its articulation of native culture into a capitalist narrative." No matter how "Asian" values are emphasized as a key to the economic growth in Asia, the rise of "Asian" capitalism signifies a transnational configuration wherever the global spread of Western-origin capitalism has made any attempt at a clear discursive demarcation of "the West" and "Asia" (and "Japan") fallacious.

The process of globalization has made the conception of rigidly demarcated national and cultural boundaries implausible and tenuous (e.g., Appadurai 1996; Hannerz 1996). The rise of the discourse of "Asian values" and Japan's cultural project of a "return to Asia" should be considered in this context. As Stuart Hall (1995, 190) neatly defines the concept: "Globalization is the process by which the relatively separate areas of the globe come to intersect in a single imaginary 'space'; when their respective histories are convened in a time-zone or time-frame dominated by the time of the West; when the sharp boundaries reinforced by space and distance are bridged by connections (travel, trade, conquest, colonization, markets, capital and the flows of labor, goods and profits) which gradually eroded the clear-cut distinction between 'inside' and 'outside.'"

As Hall emphasizes, globalization is not a new phenomenon but rather should be considered in light of the long history of Western imperialism. The experience of globalization is unequivocally marked by uneven power relations in a West-dominated modern history. However, the historical process of globalization has not simply produced the Westernization of the world. Its impact on the constitution of the world is much more heterogeneous and contradictory. The unambiguously dominant Western cultural, political, economic, and military power has constructed a modern world-system covering the entire globe (Wallerstein 1991), yet at the same time the global reach of capitalist modernity has destabilized the exclusive equation of modernity with the Western world. The experience of "the forced appropriation of modernity" in the non-West has produced polymorphic indigenized modernities in the world (Ang and Stratton 1996). One corollary of the phenomenon of ongoing asymmetrical cultural encounters in the course of the spread of Western modernity, as Ang and Stratton (1996, 22–24) argue, is that we have come to live in "a world where all cultures are both (like) 'us' and (not like) 'us,'" a world where familiar difference and bizarre sameness are simultaneously articulated in multiple ways through the unpredictable dynamic of uneven global cultural encounters.

In this dynamic context of the 1990s, Japan encounters "Asia" as a modernized cultural neighbor vis-à-vis a common but different experience of indigenizing modernity under Western cultural dominance. As the rise of other Asian economies has deprived Japan of its unique position as the only non-Western nation to achieve a high degree of industrialization and modernization, Japan needs to come to terms with the increasingly visible gap between a discursively constructed "backward Asia" and the rapidly developing economic power of geographically specific Asian nations. The trichotomy, "Asia," "Japan" and "the West," that has long governed Japanese discourses has been seriously put into question (Satō 1998; Yamamuro 1998).[18]

In this book, I will conduct an investigation into Japan's encounter with "modern" Asia through a focus on the diffusion of Japanese commercialized popular culture, especially TV dramas and popular music, in East and Southeast Asia. The development of communication technologies has facilitated the simultaneous circulation of numerous kinds of media information, images and texts, on a global level. Various (national) markets are being penetrated and integrated by powerful global media giants such as News Corp., Sony, and Disney. Globalization processes, however, have not simply furthered the spread of Americanized "global mass culture" (Hall 1991). They have also promoted the flow of intraregional media and popular culture within East and Southeast Asia. These popular cultural forms are undoubtedly deeply imbricated in U.S. cultural imaginaries, but they dynamically rework the meanings of being modern in Asian contexts at the site of production and consumption. In this sense, they are neither "Asian" in any essentialist meaning nor second-rate copies of "American originals." They are inescapably "global" and "Asian" at the same time, lucidly representing the intertwined composition of global homogenization and heterogenization, and thus they well articulate the juxtaposed sameness and difference among contemporaneous indigenized modernities in East and Southeast Asia.

The intricacy and disjunctiveness of emerging intra-Asian popular cultural flows under globalizing forces are better expressed by the term *transnational,* as opposed to *international* or *global,* for a variety of reasons. *Transnational* has a merit over *international* in that actors are not confined to the nation-state or to nationally institutionalized organizations; they may range from individuals to various (non)profitable, transnationally connected organizations and groups, and the conception of culture implied is not limited to a "national" framework. As Hannerz (1996, 6) argues, the term *transnational* is "more humble, and often a more adequate label for phenomena which can be of quite variable scale and distribution" than the term *global*, which sounds too all-inclusive and decontextualized. Moreover, the term *transnational* draws attention in a more locally contextualized manner to the interconnections and asymmetries that are promoted by the multidirectional flow of information and images, and by the ongoing cultural mixing and infiltration of these messages; it effectively disregards nationally demarcated boundaries both from above and below, the most important of which are capital, people, and media/images (Appadurai 1996; Welsch 1999).

At the same time, unlike the term *global*, the term *transnational* tends to "draw attention to what it negates" (Hannerz 1996, 6). As Michael Peter Smith (2001, 3) argues while problematizing the assumed efficacy of boundary-policing by the nation-state in the modern constitution of politics, economy, and culture, the transnational perspective at the same time explicates "the continuing significance of borders, state policies, and national identities even as these are often transgressed by transnational communication circuits and social practices." Transnational cultural flows neither fully displace nationally delineated boundaries, thoughts, and feelings, nor do they underestimate the salience of the nation-state in the process of globalization. Rather, it might more often than not be the case that "the transnational has not so much displaced the national as resituated it and thus reworked its meanings" (Rouse 1995, 380).

This point is particularly important when we look at the way in which cultural globalization has presented a ground for the recentering and reassertion of Japan's cultural power in Asia. While globalization processes have drastically facilitated the transnational cross-fertilization of popular cultural forms in many parts of the world (e.g., García Canclini 1995; Lull 1995), this boundary-violating impulse of cultural flow is nevertheless never free from nationalizing forces. In the emerging landscape of modern Asia, it is precisely through its receptivity to, ongoing cultural appropriation of, and negotiation with Western cultural influence that Japanese transnational cultural power is highlighted. The growing Japanese interest in its cultural export also tends to be informed predominantly by a historically constituted nationalistic desire for "Asia"; that is, it is articulated by a distinct "Japaneseness" in popular cultural forms, designed to raise Japan's position in Asia and to (re)assert Japan's cultural superiority.

On the other hand, the simultaneous achievement of capitalist modernity by several Asian nations has made it clear that the subtle cultural mixing of "the local" and "the foreign" (the West) is not exclusively a Japanese experience but a common feature in the formation of non-Western modernity. Activated popular cultural flows induce Japan to encounter familiar but different modes of Asian indigenized modernities in both cultural production and consumption. The transnational cultural flow in East and Southeast Asian regions is, though admittedly uneven, becoming more multilateral. The increasing intra-Asian cultural flow precipitates (asymmetrical) connections between people in Japan and those in modernized (or rapidly modernizing) "Asia," not through reified notions of "traditional, authentic culture" or "Asian values," but through popular cultural forms which embody people's skillful negotiation with the symbolic power of West-dominated global capitalism.

Being unequal in their effect, transnational media and cultural flows have had contradictory impacts on Japan's engagement with "Asia." The analysis of these cultural dynamics will highlight both the rupture as well as the continuity of Japanese condescension, as expressed in its conception of its own superior position and asymmetrical relation vis-à-vis other Asian nations. The Japanese popular cultural encounter with other Asian countries in the 1990s is overdetermined by Japanese imperial history. Nevertheless, it is more multiple, contradictory, and ambivalent than a totalizing and cavalier Japanese Orientalist conception of "Asia" would suggest.

The following chapters deal with various aspects of Japan's popular cultural "return to Asia" through discourse analysis and empirical studies, in which Japan's transnational cultural power is reasserted and articulated in terms of indigenized modernity. In chapter 1, I present theoretical reconsiderations concerning Japanese transnational cultural power. By presenting an overview of the development of Japanese active involvement in the global export economy of cultural products, I will situate the rise of Japanese cultural power in light of globalization processes and will show how the foregrounding of Japan's ascent in the global cultural flows correlates to the decentering forces of globalization.

Chapter 2 examines what I call trans/nationalism discourses, in which the transnational reach of Japanese popular culture in East and Southeast Asia is discussed and interpreted in nationalistic ways, against all the odds of disjunctive cultural flows, through a wide range of Japanese popular media texts as well as academic discussions. An essentialist configuration of Japan's sophisticated capacity to culturally indigenize the foreign, in which terms the putative Japanese national essence is imagined, has long had its place in Japanese nationalistic discourse. In the 1990s, this capacity was extrovertedly applied to the spread of Japanese popular culture in Asia. It is claimed that the appeal of Japanese popular culture lies in its subtle indigenization of American popular culture, making it suitable to "Asian tastes," and that therefore Japan has had a special leading role in constructing the sphere of Asian popular culture. The hybrid nature of Japanese popular culture is also seen to present modern, liberal facets of Japanese society to other parts of Asia. In this case, the spread of Japanese popular culture in other parts of Asia is conceived as improving Japan's image as an oppressor in Asia and thus overcomes the legacy of its history of imperial aggression in the region. I will suggest that there is an apparent ambivalence in such nationalistic claims concerning Japanese cultural export, as they occur within the context of accelerated transnational cultural flows, which have gradually made it difficult, and possibly insignificant, to specify the original source of transnationally circulated cultural products in the first place.

Chapters 3, 4, and 5 elucidate through empirical study the nature of Japanese cultural power, the decentralizing force of globalization, and the (im)possibility of transnational dialogue via popular cultural consumption. These chapters show intricate ways in which Japan's asymmetrical relation with Asia appears as regional cultural flows become intensified.

Field research was conducted in Tokyo in October 1994, from mid-January to late February 1997, and from mid-March to late April 1998; in Singapore in January 1996 and early December 1996; in Kuala Lumpur in mid-January 1996; in Taipei from mid-December 1996 to mid-January 1997 and in late May 1997; and in Hong Kong from late February to mid-March 1997. I interviewed more than 110 people who work for TV stations, in the music industry, and for publishing companies and advertising agencies in Tokyo, Taiwan, Hong Kong, Singapore, and Malaysia. The interviews posed questions concerning the promotion and reception of both Japanese popular culture in East Asia and of Southeast Asian popular culture in Japan. In Singapore and Kuala Lumpur, I also observed the production process of a star-search program, *Asia Bagus!*, coproduced by Japan, Singapore, Indonesia, and Malaysia. In addition, I conducted informal, in-depth interviews with eighteen female and three male viewers (whose ages ranged from seventeen to the late twenties) concerning Japanese TV dramas in Taipei, and with twenty-four female "fans" (whose ages ranged from the early-twenties to the fifties) concerning Hong Kong films and pop music singers in Tokyo.

These informants were selected mostly through personal introductions and therefore do not properly represent the total audience community. My purpose in interviewing these people was to identify ways in which audiences feel cultural resonance through Japanese TV dramas and Hong Kong pop stars, respectively.

Chapter 3 is particularly concerned with the "localization" strategy adopted by the Japanese media industries for entry into Asian markets, which sought to export the Japanese experience of local indigenization of Western popular culture. In spite of a dramatic increase in the export of Japanese TV programs and popular music to East and Southeast Asian markets in the early 1990s, the main strategy taken by Japanese media industries was the application of Japanese know-how in "localizing" American popular culture. Based on my interviews with Japanese producers concerning their strategies in Asian markets, I will argue that Japanese media industries, informed by the discourse of trans/nationalism, saw their strength as a capacity for indigenizing American popular culture, but that in their actual operations they have encountered more difficulty than facility with this strategy. As Howes (1996, 7) points out, discussions of globalization that do not attend to empirical contradictions and ruptures in global marketing strategies, tend to be remarkably similar in their language to the discussions of transnational corporation executives. Taking Howes's warning seriously, I will elucidate how the "localization" strategies of transnational media industries worked in contradictory ways (see Negus 1997).

What has become increasingly conspicuous in the mid-1990s is the shifting emphasis in the strategy of "localizing" Japanese popular culture in East Asian markets, away from the export of Japanese know-how and toward the direct marketing of Japanese popular culture in conjunction with local industries in East Asia. This change indicates that the intraregional flow of popular culture—collaborative industry promotion and sympathetic audience reception—has developed. Chapters 4 and 5 elaborate on this emerging phenomenon. The main issue is how asymmetrical power relations in East Asia are articulated in the favorable consumption of the media texts of neighboring countries. My focus is the media flows among Japan, Taiwan, and Hong Kong. Apart from time and funding considerations, I did not include South Korea in my fieldwork because of its restrictions on the import of Japanese popular culture.

Specifically, in chapter 4 I will discuss how Japanese cultural forms are consumed in East Asia, with a particular focus on Japanese TV dramas in Taiwan, the largest and most receptive market for Japanese popular culture. My emphasis is on the way in which several forces have been articulated together in the surging popularity of Japanese TV dramas in Taiwan during the mid-1990s and the way that Japanese cultural power productively has worked to generate a sense of cultural resonance for Taiwanese audiences in these contexts. My research in Taipei and Hong Kong suggests that many young viewers relate more easily to Japanese TV dramas and find them more attractive than American dramas, both because of cultural and bodily similarity and textual subtlety. This is neither to say that Japan has become an object of yearning in other parts of Asia, nor that a priori cultural proximity generates regionalization. Rather, under globalizing forces, the sense of cultural similarity and resonance in the region are newly articulated. It reflects an emerging sense of sharing the same temporality based upon the narrowing economic gap, simultaneous circulation of information, abundance of global commodities, and common experience of urbanization, all of which have particularly sustained a Japanese cultural presence in Taiwan.

Chapter 5 concerns itself with the other trajectory of intraregional cultural flow: the promotion, consumption, and discourse surrounding various Asian popular cultural forms in 1990s Japan. It highlights the asymmetry in intraregional cultural flow in East Asia by showing that Japanese audiences, contrary to Taiwanese audiences of Japanese TV dramas, tend to emphasize difference rather than similarity, nostalgia rather than contemporaneity, in their appreciation of other Asian popular cultures. While Japan has struggled since the early 1990s with an economic slump after the so-called bubble economy and other Asian nations have enjoyed relatively high economic growth until an economic crisis hit the region, Japanese media representation of Asian popular culture and Asian societies has been sharply marked by a nostalgic longing for a lost social vigor. This posture displays Japanese failure and refusal to see other Asians as modern equals who share the same temporality and attests to Japan's lingering double claim to a sameness with and a sense of superiority to "Asia." However, I will also show through an empirical study of Japanese female fans of Hong Kong films and pop stars that "modern" Hong Kong fascinates those fans, not least because these cultural products represent a different mode of Asian modernity, a way of negotiating with the West that produces a cultural hybrid that is perceived as even more sophisticated than the Japanese counterpart. While Japanese connections with "Asia" are tenaciously pervaded by a perceived temporal lag between Japan and the rest of Asia, a lag which prevents the Japanese from meeting the latter on equal terms, they are nevertheless becoming more complicated and ambivalent in ever-increasing transnational popular culture flows in East and Southeast Asia.

1

Taking "Japanization" seriously:

Cultural globalization reconsidered

No one would deny Japan's status as a major economic power. While its power has been relatively undermined by a prolonged economic and financial slump since the early 1990s, this only serves to highlight Japan's tremendous economic influence in the world, particularly in Asia. As Japan has become the second biggest economic power in the world, its external influence has come to be discussed in terms of the export of Japanese management and industrial relations techniques and Japanese organizational cultures (e.g., Bratton 1992; Oliver and Wilkinson 1992; Thome and McAuley 1992; Elger and Smith 1994). Such discourses started in the 1970s, when many Western scholars advocated that the West should learn lessons from the Japanese economic success (e.g., Dore 1973; Vogel 1979). Although not exclusively representing post-Fordism, "Japanization" of industrial relations and organizational cultures was discussed specifically in the search for post-Fordist industrial models, whereby "Toyotism" for example, attracted much attention as a more flexible production system than Fordism (Lash and Urry 1994; Dohse, Jurgens, and Malsch 1985; Waters 1995, 82–85).

However, it was not until the late 1980s that the significance of Japan in the global culture market began attracting wider international academic and media attention. It was a time when Sony and Matsushita were buying out Hollywood film studios and the animation film *Akira* was a hit in the Western markets. In the English-language world, many books and articles have been published on Japanese animation, computer games, and the Japanese advance on Hollywood since that time (e.g., *Mediamatic* 1991; Wark 1991, 1994; Morley and Robins 1995; Schodt 1983, 1996; Levi 1996). The Sony Walkman has even been chosen for analysis, as the most appropriate example of a global cultural product, by a British Open University cultural studies textbook, itself prepared for global distribution (du Gay et al. 1997).

Certainly, the emergence of such discourses on the spread of Japanese cultural products in the world reflects the fact that Japanese media industries and cultural forms are playing a substantial role in global cultural flows. It seems that Japanese cultural power may finally match its economic dominance. Yet crucial questions remain unanswered: what kind of cultural power (if any) is conferred on Japan? and how similar or different is it from American cultural hegemony? In this chapter, I will present a theoretical consideration of the recent rise in Japanese cultural exports and will explore how that rise might be situated within the study of cultural globalization. Rather than seeing an easy comparison between Japanese cultural exports and "Americanization," or dismissing this phenomenon as merely frivolous, I will instead suggest that it offers some new and significant insights into understanding the decentered nature of transnational cultural power.

Culturally "odorless" commodities

Even if the cultural dimensions of Japan's global influence have not been widely discussed until recently, this does not mean that Japan did not have any cultural impact before then. Rather, the hitherto assumption of Japan's lack of cultural impact testifies to a discrepancy between actual cultural influence and perceived cultural presence. The cultural impact of a particular commodity is not necessarily experienced in terms of the cultural image of the exporting nation. For example, in the realm of audiovisual commodities, there is no doubt that Japan has been a dominant exporter of consumer technologies as well as animation and computer games. From VCRs, computer games, karaoke machines, and the Walkman, to the more recent appearance of digital video cameras, the prevalence of Japanese consumer electronics in the global marketplace is overwhelming. This development has been based upon the adage "First for consumers" expressed by Ibuka Masaru, founder of the Sony Corporation (quoted in Lardner 1987, 38). After the Second World War, freed from the obligation to devote its research and development energy to military purposes, and with the support of the Japanese government, the Japanese electronics industry successfully inverted the idea of "scientific or military research first." Instead, technological development would henceforth be propelled by consumer electronics (Forester 1993, 4).

Japanese consumer technologies certainly have had a tremendous impact on our everyday life, an impact which is, in a sense, more profound than that of Hollywood films. To use Jody Berland's (1992) term, these are "cultural technologies" that mediate between texts, spaces, and audiences. New cultural technologies open new possibilities for the consumption of media texts by audiences. In turn, by promoting the market-driven privatization of consumer needs and desires, new cultural technologies open up new ways for capital to accommodate itself to the emergent communication space in the service of individual consumer sovereignty. For example, VCRs have facilitated the transnational flow of videotape-recorded programs through both legal channels and illegal piracy. This has given consumers, especially those in developing countries whose appetites for information and entertainment have not been satisfied, access to diverse programs which have been officially banned. In response, governments have changed their policies from rigid restrictions on the flow of information and entertainment to more open, market-oriented controls—for example, the privatization of TV channels (Ganley and Ganley 1987; Boyd, Straubhaar, and Lent 1989; O'Regan 1991). On the whole, this development has consequently encouraged global centralization of the distribution and production of software, as well as facilitating the further spread of American software. Despite the fear of profits being skimmed off by piracy, VCRs have helped Hollywood open up new markets and find ways of exploiting new technologies through video rental and export of TV programs to newly privatized channels (see Gomery 1988; O'Regan 1992).

At the level of the consumer, Japanese electronic technologies have promoted strongly what Raymond Williams (1990, 26) has called "mobile privatization." These consumer technologies give people greater choice and mobility in their media consumption activities in domestic, private spaces. For example, while TV and radio made it possible for individuals in their own living rooms to experience and connect with what was happening in remote places, the Sony Walkman conversely promoted the intrusion of private media into public spaces. VCRs allowed people to "time shift"—to record TV programs and watch them at a later, more suitable time. It is an interesting question why such individualistic, private technologies have been developed and have flourished in a supposedly group-oriented society such as Japan. Kogawa (1984, 1988) coined the term "electronic individualism" to characterize Japanese social relations and argued that Japanese collectivity is increasingly based upon electronic communication and therefore becoming more precarious. Although Kogawa views the contemporary Japanese situation somewhat pessimistically, he points out that it offers the dual possibilities of the emancipation of individuals via technologies and, alternatively, the sophisticated control of individuals. Indeed, as Chambers argues, the consumption of one of the most successful Japanese cultural technologies of the past decades—the Sony Walkman—is an ambivalent "cultural activity" that sways between "autonomy and autism" (1990, 2). Such an activity can be seen as a form of escapism that makes individuals feel a sense of atomized freedom from the constraints of a rigidly controlled society. It also has the possibility of substituting a privatized "micro-narrative" for collective "grand-narratives" (3). Speaking of the Chinese, Chow (1993, 398) argues that listening to a Walkman is "a 'silent' sabotage of the technology of collectivization" (for a more thorough analysis of the Walkman, see du Gay et al. 1997).

Despite the profound influence of Japanese consumer technologies on the cultural activities of our everyday life, they have tended not to be talked about in terms of a Japanese cultural presence. Hoskins and Mirus (1988) employ the notion of "cultural discount" to explain the fact that even though certain Japanese films and literature have had a Western following, the outflow of Japanese popular cultural products (particularly to Western countries) has been disproportionately small. Hoskins and Mirus describe "cultural discount" as occurring when "a particular program rooted in one culture and thus attractive in that environment will have a diminished appeal elsewhere as viewers find it difficult to identify with the style, values, beliefs, institutions and behavioral patterns of the material in question" (500). Cultural prestige, Western hegemony, the universal appeal of American popular culture, and the prevalence of the English language are no doubt advantageous to Hollywood. By contrast, Japanese language is not widely spoken outside Japan and Japan is supposedly obsessed with its own cultural uniqueness. Given the high cultural discount of Japanese films and TV programs, Hoskins and Mirus argue, Japanese cultural export tends to be limited to "culturally neutral" consumer technologies, whose country of origin has nothing to do with "the way [that they work] and the satisfaction [that a consumer] obtains from usage" (503).

Apparently, the notion of "cultural discount" does not satisfactorily explain a consumer's cultural preference for audiovisual media texts such as TV programs. Foreign programs, for example, can be seen as more attractive because they are "exotic," "different," or less "boring." The cultural difference embodied in foreign products can also be seen as less of a threat to local culture precisely because the imported products are conceived as "foreign," while those originating from culturally proximate countries might be perceived as more threatening (O'Regan 1992). The legacy of Japanese imperialism in Asia is a case in point. More importantly, Hoskins and Mirus's argument is highly West-centric. They are not aware that Japanese TV programs and popular music have been exported to East and Southeast Asia, if rarely to Europe or North America, though we also should be cautious not to mechanically explain this trend by employing "cultural discount" or "culturally proximity" in an essentialist manner (see Straubhaar 1991). I will return to this question in later chapters. For the moment, though, I will elaborate more on Hoskins and Mirus's discussion of the nature of Japan's major cultural export to the world (including Western markets).

Notwithstanding the argument about Japanese cultural export outlined above, the term "culturally neutral" seems misleading, too. The influence of cultural products on everyday life, as we have seen, cannot be culturally neutral. Any product has the cultural imprint of the producing country, even if it is not recognized as such. I would suggest that the major audiovisual products Japan exports could be better characterized as the "culturally odorless" three C's: consumer technologies (such as VCRs, karaoke, and the Walkman); comics and cartoons (animation); and computer/video games. I use the term *cultural odor* to focus on the way in which cultural features of a country of origin and images or ideas of its national, in most cases stereotyped, way of life are associated *positively* with a particular product in the consumption process. Any product may have various kinds of cultural association with the country of its invention. Such images are often related to exoticism, such as the image of the Japanese samurai or the geisha girl. Here, however, I am interested in the moment when the image of the contemporary lifestyle of the country of origin is strongly and affirmatively called to mind as the very appeal of the product, when the "cultural odor" of cultural commodities is evolved. The way in which the cultural odor of a particular product becomes a "fragrance"—a socially and culturally acceptable smell—is not determined simply by the consumer's perception that something is "made in Japan." Neither is it necessarily related to the material influence or quality of the product. It has more to do with widely disseminated symbolic images of the country of origin. The influence of McDonald's throughout the world, for example, can be discerned in terms of the bureaucratization and standardization of food; and the principles governing the operation of McDonald's can also be extended to other everyday life activities such as education and shopping (Ritzer 1993). However, no less important to the international success of McDonald's is its association with an attractive image of "the American way of life" (e.g., Frith 1982, 46; Featherstone 1995, 8). McDonald's, of course, does not inherently represent "America." It is a discursive construction of what is "America" that confers on McDonald's its powerful association with "Americanness."

Sony's Walkman is an important cultural commodity that has influenced everyday life in various ways. For this reason, du Gay et al. (1997) chose it as the cultural artifact most appropriate for a case study using the multilayered analyses of cultural studies. While taking note of the social constructedness of any national image, Sony's Walkman, they argue, may signify "Japaneseness" because of its miniaturization, technical sophistication, and high quality. Yet, I suggest, although such signs of "Japaneseness" are analytically important, they are not especially relevant to the appeal of the Walkman at a consumption level. The use of the Walkman does not evoke images or ideas of a Japanese lifestyle, even if consumers know it is made in Japan and appreciate "Japaneseness" in terms of its sophisticated technology. Unlike American commodities, "Japanese consumer goods do not seek to sell on the back of a Japanese way of life" (Featherstone 1995, 9), and they lack any influential "idea of Japan" (Wee 1997).

The cultural odor of a product is also closely associated with racial and bodily images of a country of origin. The three C's I mentioned earlier are cultural artifacts in which a country's bodily, racial, and ethnic characteristics are erased or softened. The characters of Japanese animation and computer games for the most part do not look "Japanese." Such non-Japaneseness is called *mukokuseki,* literally meaning "something or someone lacking any nationality," but also implying the erasure of racial or ethnic characteristics or a context, which does not imprint a particular culture or country with these features.[1] Internationally acclaimed Japanese animation director Oshii Mamoru suggests that Japanese animators and cartoonists unconsciously choose not to draw "realistic" Japanese characters if they wish to draw attractive characters (Oshii, Itō, and Ueno 1996). In Oshii's case, the characters tend to be modeled on Caucasian types. Consumers of and audiences for Japanese animation and games, it can be argued, may be aware of the Japanese origin of these commodities, but those texts barely feature "Japanese bodily odor" identified as such.

Japan goes global: Sony and animation

While the propensity of Japanese animators to make their products non-Japanese points to how a Western-dominated cultural hierarchy governs transnational cultural flows in the world,[2] Japan's hitherto invisible and odorless cultural presence in the world has become more and more conspicuous since the late 1980s. On the one hand, Japan has become one of the main players in the development of media globalization, by virtue of the fact that its manufacturers of consumer technologies have extending their reach into the software production business during the 1990s. It was Sony's purchase of Columbia in 1989, and Matsushita's purchase of MCA (Universal) in 1990, which dramatized the ascent of Japanese global media conglomerates through the merger of hardware and software. There was considerable reaction from within the United States against these buyouts, including claims that the Japanese were "buying into America's soul" (Morley and Robins 1995, 150). In the film *Black Rain,* Japanese costar Takakura Ken replies to Michael Douglas's antagonistic remark about Japanese economic expansion into the United States: "Music and movies are all your culture is good for. . . . We make the machines" (quoted in Morley and Robins 1995, 159). This comment apparently displays a generalized disdain by American media industries for the Japanese fascination with technology: Creative software production should not be controlled by mindless hardware manufacturers.

However, this kind of expression of the creative supremacy of American popular culture has gradually proved to be an American fantasy rather than a reflection of what is really happening. Although Matsushita retreated from Hollywood and Sony at first struggled to make a profit (see Negus 1997), Sony demonstrates that Japanese transnational corporations can make it in Hollywood, as Columbia finally achieved phenomenal box-office sales in 1997. Moreover, apart from the takeover of Hollywood by Japanese companies (as well as by European companies), there is good evidence to confirm that the era in which "the media are American" (Tunstall 1977) has ended. Japanese consumer technologies have become so sophisticated that we can talk about a "technoculture" in which "cultural information and the technical artifact seem to merge" (Wark 1991, 45). More significantly, Japan is not only increasing its capital and market share in the audiovisual global market but also its cultural presence on the global scene through the export of culturally odorless products other than consumer technologies. Japanese animation and computer games have attained a certain degree of popularity and become recognized as very "Japanese" in a positive and affirmative sense in Western countries as well as in non-Western countries. They embody a new aesthetic, emanating in large part from Japanese cultural inventiveness, and capture the new popular imagination (Wark 1994; Schodt 1983, 1996).

Since the release of Ōtomo Katsuhiro's hugely popular animation film *Akira* (1988), the quality and attraction of "Japanimation" has been acknowledged by the American market. In November 1995 the animated film *The Ghost in the Shell* was shown simultaneously in Japan, America, and Great Britain. Its video sales, according to *Billboard* (24 August 1996), reached No.1 on the video charts in the United States. According to a *Los Angeles Times* report, the export value of Japanese animation and comics to the American market amounted to $75 million in 1996 (Manabe 1997). Furthermore, three Japanese manufacturers, Nintendo, Sega and Sony, dominate the market for computer games. The popularity of Japanese game software is exemplified by the popularity of such games as Super Mario Brothers, Sonic, and Pokémon. As a director of Nintendo pointed out, according to one survey, Mario is a better-known character among American children than Mickey Mouse (Akurosu Henshūshitsu 1995, 41–42). The huge success of Pokémon in the global market since 1998 further persuades us to make a serious scholarly investigation into Japanese cultural export. Pokémon's penetration into global markets even exceeds that of Mario. As of June 2000 Pokémon game software had sold about 65 million copies (22 million outside Japan) and trading-cards about 4.2 billion (2.4 billion outside Japan); the animation series had been broadcast in fifty-one countries; the first feature film had been shown in thirty-three countries, and its overseas box-office record had amounted to $176 million; and there had also been about 12,000 purchases of character merchandise (8,000 outside Japan) (Hatakeyama and Kubo 2000). These figures unambiguously show that Pokémon has become truly a "made-in-Japan" global cultural artifact.

These examples certainly illustrate the rise of Japanese cultural products in world markets, particularly within the domain of animated software. Accordingly, we have observed an increasingly narcissistic interest in articulating the distinctive "Japaneseness" of cultural products in 1990s Japan. As early as 1992, for example, the popular monthly magazine *DENiM* ran a feature article on made-in-Japan global commodities that began "Who said that Japan only imports superior foreign culture and commodities and has nothing originally Japanese which has a universal appeal? Now Japanese customs, products and systems are conquering the world!" (Sekai ga mane-shita Nipponryū 1992, 143). In the article, global Japanese exports included food, fashion, service industry offerings, animation, and computer games (see also Noda 1990). This concern was further advanced in a book on Japanese global commodities entitled *Sekai shōhin no tsukurikata: Nihon media ga sekai o seishita hi* (The making of global commodities: The day Japanese media conquered the world). The main purpose of the book was to reconsider Japanese culture in terms of its influence in the world: "It is a historical rule that an economically powerful nation produces in its heyday global popular culture whose influences match its economic power. Such was the case with the British Empire, Imperial France, Weimar Germany and the United States of the 1950s and 1960s. What, then, has Japan of the 1980s produced for the world? Has Japan produced anything that is consumed globally and influences the lifestyle of world consumers?" (Akurosu Henshūshitsu 1995, 6). Consumer technologies, particularly the Walkman, have long been regarded as representative of Japanese global cultural commodities. The editors of the above volume remark that they originally coined the term *global commodities* in 1988 in order to articulate the phenomenal global popularity of the Walkman, but that there has been a proliferation of Japanese global commodities since then (Akurosu Henshūshitsu 1995, 6–8). Made-in-Japan global commodities discussed in the book include not only Japanese hardware commodities such as the Walkman, instant cameras, or VCRs, but also "software" cultural products such as animation and computer games, and that even the system of producing pop idols, a process that has been predominantly exported to Asia, has come more into the foreground.[3]

Euphoria concerning the global dissemination of animation and computer games prompted Japanese commentators to confer a specific Japanese "fragrance" on these cultural products. The emergence of obsessively devoted fans of Japanese animation in both Europe and the United States whose craze for Japanese animation makes them wish they had been born in Japan has been often covered by the Japanese media. Many images of Western fans playing at being would-be Japanese animation characters, wearing the same costumes and make-up, have been presented in popular Japanese magazines as evidence of the "Japanization" of the West (e.g., Nihonbunka kosupure Amerika yushutsu 1996; Amerika nimo otaku ga daihassei 1996; Furansu de kosupure kontesuto 1997; Otaku no sekai kara mejā e 1997).[4] Okada Toshio, the most eloquent spokesperson for the global popularity of

Japanese animation and computer games, further argues that Japanese animated culture and imagery has come to evoke, to a certain degree, a sense of Western yearning for "Japan" (1996, 52–56; see also Eikoku ga mitometa Nihonbunka 1996, 30–31). Comparing the passionate Western consumption of Japanese animation to Japan's and his own yearning, via the consumption of American popular culture, for "America,"—the nation of freedom, science, and democracy—Okada (1995, 43) proudly argues that to those Western fans, Japan "looks a more cool country" than the United States. More recently, the Pokémon phenomenon has provoked an increasing Japanese interest in associating its global appeal with Japanese symbolic power. Japanese scholars have observed that, increasingly, American children who love Pokémon believe Japan must be a cool nation if it is capable of producing such wonderful characters, imaginaries, and commodities (Kamo 2000; Sakurai 2000).

Is the world being "Japanized"?

It remains a contentious issue, however, what power status (image of power) the global spread of Japanese animations and computer games may have granted to Japan. How do these products evoke a distinctively Japanese way of life to consumers and audiences? The cultural presence of a foreign country is often interpreted as a threat to national identity and/or to the national interest, or as a sign of the foreign country's status as an object of yearning in the recipient country. In either case, it marks the foreign country's cultural power. Here, the notion of Americanization and cultural imperialism has long informed discussion of the cultural imposition of a dominant country over others. As Said (1994, 387) argues, "Rarely before in human history has there been so massive an intervention of force and ideas from one culture to another as there is today from America to the rest of the world." The unprecedented global reach of American power is all-inclusive, a complex of political, economic, military, and cultural hegemony. In the Cold War era, it is well known that the United States strategically disseminated an American model of a modern, affluent, open, and democratic society to win the ideological battle against the Communist bloc. Mass media and consumer culture were the major vehicles of "Americanization."

American political scientist Joseph Nye (1990, 188) argues that a significant factor that confers on the United States a global hegemony is its "soft co-optic power," that is, the power of "getting others to want what you want" through symbolic power resources such as media and consumer culture: "If [a dominant country's] culture and ideology are attractive, others will more willingly follow" (32). In contrast, Nye contends that Japan is a one-dimensional economic power and its consumer commodities, no matter how globally disseminated, still lack an associated "appeal to a broader set of values" (194)—and thus are culturally odorless.

This is not simply due to the fact that since the end of World War II, Japan has had no manifest policy of political, military, or ideological/cultural exertion of its transnational power. More importantly, what is implied here is that there is an inherent difficulty in comparing the advent of Japanese animations or computer games to an "Americanization" paradigm as suggested earlier. This is not to say that Japanese animation does not embody any specific cultural characteristics that originate in what we call "Japanese culture." American fans of Japanese animations are inescapably "dependent upon Japanese culture itself" (Newitz 1995, 12; Kamo 2000).[5] But to interpret the global success of Pokémon and other Japanese cultural products as the mirror image of the global process of "Americanization" is fallacious. Looking beneath the surface of these celebratory views of Western perceptions of the coolness of Japanese culture, we find a basic contradiction: the international spread of mukokuseki popular culture from Japan simultaneously articulates the universal appeal of Japanese cultural products and the disappearance of any perceptible "Japaneseness," which, as will be discussed later, is subtly incorporated into the "localization" strategies of the media industries. The cultural influence of Japanese animation and computer games in many parts of the world might be tremendous, but it tends to be an "invisible colonization" (Bosche 1997).[6]

One cultural critic, Ōtsuka Eiji (1993), thus warns against any euphoria concerning the global popularity of Japanese animation, arguing that it is simply the mukokuseki (the unembedded expression of race, ethnicity, and culture), the "odorless" nature of animation, that is responsible for its popularity in the world. Likewise, Ueno (1996b, 186) argues that "the 'Japaneseness' of Japanimation can only be recognized in its being actively a mukokuseki visual culture." If it is indeed the case that the Japaneseness of Japanese animation derives, consciously or unconsciously, from its erasure of physical signs of Japaneseness, is not the Japan that Western audiences are at long last coming to appreciate, and even yearn for, an animated, race-less and culture-less, virtual version of "Japan"?

It is one thing to observe that Pokémon texts, for example, are influencing children's play and behavior in many parts of the world and that these children perceive Japan as a cool nation because it creates cool cultural products such as Pokémon. However, it is quite another to say that this cultural influence and this perception of coolness is closely associated with a tangible, realistic appreciation of "Japanese" lifestyles or ideas. It can be argued that the yearning for another culture that is evoked through the consumption of cultural commodities is inevitably a monological illusion. This yearning tends to lack concern for and understanding of the socio-cultural complexity of that in which popular cultural artifacts are produced. This point is even more lucidly highlighted by the mukokuseki nature of Japanese animation and computer games.

As mentioned earlier, Japanese exports to other parts of Asia are not re-stricted to culturally odorless products but include popular music, TV dramas, and fashion magazines, in all of which textual appeal has much to do with visible "Japaneseness." Though Japan's cultural presence is thus differently but more clearly manifested in the region, the comparison of Japanese transnational cultural power in Asia to its American counterpart nevertheless raises serious doubts. In interpreting the popularity of Japanese popular culture in Asian regions, some Japanese conservative intellectuals argue that Japan has replaced the United States as an object of yearning (e.g., Morita and Ishihara 1989). However, this is refuted by the fact that it matters not that Japanese animations and TV programs are eagerly consumed. It is argued that a sense of yearning for Japan is still not aroused in Asia, because what is appreciated, unlike American popular culture, is still not an image or idea of Japan but simply a materialistic consumer commodity. A critical Japanese scholar of Asian Studies, for example, is unequivocal in his dismissal of the spread of Japanese consumer culture as a mere extension of the Japanese economy. He argues that "Japanese culture is not received in other Asian countries with the same sense of respect and yearning as American culture was received in postwar Japan" (Murai 1993, 26). Though the Asian popu-larity of Japanese animation, such as *Doraemon,* according to Murai, symbol-izes a convenient and enjoyable Japanese consumer culture, Japanese cultural influence is nevertheless much weaker than Japanese economic influence.

Similarly, in his introduction to an edited volume on the Japanization of Asia, Igarashi Akio gives a concise overview of the "Japanization" phenom-enon and then wonders whether the Japanese attention to the spread of Ja-pan's popular culture in Asia merely reflects "a simplistic nationalism among the Japanese, a surplus of self-consciousness," as there might actually be no distinctive Japanese cultural influence to be found in the "Japanization" phenomenon (Igarashi 1997, 15). While the notion of "Americanization" includes broad cultural and ideological influences, such as ideas of American democracy and the American way of life based upon affluent, middle-class material cultures, Igarashi argues that "Japanization" only embodies consumer culture and thus represents "more materialistic cultural dissemination" (6). A similar observation is made by a Singaporean scholar, Wee Wan-ling (1997). He warns us not to confuse the presence of Japanese consumer commodities, animation, and popular music in Singapore with a "Japanization" signifying a substantial influence on ideas. Congruent with the view regarding Japanese imperialism's cultural power over other Asians as derivative, this argument expresses a difficulty in seeing specifically "Japanese" influence in the spread of Japanese popular and consumer culture in other parts of Asia. What is experienced through Japanese popular culture is actually a highly materialistic Japanese version of the American "original."

Global cultural power reconsidered: Decentered transnational alliances

Certainly, any attempt to interpret the increase in the export of Japanese popular culture in terms of an "Americanization" paradigm would misjudge the nature of Japanese cultural power in the world. There is apparently a different logic of global cultural influence operating here. However, I would argue, it is possible and perhaps productive to take the awkwardness denoted by the notion of "Japanization" as an opportunity to reconsider the meaning of transnational cultural power which has long been understood in terms of "Americanization," and to appreciate the precarious nature of transnational cultural consumption (Appadurai 1996; Howes 1996), rather than to dismiss the pervasiveness of Japanese influence. The rise of Japanese cultural export can, I suggest, be read as a symptom of the shifting nature of transnational cultural power in a context in which intensified global cultural flows have decentered the power structure *and* vitalized local practices of appropriation and consumption of foreign cultural products and meanings. In this sense, it does not seem entirely contingent that the manifestation of Japanese cultural power has occurred in the last decade. This is a period during which the historical process of globalization, as defined by Hall

(1995), has been accelerated by several interconnected factors. These include the global integration of markets and capital by powerful transnational corporations; the development of communication technologies which easily and simultaneously connect all over the globe; the emergence of an affluent middle class in non-Western countries, especially in Asia; and the increasing number of people moving from one place to another by migration and tourism. Theoretical reformulation has become imperative in order to cope with these globalizing forces that make transnational cultural flow much more disjunctive, non-isomorphic, and complex than what the center-periphery paradigm allows us to understand (Appadurai 1990).

The expansive force of globalization, the transmission of cultural forms from the dominant to the rest via communication technologies and transportation systems, has brought about a "time-space compression" (Harvey 1989), or the shrinking of the distance between one place and another. As the merger and cooperation of transnational corporations of different countries of origin intensifies, various markets are increasingly integrated and interrelated. This, together with the development of communication technologies, leads to an increasing simultaneity in the cultural flow of information, images, and commodities emanating from a handful of powerful nations, including Japan, to urban spaces across the globe. The speed and quantity of the global distribution of cultural commodities has been rapidly accelerating. The recent simultaneous popularity, and quick decline, of Spice Girls and Tamagotchi (a tiny digital pet) in many parts of the world testify to this trend. Under these developments, discourse on globalization has tended to facilitate myths of global coherence (Ferguson 1992) by its evocation of global synchronization or a utopian view of world unity, in the same way that Macluhan's famous term *global village* connotes a sense of bonding, togetherness, and immediacy.

However, media globalization does not simply promote the global reach of Western media and commodities. It also facilitates "the de-centering of capitalism from the West" (Tomlinson 1997, 140–43) through increasing integration, networking, and cooperation among worldwide transnational media industries, including non-Western ones. For transnational corporations to enter simultaneously those global, supranational, regional, national, and local markets, the imperatives are the establishment of a business tie-up with others at each level—whether in the form of a buyout or collaboration—along with the selection of new cultural products that will have an international appeal.

It is thus important to place the significance of Japanese inroads into Hollywood, as well as the international popularity of Japanese animation and computer games, within a wider picture of transnational media and market interconnections as well. The rise of Japanese media industries articulates a new phase of global cultural flow dominated by a small number of transnational corporations (Aksoy and Robins 1992). These moves testify to the increasing trend of global media mergers which aim to offer a "total cultural package" of various media products under a single media conglomerate (Schiller 1991).[7] After all, the reason Sony and Matsushita bought into Hollywood was not to dominate American minds, but rather to centralize product distribution. The purpose was to construct a total entertainment conglomerate through the acquisition of control over both audiovisual hardware and software. It was based upon the sober economic judgment that "it is cultural distribution, not cultural production, that is the key locus of power and profit" (Garnham 1990, 161–62). The incursion can be seen as a confirmation of the supremacy of American software creativity and therefore of Japan's second-rate ability as a software producer. Japanese trading companies such as Sumitomo and Itochu also invested in American media giants (e.g., Sumitomo–TCI or Itochu–Time Warner). This suggests that Japanese cultural influence and presence in the world is still overshadowed by its economic power (Herman and McChesney 1998, 104). Seen this way, the purpose of the Japanese takeover was not to kill the American soul; on the contrary, it was to make Hollywood omnipresent. Japanese ingenuity in hardware production and American genius in software go hand in hand because (Japanese) consumer technologies work as "distribution systems" for (American) entertainment products (Berland 1992, 46). These Japanese companies strengthen American cultural hegemony by investing in the production of Hollywood films and by facilitating their distribution all over the globe.

Conversely, finding a local partner is particularly important in facilitating the entry of non-Western media industries and cultural products into Western markets. Morley and Robins (1995, 13) point out three strategic patterns of activities for global media corporations: producing cultural products; distributing products; and owning hardware that delivers products. Penetration of transnational media industries into multiple markets needs the combination of at least two of the above three, particularly production and distribution, both of which are dominated by American industries. If Sony's encroachment on Hollywood articulates Japanese exploitation of

American software products in order to become a global media player, media globalization also promotes the incorporation of Japanese, and other non-Western, media products into the Western-dominated global distribution network. Japanese media industries and cultural products cannot successfully become transnational players without partners. The most serious shortcoming of the Japanese animation industry, despite mature production capabilities and techniques, is its lack of international distribution channels. Western (American) global distribution power is thus indispensable to make Japanese animation a part of global popular culture. The process can be called an "Americanization of Japanization." For example, it was the investment and the distribution channels of a British and American company, Manga Entertainment (established in 1991 and part of the Polygram conglomerate) that made *The Ghost in the Shell* a hit in Western countries. Similarly, in 1995, Disney decided to globally distribute Miyazaki Hayao's animated films. Miyazaki gained prestige from Disney's decision, which helped turn his animated *Mononokehime* into a phenomenal hit in Japan in 1997. As the producer of the film acknowledged, the fact that Hayao's animations are highly appreciated by the global animation giant, Disney, worked well as the publicity for giving the film an international prominence (Mononokehime, datsu Miyazaki anime de 100 okuen 1998).[8]

The global success of Pokémon also has much to do with America's intervening partnership. Most manifestly, Warner Bros., one of the major Hollywood studios, handled the global distribution of *Pokémon: The First Movie,* as well as televising Pokémon on its own U.S.-wide channel. No less significant is how Pokémon has been localized, or Americanized, "to hide its 'Japaneseness'" (Invasion of the Pocket Monsters 1999, 68–69) as part of a global promotion strategy. Significantly, it is the remade-in-the-U.S. version of Pokémon that has been exported to other parts of the world (except Asia). Thus, the successful marketing of Pokémon as a global character owes much to American intervention (handled by Nintendo of America), which testifies to another "Americanization of Japanization." Japanese animation's inroads into the global market articulate the ever-growing global integration of markets and media. The examples discussed above clearly show that the Japanese animation industry is becoming a global player only by relying on the power of Western media.[9]

Global–local complexity: From cultural imperialism to globalization

Decentered processes of cultural globalization have also accompanied a significant theoretical shift—the questioning of the "cultural imperialism" thesis—in studies of asymmetrical transnational cultural flows in the last decade. The cultural imperialism thesis emphasizes the unidirectional flow of culture from the dominant (in most cases equated with the United States) to the dominated. It argues that American popular culture, combined with economic and political hegemony, is disseminated all over the globe, instilling American consumerist values and ideologies. The cultural imperialism thesis, as mentioned earlier, tends to describe the relationship between the West (America) and the Rest as one of unambiguous cultural domination and exploitation (e.g., Hamelink 1983; Mattelart, Delcourt, and Mattelart 1984; Schiller 1969, 1976, 1991). But the thesis neglects analysis of empirical evidence of audience reception in subordinate cultures, and that is particularly problematic. In considering the global cultural flow and foreign cultural influence in a particular region, "cultural domination" is in many cases a discursive construct rather than the reflection of the subordinate people's actual experience. This is what Tomlinson (1991) convincingly discusses in his book on cultural imperialism and what other excellent studies on the discourse of "Americanization" also demonstrate (e.g., Kuisel 1993). The cultural imperialism thesis bases its argument of domination on a political economy approach and does not pay adequate attention to whether, and how, audiences are culturally dominated through the act of consuming media texts from the center. The thesis explicitly or implicitly sees audiences as passive "cultural dupes" who, apparently without a critical cultural lens, automatically absorb any messages and ideologies from the dominant center. However, such a simplifying view of cultural exchange has been refuted by many ethnographic studies which show that audiences actively and creatively consume media texts and cultural products (e.g., Morley 1980, 1992; Radway 1984; Ang 1985).

Perspectives of globalization, in reconsidering the nature of transnational cultural unevenness highlighted by cultural imperialism discourses, instead stress that what is occurring is not simply homogenization through the global distribution of the same commodities, images, and capital from the Western (and Japanese to a lesser extent) metropolitan centers. Such dissemination also produces new cultural diversity (e.g., Hall 1991; Robins

1997). The term *transculturation* refers to this process of globalization, in which the asymmetrical encounter of various cultures results in the transformation of an existing cultural artifact and the creation of a new style. Mary Louise Pratt (1992, 6) states this succinctly when she writes, "While subjugated peoples cannot readily control what emanates from the dominant culture, they do determine to varying extents what they absorb into their own and what they use it for."

Although Pratt uses this concept to analyze colonial encounters in a "contact zone" through the reading of Western imperial travel writings, the concept of transculturation is helpful for us to understand that it is through engagement with West-dominated global cultural power that non-Western modernities articulate their specificity (Hall 1995). In contrast to the homogenization thesis, this view is concerned more with sites of local negotiation. It suggests that foreign goods and texts are creatively misused, recontexualized in local sites, differently interpreted according to local cultural meaning. Something new is produced in the unequal cultural encounter by mixing the foreign and the local (e.g., Hannerz 1992; Lull 1995; Ang 1996). The ascent of Japanese transnational cultural power should be considered in the context of this wider vista of theoretical paradigm shifts, which attempt to attend simultaneously to the homogenizing forces of globalization and to transformative local practices in the formation of non-Western indigenized modernity, so as to understand the question of transnational cultural power.

The shift from an emphasis on center–periphery relations to a diffusion of cultural power marks the relative decline of the main actor, the United States. It is often pointed out that, contrary to the logic of cultural imperialism, U.S. TV programs are not as popular as "local," or domestically produced, programs in many countries (e.g., Siji 1988; Lee 1991; Straubhaar 1991; Tomlinson 1991). The unambiguous American domination of global culture is also put into question by the rise of other global players such as Brazil (e.g., Sinclair 1992; Tomlinson 1997). Tunstall (1995, 16), the author of *The Media Are American* (1977), argues that American media are still influential but no longer dominant: "The United States is the only media superpower, but it is a media superpower in gradual decline against the world as a whole." Tunstall argues that American TV programs are becoming less popular in the world not because their quality is degrading but, rather, because there exists a process of local indigenization of original American TV formats, a point I will return to later.

This does not mean that the United States has lost its cultural hegemony. Even if the global popularity of American TV programs has declined, American cultural power is still articulated in the recognition that media and cultural forms which originate in America have been fully globalized (Morley and Robins 1995, 223–24). As Bell and Bell (1995, 131) argue, " 'America' has rather come to symbolize the very processes of social and cultural modernization themselves." Likewise, Yoshimi (1997), in his studies of the "Americanization" of Japan, argues, with a particular emphasis on Tokyo Disneyland, that "America" shifted from a symbol to an invisible system in the 1980s. While the American way of life has lost its manifest appeal in Japan, according to Yoshimi, the Japanese cultural scene has been saturated with the logic of American consumer capitalism. Baudrillard also declares that "America is the original version of modernity and Europe is the dubbed or subtitled version" (1988, 76). Although admitting that American hegemonic power is in decline, Baudrillard argues that the decline merely shows the changing nature of power: "It [America] has become the orbit of an imaginary power to which everyone now refers. From the point of view of competition, hegemony, and 'imperialism,' it has certainly lost ground, but from the exponential point of view, it has gained some" (107). According to Baudrillard, American power has entered a new stage of "hysteresis," which is "the process whereby something continues to develop by inertia, whereby an effect persists even when its cause has disappeared" (115). America is now ubiquitous as the unmarked model for (post)modern culture.

It is an open question if this transformation of the nature of America's global cultural influence is the pinnacle of Americanization or the demise of Americanization. Smart (1993) criticizes Baudrillard by arguing that an exclusive comparison between Europe and America leads to a failure to realize the limits and decline of all-powerful Western/American modernity. Baudrillard is, deliberately or not, "indifferent to the possibility that America may no longer be the model for business, performance, and international style, no longer the 'uncontested and uncontestable' model of modernity" (Smart 1993, 66). While Smart emphatically refers to Japan as an emerging model of postmodernity, the critical issue here is not the substitution or addition of new cultural centers but overcoming a nation-centric view of global cultural power. At the high point in the development of modernization theories, discussions of non-Western modernization either stressed divergence or convergence with the Western model. Or conversely, Western countries were thought to follow the Japanese modernization model as a process of reverse-convergence (Dore 1973; see also Mouer and Sugimoto 1986). However, the late twentieth century is marked by the fact that there is no absolute societal model to follow (Scott 1997).

The disappearance of an absolute center of global power is often interpreted as evidence that Americanization has not melted into air but into global capitalism. Spark (1996, 96–97) makes the point astutely, referring to the British context: "Americanization might better be considered as only the evidential characteristic of modern consumer capitalism, with the appellation 'American' referring only to the prime, originating characteristics of the model. In this sense, America is not acting to subordinate foreign cultures: the process is one of globalized modernization, and as the experience of the British with America reveals, it is reciprocal." Sklair (1995, 153) extends Spark's point further when he criticizes the view that media and cultural imperialism tend to be equated with "Americanization": "It implies that if American influence could be excluded, then cultural and media imperialism would end. This could only be true in a purely definitional sense. Americanization itself is a contingent form of a process that is necessary to global capitalism, the culture-ideology of consumerism."

Sklair's argument captures the fundamental force of globalization, that generated by the logic of the ever-expanding reach of capital, and few would disagree with this point (Tomlinson 1997, 139–40). However, this argument seems too sweeping a generalization of transnational cultural flows to capture the contradiction and ambivalence articulated in local practices. Hall is more sensitive to the decentralizing feature of global capitalism. He coins the term *global mass culture* to characterize the emerging global diffusion of media images. While acknowledging American and Western hegemony in this process, Hall points out that this is a "peculiar form of homogenization" which does not destroy but rather respects cultural differences in the globe: "[Global mass culture] is wanting to recognize and absorb those differences within the larger, overarching framework of what is essentially an American conception of the world." Capital does not try to obliterate differences but to "operate through them" (1991, 28). Unprecedented concentration of capital in transnational corporations has generated another feature of decentralization, where the recognition of cultural diversity and difference is increasingly exploited by transnational corporations.

Globalization as structuring differences

The theoretical shift from cultural imperialism to globalization thus goes together with a turn from the notion of a straightforward globally homogenizing cultural dominant toward the idea of an orchestrated heterogenization under the sign of globalizing forces; from an emphasis on content to an emphasis on the form of cultural products, which structure diversity and difference in the ever-increasing interconnection of the world (e.g., Wilk 1995; Hannerz 1996; Robins 1997). Globalization brings about, as Hannerz (1996, 102) put it, "an organization of diversity rather than a replication of uniformity," or a "repatriation of difference," which is produced by the local absorption and indigenization of homogenizing forces.

A dichotomous view of global–local would fail to acknowledge the complex, juxtaposed and fractured nature of cultural globalization. We should consider, instead, what Morley and Robins (1995, 116) call the "global–local nexus": "Whilst globalization may be the prevailing force of our times, this does not mean that localism is without significance. . . . Globalization is, in fact, also associated with new dynamics of *re*-localization. It is about the achievement of a new global–local nexus, about new and intricate relations between global space and local space" (emphasis in original). The conception of globalization as an organizing force of new diversity and particularity is also argued by Robertson (1992, 1995). He refers to globalization in terms of the form in which global interconnection is structured and a new kind of particularism is globally institutionalized (1995, 38). Robertson is cautious to distance his view from the "naive functionalist mode" of integration. He emphasizes that homogenization and heterogenization, like globalization and localization, are "complementary and interpenetrative" phenomena (40).

Newly articulated particularism or localism in the local negotiation with globalizing forces testifies to the spread of common forms in which difference and diversity can be claimed. In this sense, while the concept of "hybridity" that tries to deconstruct the essentialization of "original" has gained intellectual currency, it should not simply be read as a celebration of the creative practices of the dominated. It indicates that global homogenizing power is a constitutive and generative part of any local cultural practice (e.g., Hall 1991, 1992; García Canclini 1995; Lull 1995). Arguing that the hybridization perspective should shift our conception of culture from a territorial/static mode to one of a translocal/fluid movement, Pieterse (1995) defines globalization as an ongoing production of a "global mélange" through hybridization processes. He distinguishes structural hybridization, where the production of various hybrid forms is facilitated by "the increase in the available modes of organization" (50), and cultural hybridization, where such hybrid forms represent "new translocal cultural expressions" (64). The ever-increasing hybridization in these two processes actually testifies to "transcultural convergence," as Pieterse argues that "the very process of hybridization shows the difference to be relative and, with a slight shift of perspective, the relationship can also be described in terms of an affirmation of *similarity*" (60, emphasis in original).

Likewise, in discussing the discourse of Japanese cultural uniqueness in the wider context of globalization, Morris-Suzuki (1998b, 164) emphasizes the "formatting of difference," by which she means "the creation of a single underlying common framework or set of rules which is used to coordinate local subregimes" as a significant structuring force of globalization. Difference can be convincingly and successfully advocated precisely because of the diffusion of a common format. As I will discuss in detail in chapter 4, if it can be argued that the hegemony of the global cultural system is articulated in globally shared "forms" (Wilk 1995), the latter also promote the production of multiple, distinct indigenized modernities in the world. In sum, a convincing analysis of the unevenness of global interconnectedness should go beyond a global–local binary opposition. The operation of global cultural power can only be found in local practice, whereas cultural reworking and appropriation at the local level necessarily takes place within the matrix of global homogenizing forces.

The Japanese cultural presence under a global gaze

The decentralizing forces of globalization open the way for Japanese transnational cultural power to be seen in a different light from that of "Americanization." The increasing emphasis on the decentralization of global cultural power does not mean there are no longer dominant centers. The suppliers of transnational cultural products and "forms"—which make creative local hybridization possible—are still limited to a small number of centers. Cultural commodities and images are predominantly produced by a small number of wealthy countries, including Japan, and many parts of the world still cannot even afford to enjoy global cultural consumption (Sreberny-Mohammadi 1991). From an American point of view, the globalization process might testify to the decentralization and decline of

American/Western power. From a Japanese point of view, however, it represents a recentralization by means of which new globally powerful nations such as Japan have successfully repositioned themselves.

Nevertheless, it should be reiterated that this reconfiguration of transnational cultural power is occurring in the context in which uneven distribution and circulation of such cultural products are becoming more difficult to trace and the origins of images and commodities become increasingly insignificant and irrelevant. Ang (1996, 13) argues that there has been a significant shift in audience reception of TV texts in the postmodern age, in that audiences are expected to be active, not simply in theory but in their real-life situations, producing meaning out of multifarious media texts. Likewise, it can be argued that the local needs to be creative in articulating difference by indigenizing the global. With the proliferation and accelerated speed of globally circulated images and commodities, the local transculturation process has come to be a quotidian site where the local negotiates and appropriates the global rather than that of the unambiguous cultural domination by the center of the periphery (see Hannerz 1991; Miller 1992).

Although we cannot be too cautious in generalizing this picture on a global scale, gradually disappearing in this process is the perception, not the fact, of derivative modernity, the sense that "our" modernity is borrowed from a modernity that happened elsewhere (see Chatterjee 1986; Chakrabarty 1992). Ubiquitous modernity, in contrast, is based on a sense that "our" modernity is the one that is simultaneously happening everywhere. To put it differently, the Western gaze, which has long dominated the material and discursive construction of non-Western modernity, is now melting into a decentered global gaze. To use Lash and Urry's (1994, 29) words about the nature of current cultural power emanating from the core to the rest, "It is there, it is pervasive, but it is not the object of judgement—one does not assent to it or reject it." This might sound exaggerated. Needless to say, there are still clear-cut protests against American global cultural hegemony and strong anti-America sentiments in many parts of the world. Indeed, "America" still stands as a significant (hated) center. Nevertheless, at the least, the age of "Americanization," in which cross-cultural consumption was predominantly discussed in terms of the production of a sense of "yearning" for a way of life and ideas of a dominant country, seems to be over. Global cultural power does not disappear but is now highly dispersed.

It is the shift from a Western gaze to a decentered global gaze, manifested in the process of indigenizing modernity, that the new meaning of "Japanization" thrives on. Japanese cultural power has paradoxically become visible and conspicuous, as the absolute symbolic center no longer belongs to a particular country or region and transnational cultural power is deeply intermingled with local indigenizing processes. Transnationally circulated images and commodities, I would argue, tend to become culturally odorless in the sense that origins are subsumed by the local transculturation process. By appropriating, hybridizing, indigenizing, and consuming images and commodities of "foreign" origin in multiple unforeseeable ways, even American culture is conceived as "ours" in many places. McDonald's is so much a part of their own world that it no longer represents an American way of life to Japanese or Taiwanese young consumers (Watson 1997).

The multiplicity of indigenized modernities brought about by local creative practices has, for one thing, spotlighted the Japanese experience of transculturation as an exemplar to be followed by other non-Western countries. As mimesis has become associated less with second-hand cheapness and superficiality than with creativity and originality (Taussig 1993), the borrowed nature of Japanese cultural power has come to be seen as not totally groundless. Tunstall (1995) suggests, in arguing the relative decline of American media power in the world, that the Japanese mode of indigenization of American original media products can be seen as a pattern in the development of non-Western TV industries, which, he predicts, other non-Western countries such as China or India will follow. Local indigenization and consumption is, moreover, consciously incorporated into the global marketing strategy of Japanese transnational corporations, as is the case with Sony's articulate strategy of "global localization" (see Aksoy and Robins 1992; Barnet and Cavanagh 1994; du Gay et al. 1997). The Japanese capacity for indigenizing the foreign is reevaluated in globalization theories, and Toyotism has been replaced by Sonyism (Wark 1991). Sony's strategy of globalization has come to signify a new meaning of "Japanization." As Featherstone (1995, 9) argues, "If the term Japanization of the world means anything it is in terms of a market strategy built around the notion of *dochaku,* or "glocalism." The term refers to a global strategy which does not seek to impose a standard product or image, but instead is tailored to the demands of the local market. This has become a popular strategy for multinationals in other parts of the world who seek to join the rhetoric of localism."

I will argue in later chapters that the exclusive association of Japanization with glocalism looks tenuous and essentialist (see chapters 2 and 3). Suffice it to say here that Featherstone's observation is derived from the fact that the Japan-originated marketing strategy of "global localization"—or "glocalization"—has come to be credited as a leading formula for global corporations in the 1990s in place of "global standardization" (Robertson 1995). Profits brought about by cultural power are becoming articulated less in association with the symbolic and ideological domination by the powerful nation-state and more with local camouflaging which smoothes the economic expansion of transnational corporations.

Power reconfigured in the intraregional cultural flow

As suggested earlier, the ascent of Japanese transnational cultural power is most conspicuously illustrated in the specific cultural geography of East and Southeast Asia, as the export of Japanese popular culture to Asia includes a wide range of products such as Japanese TV dramas, pop idols, character goods, and fashion magazines, most of which have rarely found receptive consumers in the West. Although the wide range of Sony's transnational activity can be called "global" and the strategy of "global localization" is deployed in multiple locales in the world, the application of the strategy to the production of popular music and TV programs is clearly limited to the Asian region. Even animations, which are well received in the West, are more eagerly consumed in Asia, and some animations and comics are only exported to Asia (e.g., Ono 1992, 1998; Kawatake 1995). East and Southeast Asian markets were at the receiving end of almost half of the total number of Japanese TV program exports in 1995 (Japanese Ministry 1997). These facts suggest that a Japanese mode of indigenized cultural modernity embodied in popular cultural production is not simply the model for a localizing strategy. Japanese cultural products themselves have come to hold a certain symbolic appeal to other Asian nations—which can be conceived neither as merely "odorless," nor as nonderivative of American cultural power, nor as comparable to the Americanization paradigm—in the context of the proliferation of non-Western indigenized modernities, which we need to examine with a different analytical tool.

The specificity of the spread and consumption of Japanese popular and consumer culture in Asia reminds us of one important caveat: unsubstantiated use of the two-relational concepts "global" and "local" as empty categories would risk overexaggerating the reach and the impact of transnational cultural flows (Ferguson 1992; Chua 1998). It would underestimate "the historical and cultural situatedness of spaces traversed by [disjunctive cultural] flows" (Ang and Stratton 1996, 28). Even if it has become a common view that globalization processes are too chaotic, decentralizing, and disjunctive to be explained by a center–periphery model (e.g., Lash and Urry 1994; Appadurai 1996), as Ang and Stratton (1996) argue, we should not assume that such flows totally replace the old power relations, as the current cultural flows are always already overdetermined by the power relations and geopolitics embedded in the history of imperialism and colonialism. While, together with the dissolution of the cultural and economic imperialism perspective, fifty years would seem long enough for former colonies, South Korea and Taiwan, to become more tolerant toward, if not to forget, the legacy of Japanese imperialism,[10] this does not mean that Japanese cultural power has altogether vanished. Focusing on supra–national regional flows presents a productive way to analyze how globalization re-inscribes Japanese transnational cultural power in a new configuration of more complex, multiple and intersecting power relations in Asia.

The concentration of Japanese cultural export in East and Southeast Asian regions testifies to another facet of the decentralizing globalization process, in which local practices increasingly acquire another importance: the relative decline of American cultural power has brought about the capitalization of intraregional cultural flows, with the emergence of regional media and cultural centers such as Brazil, Egypt, Hong Kong, and Japan (e.g., Straubhaar 1991; Sinclair, Jacka, and Cunningham 1996b; Lii 1998). Given the limited reverse cultural flow from these non–Western semicenters to Western metropoles, the rise of non–Western economic power and its transnational corporations in the global arena has not seriously challenged the Western-dominated "power geometry" (Massey 1991). Nevertheless, the analysis of intraregional cultural flows would highlight alternative patterns of transnationalization of media and popular culture, compared to the sweeping view which equates globalization with Americanization, by turning our attention to another significant facet of "locality"—the transnational appeal of a non–Western mode of indigenized modernity for culturally and/or geographically contiguous nations.

Of particular concern for this book is the question of how transnational cultural power is embedded in the perception of cultural distance, which is in a state of flux under globalization processes. Complexity articulated in the intensification of intraregional cultural flows is closely related with the ambiguity of the meaning of cultural intimacy and distance associated with "locality," in which audiences are thought to find pleasure through the consumption of cultural products from supposedly culturally similar nations (Straubhaar 1991; Sinclair, Jacka, and Cunningham 1996a). The reservation about claims for Japanese cultural power in Asia occurs not simply because Japanese cultural products are supposed to lack the signification of substantially Japanese ideas and lifestyles or because of a lingering, unambiguous, Western cultural hegemony. Japanese cultural power in Asia, I suggest, also tends to slip into a seemingly power-free perception of cultural similarity and local intimacy which is derived from the narrower temporal and spatial distance perceived among East and Southeast Asian countries than is the case with the latter's relation to the West.

However, it should be stressed that the sense of "cultural proximity" (Straubhaar 1991) is never a given attribute equally embodied in cultural products in a specific region and experienced by various strata of people. Rather, the production of locality (see Appadurai 1996, 178–99) itself is to be considered as a site at which a regional cultural power is articulated. The perception of cultural distance among non-Western nations has tended to be swayed by their relative temporal proximity to Western modernity, the standard by which the developmental ranking of the non-West has been determined (see Fabian 1983). As an apt illustration, such a developmental yardstick was earlier exploited by Japanese imperialist ideology to confirm Japan's superiority to other racially and culturally "similar" Asian nations and justify the Japanese mission to civilize Asia (e.g., Duus 1995; Oguma 1995).

The recent spread of Japanese popular culture in other Asian nations in turn suggests a possibility that the diminishing temporal lag between them (re)activates the sense of spatial affiliation in the region. A certain degree of economic growth might have brought about commonalities underlying the formation of modern Asian cultures. However, as the increase in Japanese export of media and cultural products shows, it also produces the asymmetry in which the Japanese mode of indigenized cultural modernity embodied in popular cultural forms becomes more appealing in other parts of Asia. As I will show in chapters 4 and 5, the different ways in which Taiwanese and Japanese perceive cultural and temporal distance in consuming other Asian cultural products—one marked by a sense of coevality, the other by a sense of nostalgia—demonstrate that unequal cultural power relations are deeply inscribed in one's spatial-temporal experience of "familiar difference" in the popular cultural products of cultural neighbors. While the consumption of Japanese popular culture in other Asian nations might not produce the same kind of a sense of yearning for Japan as does (or did) its American counterpart, Japan's relatively dominant position in intra-Asian cultural flows is noted in the fact that Asian consumption of Japanese popular culture generates a positive sense of cultural immediacy.

Although offering stimulating new insights into the investigation of de-centered global cultural power relations, intraregional cultural interaction is an underexplored area in the study of cultural globalization. In recent years, theories of modernity and modernization have been criticized for their Eurocentric perspective. Now that many non-Western countries have achieved a certain degree of modernization, it has been fully, though belatedly, recognized that spatial differences were unjustifiably subsumed by the developmental temporality of Western modernity and that equal emphasis should be placed on space so that academics engage seriously with plural modernities, (e.g., Featherstone, Lash, and Robertson 1995). Although globalization perspectives surely complicate the straightforward argument for the homogenization of the world based on Western modernity, the arguments for transculturation, heterogenization, hybridization, and creolization still tend not to transcend the West–Rest paradigm. Global–local interactions are predominantly studied in terms of how the Rest resists, imitates, or appropriates the West. There have been fascinating analyses of (non-Western) local consumption of Western media texts (e.g., see Miller 1992, 1995), which go beyond a dichotomized perspective of the global and the local and explore how non-Western countries "rework modernities" (Ong 1996, 64). Nevertheless, even in these examples, "global" still tends to be associated exclusively with the West.

Likewise, the rise of non-Western cultural centers of power such as Japan and Brazil often has been pointed out to refute a straightforward view of Western cultural domination and to support an argument for decentralized Western cultural hegemony (e.g., Morley and Robins 1995; Barker 1997; Tomlinson 1997). However, how such emerging non-Western semicenters exert cultural power through their dynamic interaction with other non-Western modernities has been seriously under-explored. The following chapters aim to take a further step in the analysis of decentered global cultural power relations by exploring from a Japanese perspective the dynamic and asymmetrical relations between Asian modernities.

2

Trans/nationalism: Discourses on

Japan in the global cultural flow

It has become commonplace to argue that national identity is never naturally given but is rather discursively constructed, invented, and imagined, a conception that has been developed out of excellent studies of the origin of national identity or nationalism (e.g., Hobsbawm and Ranger 1983; Anderson 1983). It is argued that the precariousness of national identity is becoming more visible and conspicuous as a result of globalization processes which have interconnected the world in multiple, contradictory, and disjunctive ways (e.g., Hall 1992).

The concept of "hybridity," developed in postcolonial theories, brings to light the doubleness and in-betweenness of national/cultural identity formation. Hybridity usefully counters exclusivist notions of imagined community, as well as the essentialism and "ethnic absolutism" involved in ideas of cultural "purity" and "authenticity." It creates "the 'third space' which enables other positions to emerge. . . . It displaces the histories that constitute it, and sets up new structures of authority, new political initiatives, which are inadequately understood through received wisdom" (Bhabha 1990, 211). The concept fruitfully displaces our conception of clearly demarcated national/cultural boundaries, which have been based upon a binary opposition between "us" and "them," "the West" and "the Rest," and the colonizer and the colonized, with a postcolonial perspective which "oblige(s) us to re-read the binaries as forms of transculturation, of cultural translation, destined to trouble the here/there cultural binaries forever" (Hall 1996a, 247).[1]

In the study of transnational cultural flows, the concepts of hybridity and hybridization, together with others such as creolization (Hannerz 1991) and indigenization (Appadurai 1996), also articulate the dynamic, ongoing, uneven but creative process of cultural interconnection, transgression, appropriation, reworking and cross-fertilization.[2] The accelerating flow of media images and people all over the globe not only generates the multiplicity of differences within a nation but also highlights the porousness of any apparently bounded cultural entity. As Hannerz (1996, 18) argues, "That image of a cultural mosaic, where each culture would have been a territorial entity with clear, sharp, enduring edges, never really corresponded with realities" (see also Gupta and Ferguson 1992; Buell 1994).

More recently, as discussed in the introduction, the term *transnationalism* has come to be commonly used to describe such a situation facilitated by globalization processes, "a condition by which people, commodities, and ideas literally cross—transgress—national boundaries and are not identified with a single place of origin" (Watson 1997, 11). As exemplified by the analysis of cultural politics concerned with diasporas, the notion of transnationalism draws attention to the ways in which the intensifying scale and speed of the transnational flows of people, capital, and media has disregarded, though not entirely, the efficacy of clearly demarcated national boundaries and identities, from below as well as from above. It highlights new modes of unevenness, connection, and imagination crisscrossing the world that we need to come to terms with (e.g., Smith and Guarnizo 1998; Grewal, Gupta, and Ong 1999).

However, this does not mean that the "national" has become insignificant. On the contrary, its persisting significance is newly articulated precisely through transnational movements (Smith 2001). This chapter discusses this dynamic in the Japanese context by attending to how the discussion of cultural hybridization and transnational cultural flows has been generated by and has even fuelled a strong nationalist impulse of claiming a distinct and superior "Japaneseness." I will critically examine this set of reactionary discourses, what I call *trans/nationalism*, which has desperately tried to contain the emergent state of transnationality within the national framework and thinking in contemporary Japan. After giving an overview of the historical evolution and transformation of Japanese and Western (English-language) discourse in terms of its capacity for cultural hybridization before and after the collapse of the Japanese empire, I will discuss how that language became assertively extroverted again in the 1990s in tandem with the growing narcissistic urge to (re)claim Japanese cultural prominence through the spread of Japanese popular culture to other parts of Asia. Previously, I have discussed the emergence of self-congratulating views of the worldwide consumption of Japanese "odorless" cultural forms, or muko-kuseki (in the sense of the disappearance or erasure of obvious national/

cultural characteristics), such as animation and computer games. A form of trans/nationalism has differently manifested itself with regard to the favorable reception of Japanese popular culture in East and Southeast Asia since the 1990s. It is strongly overdetermined by Japan's imperialist history and intertwined with its postcolonial desire for "Asia." The nationalist discourse in this case disregards the complexity inherent in transnational cultural flows and consumption by claiming a likable modern "Japaneseness" in mukoku-seki cultural forms (this time, in the sense of "culturally hybridized" forms set against "traditional" ones). Here, the transnationalization of Japanese popular culture has not simply regenerated a conception of Japan's leading position in Asia, it is also conveniently regarded as helping Japan suppress and overcome its historically constituted, problematic, and uneven relationship with other Asian nations. In sum, the transnational intersects with the postcolonial under the influence of the media globalization process.

Imagining Japan as a hybrid nation

In the course of Japan's modern history, in which West-centric transnational and cross-cultural encounters, conflicts, and connections have been accelerated at various levels, a particular self-image of the Japanese national essence has been developed so as to construct a modern national identity in the face of Western domination. Japan is said to be a vociferously assimilating cultural entity: The Japanese modern experience is described in terms of appropriation, domestication, and indigenization of the foreign (predominantly associated with the West) in a way that reinforces an exclusivist notion of Japanese national/cultural identity. It is in this sense that I argue that the Japanese capacity for cultural borrowing and appropriation does not simply articulate a process of hybridization in practice, but it is strategically represented as a key feature of Japanese national identity itself. This mode of self-representation, which I am calling "strategic hybridism," is a principal form of Japan's trans/nationalism discourses. Friedman (1994, 209) argues that, "The establishment and maintenance of creole identity are a social act rather than a cultural fact." Japanese hybridism aims to discursively construct an image of an organic cultural entity, "Japan," that absorbs foreign cultures without changing its national/cultural core. As Yoshimoto (1994, 196) suggests, the problematic of hybridism arises from the nationalistic reconciliation of two "contradictory principles of cultural production—obsession with native uniqueness and the indifference of origins." Foreign origin is supposed to be purged by the Japanese tradition of cultural indigenization. Japan's hybridism strategically attempts to suppress ambivalence generated by the act of cross-fertilization, relentlessly linking the issue of cultural contamination with an exclusivist national identity, so that impurity sustains purity.

Hybridism thus essentializes hybridity and hybridization as an organic and ahistorical aspect of Japanese national/cultural identity. Hybridism is based upon the concentric assimilation of culture, while hybridity emphasizes the incommensurability of cultural difference. Hybridism assumes that anything foreign can be domesticated into the familiar, whereas hybridity assumes an "awareness of the untranslatable bit that lingers on in translation" (Papastergiadis 1995, 18). Hybridity thus destabilizes the very notion of identity, whereas hybridism does not create such a liminal space in which fixed and exclusive national/cultural boundaries can be blurred. Rather, it reinforces the rigidity of these boundaries. Hybridism might be called a fluid essentialism. The snare of a static essentialism is to imagine a "pure, internally homogeneous, authentic, indigenous culture, which then becomes subverted or corrupted by foreign influences" (Morley 1996, 330). In a fluid essentialism, by contrast, identity is represented as a sponge that is constantly absorbing foreign cultures without changing its essence and wholeness.

The manner in which Japan's cultural encounters and indigenization of the foreign (the West) is talked about changes according to the historical context. Within Japan, assimilation of foreign cultures has not always been viewed positively. It has also precipitated relatively negative, self-defensive, or ironical discourses on cultural borrowing. Since the mid–nineteenth century, the threat of colonization by the West has forced Japanese leaders to try hard to emulate Western modernity. Rapid and selective Westernization was at one time official policy (Westney 1987). At the same time, in the face of apparent Western domination, the search for, and claim of, an "uncontaminated" Japanese essence became an imperative for the construction of a Japanese national/cultural identity. Westernization had to be balanced by Japanization. The slogan, *"wakon yōsai"* (Japanese spirit, Western technologies)—a modified version of the mid–nineteenth-century *"wakon kansai"* (Japanese spirit, Chinese technique) which articulated Japan's cultural indebtedness to China—was a manifestation of this need (Kawamura 1982; Wilkinson 1991). The search for a national "essence" in the sphere of race, culture, and language has been a recurrent theme in modern Japanese history (Minami 1994). Indeed, indigenous discussion of Japanese culture is notorious for an obsessive claim of racial/ethnic purity and homogeneity (e.g., Dower 1986; Yoshino 1992; Mouer and Sugimoto 1986; Iwabuchi 1994). Thus, the search for, and construction of, a pure "Japaneseness" has gone hand in hand with the acceptance of significant Western influence.

During the twentieth century, however, a defensive view of cultural borrowing and an associated discourse on Japanese racial purity and superiority have been juxtaposed with a more confident and aggressive one, particularly as Japan became an imperial power in the early part of the century (Oguma 1995). The Japanese capacity for assimilation (*dōka*) of the foreign without changing the Japanese essence has been promoted and characterized as a great quality of Japaneseness which justified Japanese colonial rule of other Asian nations. Numerous prominent scholars and political leaders such as Shiratori Kokichi or Gotō Shinpei have maintained that this capacity is not only a characteristic of Japanese culture and civilization but is evidence of Japanese superiority to the West (see Oguma 1995; Kang 1996). An official statement of nationalist ideology, *Kokutai no Hongi* (Cardinal principles of the national entity of Japan), published and distributed to Japanese schools at all levels in 1937 as a teaching guide on the distinctiveness of the Japanese nation, demonstrates that the Japanese capacity for assimilating the foreign was clearly defined as a unique Japanese characteristic.

> Our present mission as a people is to build up a new Japanese culture by adopting and sublimating Western cultures with our national entity as the basis, and to contribute spontaneously to the advancement of world culture. Our nation early saw the introduction of Chinese and Indian cultures, and even succeeded in evolving original creations and developments. This was made possible, indeed, by the profound and boundless nature of our national entity; so that the mission of the people to whom it is bequeathed is truly great in its historical significance. (Hall 1946, 183)

It should be noted that the Japanese capacity for assimilation is discussed from the perspective of the racially mixed origins of the Japanese people as well as the history of importing foreign cultures in prewar Japan. This point is particularly important when we consider how the image of the Japanese fusion of East and West was firmly incorporated into Japanese imperial ideology, which regarded Japanese sovereignty over Asia as a national mission. In the first part of twentieth century, Japan, as a colonizing center, was concerned with the assimilation of non-Western (Asian) racial and cultural

Others into the empire, as well as with the management of the absorption of Western ideas, technologies, and culture. As Oguma (1995) shows in detail, there were competing arguments in prewar Japan, evoked by Western scientific discourse, about the racial origin of the Japanese. Some advocated Japanese racial purity, stressing the blood linkage of the nation to an uninterrupted Imperial family line (Morris-Suzuki 1998b, 88–90).[3] A no less powerful argument in prewar Japan emphasized the hybrid racial origin of Japanese: Japan was a nation formed by the mixture of Northern and Southern Asian races in ancient times, followed by a vast number of Chinese and Koreans, who settled in Japan from the late fourth century to the early eighth century and introduced the culture of the continent to the country (Oguma 1995; Morris-Suzuki 1998b, 90–95).

Discourse on the racially mixed origins of the Japanese was readily appropriated to justify Japanese colonial rule over other Asian nations; since Japan had long successfully assimilated foreign (Asian) races as well as their cultures, Japan was endowed with the capacity to harmoniously assimilate colonial subjects in Taiwan and Korea. Therefore, so the argument went, Japanese colonial rule and assimilation policy, unlike those of its Western counterparts, was not based on racism (see, e.g., Peattie 1984; Oguma 1995; Duus 1995; Morris-Suzuki 1998b). Needless to say, this ideology of Japanese racial hybridism sharply contradicted the reality of Japanese colonial rule and its harsh racial discrimination against Koreans and Taiwanese (Weiner 1994; Komagome 1996).[4]

Postwar twist to introverted symbolic hybridism

Affirmative self-evaluation of Japan's assimilation of the foreign continued after the end of World War II and on into the second half of the twentieth century. However, there was a fundamental difference between prewar and postwar Japan. After the war, Japan no longer had to consider racial and ethnic differences within the nation to claim Japanese uniqueness. Japan's defeat in World War II and its consequent occupation by the Allied Forces, led by the United States, allowed Japan to avoid seriously confronting the consequences of its own imperialism/colonialism. The postcolonial moment for Japan was articulated predominantly by its subordinate position to the United States: Japan was a victim, not an oppressor. While as an imperial/colonial power Japan had been forced to face seriously the cultural and ethnic difference within the empire of the prewar era, postwar Japan was free of this burden. It was allowed to forget its colonizing past and to become obsessed with claiming its racial purity and homogeneity through the binary opposition of two culturally organic entities, "Japan" and the "West." Through this collusive "othering," Japanese cultural uniqueness became exclusively associated with an homogenous Japanese nation (Iwabuchi 1994).

Thus, the loss of Japanese imperial power in Asia was accompanied by an introverted shift of emphasis in discourse on Japan's hybridity, from a discourse of racial/ethnic assimilation to one of symbolic/cultural mixing. Japan's hybridism changed from an outwardly directed state ideology of Japanese imperialism and colonialism to an inwardly oriented nationalistic discourse on Japanese cultural hybridity.

Prominent critical commentator Katō Shūichi's two essays on *zasshu bunka* (the hybridity of Japanese culture) (1979, 5–46), originally published in 1955, initiated the postwar discourse on Japanese cultural hybridity. Katō's main point was not to evoke nationalistic sentiment but to find a third way of seeing Japanese culture, that is, a way beyond the two extreme views of purity: a self-disparaging view of modernity as "pure" Westernization, or, alternatively, a nostalgic nationalistic turn to the concept of traditional "purity." Katō tried to affirm the hybrid formation of Japanese culture, which could be seen in everyday life as a counterargument to the ethnocentric discourse of an uncontaminated "authentic Japanese culture."

However, Katō's critique failed to discern the similarity of the two purities in terms of their nationalistic orientations. As Yoshimoto (1994, 196) argues, "To the extent that the impulse to modernize and Westernize Japan is inseparable from a strong nationalistic sentiment, what first appear to be two opposite manifestations of Japanese obsession with purity are only two different modes of Japanese nationalism." Recognizing the similarity between these two modes of nationalism exposes the flaw in Katō's claim of transcending Japanese "purity." Katō's failure to realize the common nationalistic orientation of the two views of purity in his argument for a Japanese hybrid culture seemed to testify that he somewhat shared with them an essentialist assumption of Japanese "national culture." Katō saw the Japanese way of actively adopting Western things and ideas as unique in comparison with other Asian countries, which he thought directly imported "the West." The comparison he made was not based on a rigorous analysis. Rather, on intuitive comparison of the outlook of Singapore and Kobe was convincing enough to make him conclude that Japanese culture is fundamentally and typically hybrid, because only Japan absorbs Western influence in a way that suits local contexts. While Katō suggested the impossibility of "purifying" Japanese hybrid culture in terms of either "authentic tradition" or "Western modernity," he did not radically deconstruct the essentialist assumption of "Japanese culture," so that in spite of his intent, his critique risks turning to another discursive purification of Japanese culture.

Historical context should also be taken into consideration in evaluating Katō's arguments. His articles were published in 1955 in two prestigious opinion magazines, *Shisō* and *Chūō Kōron*. This was just after the end of the postwar occupation and at the beginning of Japanese economic recovery. In this sense, his affirmation of Japanese hybridity (*zasshusei*) reflected the recovery of a confidence by the Japanese in their own culture (Minami 1994; Aoki 1990). The Japanese practice of indigenizing the foreign without changing its cultural core has continued to be a recurrent theme of Japanese scholarly investigation in postwar Japan (e.g., Maruyama 1961, 1991; Tsurumi 1972; Kozakai 1996). While these authors are not necessarily celebratory of Japanese cultural borrowing, it is above all in the decades after Japan attained the status of a leading economic power, particularly since the 1980s, that the positive image of assimilator has gained currency in Japan. This was the moment when the nationalist slogan of *kokusaika* (internationalization) became prevalent in Japan (Befu 1987; Yoshimoto 1989; Iwabuchi 1994). Japan's increasing engagement with foreign (predominantly Western) people and cultures enhanced the drive for embracing the Japanese skill of absorbing the West without losing the definite demarcation between "us" and "them." As Ivy argues, "The foreign—because of its very threat—must be transformed into a manageable sign of order" (1995, 3). The confrontation with cultural difference is subtly replaced by the pleasurable consumption of foreign cultures that are destined to be indigenized into Japanese soil. As Ivy succinctly describes it, "The image of Japan as the great assimilator arises to explain away any epistemological snags or historical confusion: Japan assimilates, if not immigrants and American automobiles, then everything else, retaining the traditional, immutable core of culture while incorporating the shiny trappings of (post)modernity in a dizzying round of production, accumulation, and consumption" (1).

In this context, the practice of cultural appropriation, or Japan's "genius for simulacra" (Buell 1994), has become a well-accepted feature of the prosperous Japanese nation; so much so that many people in Japan now hold the view that the capacity for absorption and indigenization of foreign cultures is uniquely Japanese. In his study on the consumption of Nihon-jinron (essentialist discourses on Japanese uniqueness), Yoshino (1992, 114) found that almost half of his seventy-one respondents agreed with the view that "the active receptivity of the Japanese towards foreign cultures, as well as their ability to blend them with Japanese culture to create a distinctive form of culture, (is) [another] example of Japanese uniqueness."

Even at Tokyo Disneyland, we find this familiar narrative of Japan's long history of cultural appropriation. As Brannen (1992) discussed in detail, an exhibition called "Meet the World," an original Japanese attraction at Tokyo Disneyland, teaches Japan's history in terms of Japan's encounter with Others and the way Japan has successfully indigenized foreign cultures to create a unique culture out of foreign input. The attraction confidently tells visitors that even before encountering the West, Japan had a long history of cultural borrowing from China, as mentioned earlier. Japan's long tradition of cultural indigenization is celebrated as the secret of Japan's prosperity and as the core of Japan's national sense of Self.

Japan as a champion of globalization

In the same postwar period, the spectacle of Japan's domestication of foreign culture, particularly the way that Japan has successfully purged the impurity of foreign contamination in the process of cultural indigenization and thus maintained rigidly demarcated boundaries between Japan and the West, has become an object of intrigue and analysis in the Western academy . It is my contention that Western (critical) analyses of Japan's domestication of the West have merely perpetuated notions of Japan as a great assimilator. West-ern discourses have colluded in lifting Japanese strategic hybridism to the level of a recognized national essence. This is not to underestimate the strong impetus to cultural hybridization in modern Japan. Rather, I would argue that the unquestioning acceptance of the efficacy of Japan's skilful boundary-making in opposition to the foreign, whether under the name of domestication, indigenization or self/counter-Orientalism, tends to result in an essentialist celebration of the object of analysis and in conceiving of "Japan" as a porous yet stable, unchanging entity. Thomas criticizes Bhabha's concept of hybridity for its strange denial of the autonomy of the colonized, which tends to reify "a general structure of colonial dominance" by seeing resistance and subversiveness themselves as "deeply conditioned by it [colonial enunciation]" and "expressed on the ground defined by the oppressor" (Thomas 1994, 56–57; see also Parry 1987, 1994). Conversely, the prevailing analysis of Japan's hybridism should be criticized for too much emphasis on intentional counter-Western-domination enunciation and for the apparent success of nationalist strategies of "decontamination."[5]

As a non-Western society that has achieved a degree of modernization comparable to or higher than the West, Japan appears to be an extreme example of successful domestication of the West. It therefore is seen as subverting the very assumption of a Western Orientalism. Japan-meets-the-West becomes the theme, under the aegis of which all questions tend to revolve around whether Japan "domesticates" the West or is "colonized" by the West. The edited collection, *Remade in Japan*, deals solely with Japan's "domestication of the West." The introduction sees "the Japanese as engaged in an ongoing creative synthesis of the exotic with the familiar, the foreign with the domestic, the modern with the traditional, the Western with the Japanese" (Tobin 1992a, 4). In a wider context, this view corresponds to a critique of the "cultural imperialism thesis" in which the non-West is a mere victim of Western cultural domination (Tomlinson 1991). Such a position can also be put in the context of recent anthropological interest in the local consumption of global (Western) cultural products (e.g., Miller 1992, 1995; Howes 1996).

Nevertheless, despite its innovative insight in alignment with a recent theoretical shift in the study of consumption, *Remade in Japan* is quite distinctive in its strong emphasis on Japan's adept demarcation of the boundary between "Japan" and "the West." While offering intriguing analyses of Japanese "domestication of the West," most of the essays in the book do not attend to the dynamic socio-cultural transformations engendered by cultural hybridization and/or the internal cultural politics of difference pertaining to race, ethnicity, gender, and class. Consequently, the arguments tend to be based upon the presumed demarcation of a fixed and absolute boundary between "Japan" and "the West"—thus risking reproducing some essential difference between these two entities. While giving a detailed analysis of the importation of Disneyland into Japan, for example, Mary Yoko Brannen (1992, 219) concludes that "the process of assimilation of the West, the recontexualization of Western simulacra, demonstrates not that the Japanese are being dominated by Western ideologies but they differentiate their identity from the West in a way that reinforces their sense of their own cultural uniqueness and superiority, or what we might call Japanese hegemony." Furthermore, she declares that the process is "a specifically

Japanese form of cultural imperialism," in which the assimilation of the foreign is successfully appropriated for "continually reinforcing the distinction between Japan and the Other, keeping the exotic exotic" rather than just "domesticating" it or making it familiar (Brannen 1992, 227). Too much preoccupied with a rivalry between Japan and the West in analyzing Japanese experience of cultural indigenization, Brannen's argument regards the Japanese cultural and historical context as given and everlasting. As corollary of this, it seems as if "the West" is domesticated and indigenized into a "Japan" whose essence never changes and where a stable hybrid "Japaneseness" is constantly reproduced (Yoshimi 1997, 212). We should think seriously whether this kind of analysis of Japanese domestication of the West actually lends itself to keeping Japanese "Japanese."[6]

Thus, the exclusive attention to the binary opposition "Japan" and "the West" conspires with Japan's postwar hybridism, which exploits Japan's difference in a unitary mode of opposition to "the West." It not only homogenizes the two cultural entities but also directs our attention away from the doubleness of the Japanese (post)colonial experience as a non-Western colonizer. The relative marginalization of postcolonial discourse in Japan until recently might have been the other side of the predominance of other "posts"—postwar, postmodern, poststructuralism—all of which are, in Japan's case, products of an exclusive engagement with the West.

With the development of globalization theories, Japan's long history of appropriating foreign dominant cultures has gained further prominence as a conspicuous counterexample to academic conceptions of self-sustaining "society" and "culture." With the increasing emphasis on relational, spatial, and processual aspects of "society," society's conceptualization as an unambiguous unit of analysis has recently been called into question, particularly in sociology. Mike Featherstone (1995, 137) argues that sociology had tended to see society as an integrated whole and has underestimated "inter- and trans-societal processes" in favor of the intrasocietal dimension. This critique of the image of society is similar to that of anthropology's central concept of "culture," which tends to foreground the "inherent patterning to culture" where there is little sense of intercultural transculturation. In emphasizing the global interconnectedness of societies and cultures, Featherstone refers to Japan as a representative counterexample. Although widely regarded as a closed country until the mid–nineteenth century, he argues, Japan was never closed but always connected to the outside world through cultural appropriation, particularly from China: "The cultural borrowings and syncretisms which have resulted from this process . . . cannot but put a big question mark against the long-held notions of culture within sociology and anthropology which emphasize organic or aesthetic unity" (135).

Featherstone's discussion of "the death of society," by which is meant a limit to conceiving "society" as a clearly demarcated unit of sociological analysis, is well taken. Still, Featherstone tends to ignore the extent to which Japan's construction of an exclusivist national identity has been based precisely upon a particular narrative of its history of intersocietal relativization and cultural borrowings (Iwabuchi 1994). The issue at stake is again whether or not Japan's practice of constructing a national identity based upon cultural borrowing amounts to the postulation of a transhistorical cultural essence for Japan, and whether the image of Japan's capacity for assimilating the foreign tends to be reified as an ahistorical essence. Without critically attending to this risk, Featherstone's deconstruction of the assumption of an "inherent patterning to culture" paradoxically accompanies another essentialized patterning of cultural hybridization in Japan.[7]

More significantly, unlike the domestication thesis, some globalization perspectives tend to conceive Japan's experience of appropriating foreign dominant cultures not simply as a domestic Japanese trait but as a possible model for other nations. Jean Baudrillard, for example, articulates a postmodern image of Japan. He mentions in passing that Japan represents a "weightless artificial satellite," which is concerned neither with origin nor authenticity but knows "how to exploit that situation to the full," and that the future of the world will belong to such a weightless satellite (Baudrillard 1988, 76). Although we cannot generalize Baudrillard's conception as the Western image of Japan, it appears that Western evaluations of the Japanese genius for hybridization have become even more positive along with a new interpretation of the historical dynamic in the age of globalization. This has much to do with theoretical shifts from modern to postmodern, from production to consumption, and from a view of societies as separate entities to one of global interconnectedness. David Morley (1996, 351), for example, referring to Claxton's discussion of Singer's *History of Technology,* argues that the rise of Western modernity was heavily based on imitation and improvement of Near Eastern [*sic*] techniques, and this "can be seen to be in close parallel with the relation of Japanese to Euro-American technologies in the late twentieth century, in which the originally inferior imitators finally surpass their erstwhile 'masters.' "

Likewise, Roland Robertson suggests that the answer to the secret of "Japan's high degree of careful selectivity concerning what is to be accepted or rejected from without" lies in "the new globality-globalization problem." Robertson argues that "whereas the old, but still surviving way of considering Japan was in terms of its externally stimulated internal transformation along an objective path of modernization, the new, more appropriate form of consideration should take as its starting point Japan's relatively great capacity not merely to adapt selectively to and systematically import ideas from other societies in the global arena but also, in very recent times, to seek explicitly to become, in a specifically Japanese way, a global society" (1992, 90) Robertson further emphasizes the significance of Japan's capacity as a model for emulation: "Japan is of great sociological interest not because it is 'unique' and 'successful,' but because it fulfills the function in the contemporary world of the society from which 'leaders' of other societies can learn how to learn about many societies. *That* is what makes Japan a global society, in spite of claims to the contrary" (86; emphasis in original). With the ascent of globalization theory, Japanese cultural hybridization takes center stage, as "Japan is an effective generator of specific conceptions of world order" (96).

From culture to civilization: Reevaluating cultural hybridization

In the 1990s the increasing attention to Japan's history of cultural absorption of the foreign as a corrective to the Eurocentric view of history and globalization in Western scholarship again has an interesting convergence with an emerging Japanese discourse on the transnational influence of its sophisticated hybridizing capacity. With the extroverted shift in its cultural orientation, Japan's hybridism this time is talked about within Japan not in terms of Japanese culture but in terms of Japanese civilization.[8] Japanese civilization theory was first espoused by a leading ethnologist, Umesao Tadao in his 1957 article, "Bunmei no seitai shikan" (Civilization from the perspective of ecological history), published during the same period as Katō's papers on hybrid culture. Rejecting a Eurocentric view of evolution and the associated dichotomy of West and East, Umesao organizes Eurasian civilizational geography into two regions. Japan and Western Europe, situated on the fringes, make up the first region; the desert areas of central Eurasia, including China, India, and Russia, constitutes the second region. Umesao's argument is that the similarities between Japan and Western Europe in terms of their ecological history produced a parallel civilizational evolution. Umesao insists that Japan does not therefore belong to Asia, as it is much closer to Western Europe by the yardstick of the historical process of civilizational evolution from agricultural civilization to industrial civilization. By dissociating Japan from "backward" Asia, Umesao's argument, like Katō's, tried to positively reevaluate Japanese culture/civilization, which had been negatively regarded as a cheap imitation of the West since Japan's defeat in World War II (Aoki 1990, 70–76).

Umesao's work undoubtedly has had a great influence on contemporary civilization theory, particularly in its eagerness to place Japanese civilization on a par with Western civilization by rejecting the Eurocentric world view as well as the teleological Marxist view of social evolution (Morris-Suzuki 1998b, 142–43). As we have seen in the introduction, however, inspired by the advance of a "clash of civilizations" thesis and the rise of Asian economic and political power that accordingly deprived Japan of its unique experience vis-à-vis the West, in the 1990s Japanese civilization has been more eagerly and assertively discussed. While there is diversity in the arguments and approaches of civilization theories in Japan, there are some common assumptions. Although emphasizing historical dynamics and spatial differences in the creation of multiple civilizations, the notion of "civilization" in these discussions is derived from the essentialist view of organic culture (Morris-Suzuki 1998b, 152). Like the hybridism discourse, Japanese civilization theories take the existence of clearly demarcated integrated cultural entities as given. More significantly, there is also a general agreement among Japanese scholars in regard to the difference between culture and civilization. While "culture" is the way of life of a social group, "civilization" articulates a higher stage which a particular culture has reached in the course of historical evolution (e.g., Ueyama 1990, 42–43; Kawakatsu 1991, 22–24; Hirano 1994, 31; see also Morris-Suzuki 1998b, 143–44). This view is clearly expressed by the well-known cultural critic Yamazaki Masakazu when he distinguishes culture and civilization: "Culture is a way of life, a conventional order, physically acquired and rooted in subliminal consciousness. Civilization, in contrast, is a consciously recognized ideational order. . . . Cultures die hard, but their spheres of dominance are limited. Civilizations can become widespread, but they may be deliberately abandoned" (Yamazaki 1996, 115). "Culture" thus signifies something particularistic, but "civilization" has much to do with universal principles which can be willingly adopted by other cultures and civilizations.

This shift in attention from particularistic culture to universal civilization has accompanied an important transformation of the conception of hybridism. The main concern of Japanese civilization theorists in the 1990s is less with discerning a parallel between Japan and the West than with advocating a distinct and exportable Japanese civilizational pattern. If civilization and culture are to be distinguished in terms of the capacity for external influence, the term *civilization* must connote an active extroversion endorsed by confidence in its own cultural export capacity, where *culture* connotes something more introverted (Tsunoyama and Kawakatsu 1995, 231). In other words, the articulation of Japanese civilization theories in the 1990s is strongly motivated by the desire to put Japan at the center of human history, to present Japanese civilization as a new guiding principle of global history. As Morris-Suzuki (1998b, 178) argues, the shift reflects a growing belief that "the distinctive features of Japanese society are no longer merely national issues, but offer a pattern for others to follow, just as the patterns of Egyptian, Greek, or Roman civilization once shaped the development of wide realms of world history."

It is in terms of this emerging concern with civilization's capacity for expansive spatial spread that famous civilization theorist, Ueyama Shunpei, who edited seven volumes on the history of Japanese civilization, attracted criticism from other scholars of Japanese civilization theory. Ueyama distinguishes Japanese and Western civilization in terms of their propensities to cross-cultural influence. Western societies are marked by a "convex culture," willing to exert influence on others. Japanese culture is a "concave" culture, receptive to foreign influences (Morris-Suzuki 1998b, 144–45). Ueyama's view, however, attracted much criticism from other civilization theorists. Tsunoyama (1995, 32), for example, argues that unlike Umesao, who insisted on the parallel development of Japanese and European civilization, Ueyama's evaluation of "concave" Japanese culture reduces Japanese industrial civilization to that of a follower of European civilization. Likewise, Kawakatsu (1991, 23–24) refutes Ueyama's (1990) attempt to articulate a distinct Japanese civilization through the development of the Japanese Emperor system, arguing that the Emperor system is too particularistic to be analyzed in a civilizational framework. For Tsunoyama and Kawakatsu, no civilization can be secondary to others, and all civilizations inevitably have a significant transnational impact.

Thus, it is suggested that one of the core principles of Japanese civilization to be emulated in the world is Japan's capacity for assimilating the best from other cultures and civilizations. Kawakatsu (1991, 244–47) argues that, unlike other nations, which have resisted absorbing foreign civilization, Japanese civilization has a superior capacity for taking the best out of foreign civilizations. The time has come, according to Kawakatsu, for Japan to conceive foreign cultural influence not in terms of either worshiping or denying Western influence. Japan should positively regard its own capacity for cultural mixing so that it can present itself to the world as a distinguished model of making good use of the world's diverse civilizations. Japan is, Kawakatsu (1995, 81–82) argues, a living museum and a great laboratory in which world civilizations coexist.

Japanese popular culture and an Asian civilization

The shift from culture to civilization, from inward hybridism to outward hybridism, newly generates Japan's claim for its cultural superiority through asserting commonality with other Asian nations. This urge is strongly inscribed, as I discussed in the Introduction, by an historically constituted ambivalence of the Japanese conception of "Asia," a cultural geography that offers Japan at once a shared identity with other parts of Asia and is also the source of Japanese feelings of superiority (Tanaka 1993). What is new this time is the observation that the Japanese popular culture exports, such as TV dramas, animation, and popular music, demonstrate Japanese cultural hegemony in the region, while at the same time inferring a sameness between the Japanese and Asian populaces.

Japanese nationalists easily translate this spread of Japanese popular culture to other parts of Asia into the "Asia-yearning-for-Japan" idea, which confirms the shift of power from the United States to Japan that took place in the 1990s. The most eloquent right-wing Asianist in Japan, Ishihara Shintaro, asserted in *Japan that Can Say "No"!,* a book that posits the rise of Japanese power and the decline of American power: "Japanese popular songs are sung throughout East and Southeast Asia, a phenomenon similar to the impact of American pop music on Japan after World War II. We hummed the Top Ten tunes, became fascinated with the American way of life, and created a U.S.-style mass consumption society" (Morita and Ishihara 1989, 151). This view displays a belief that Asian people are now yearning for Japanese affluence, technology, and popular culture in exactly the same way that the Japanese people in the postwar era yearned for the American way of life. It tends to stress an evolutionary time lag between

Japan and Asia: Asia is behind Japan but is becoming like "us." In the controversial *Voice of Asia* (1995), Ishihara again observed the spread of Japanese popular culture in Asia but subtly shifted the book's emphasis from one of Japanese cultural superiority to one of Asian commonality. Ishihara calls this a manifestation of the "natural" commonality shared by Asians: "Our popular culture strikes a sympathetic chord across Asia. No hard sell is necessary: the audience is receptive" (Mahathir and Ishihara 1995, 88). The unambiguous claim of Japanese cultural superiority to other Asian countries is, again, camouflaged by apparent cultural commonality.

As Ching (2000) points out, there is a certain similarity between the prewar pan-Asianism exemplified by Okakura Kakuzo's (known as Okakura Tenshin) (1904) saying "Asia is one" and the 1990s neo-Asianism uttered by Ishihara. Nevertheless, as the object of such discourse significantly shifts from aesthetics or high culture to commercialized popular culture, the existence of primordial racial and cultural sameness becomes less persuasive to elucidate the commonality between Japan and Asia. Instead, the experience of absorption of Western modern civilization and the practice of cultural indigenization of Western/American cultural influences are brought more into focus.

In this respect, it should be noted that an essentialist view of "Asian value" discourse has attracted as much criticism as approval in Japan. Yamazaki (1996) argues, for example, that history shows how Asia has been marked by the existence of incommensurable cultural differences, without any civilizational umbrella which might have brought coherence to Asian regions, until the spread of Western modern civilization offered a common ground, if not common attributes or values, to Japan and other Asian cultures. If the notion of "Asia" has any substantial meaning at all, Yamazaki (1996, 112–13) argues, it is based not upon traditional, authentic values and culture but on the contemporaneous experience of modernization. Saeki Keishi (1998, 26), a prominent economist, succinctly paraphrases Yamazaki's point: "Asian modernity should not be regarded as a stage of the teleological civilizational evolution. It might be characterized by the greediness to absorb anything universal, irrespective of its origin, in a twinkling and to assimilate and hybridize various foreign things with its own 'culture' according to the yardstick of convenience and pleasure." It is the keen indigenization of Western modern civilization that is giving birth to a shared (East) Asian civilization for the first time in history.[9]

Accordingly, the urban, middle-class, consumer culture widely discerned across Asia is referred to as proof of the "Asianization of Asia." A noted newspaper journalist, Funabashi Yoichi (1993, 77) argues that the Asianism observed in several Asian societies in the 1990s is marked by the fact that Asian societies have begun defining "Asia" in a positive way, not just as the shadow of Western modernity, and that this is less a "re-Asianization" than an "Asianization." This is because the search for Asian identity is "predominantly affirmative and forward-thinking, not reactionary or nostalgic." Such "Asianness" is more a "workaday pragmatism, the social awakening of a flourishing middle class" (Funabashi 1993, 75). Such "Asianness" is, it is suggested, now primarily articulated in the shared pursuit of urban consumption of Americanized (Westernized) popular culture. As Funabashi further argues, "Asia, which lacks a common heritage of aristocratic class culture, has increasingly become a hotbed of middle-class globalism" where the cultural links between the middle classes of various Asian countries are strengthening through the development of consumerism and electronic communication technology (78). It is supposed that this "nouveau riche Asianness" is taken positively by Japan because it signifies "the birth of the real Asia" (Ogura 1993) and "the first commonness in the history between Japan and Asia" (Aoki 1993).

In this claim of a shared popular and consumer culture in Asia, the idea of a shared consumer culture among Asians has still tended to be utilized by some intellectuals as a reactionary alibi for secondarily confirming the existence of, or justifying the search for, shared Asian values, such as Confucian values, a strong work ethic, or collectivism, all of which are at odds with hedonistic consumerism. For example, one of the most eloquent Japanese Asianists, Ogura Kazuo (1993), cites the influence of American popular culture as a common ground for Asian societies, but quickly makes his point that in order to make "the real Asia" more substantial, Asian people should search for features of the "Asian spirit" which could be offered to the rest of the world as universal values, some of which may be diligence, discipline, and group harmony. This search should be done through a reexamination of traditional values and through the education of Westernized youth who are ignorant of Asian culture.

More importantly, the spread of a common culture cited as evidence of an "Asianization of Asia" often means the prevalence of Japanese popular culture in Asia. Funabashi (1995, 223–24), for example, argues that "increasing interaction with Asia and the sharing of popular culture have revealed to the

Japanese people the mutual interests they share with other Asians." However, he refers to the popularity of Japanese cultural products, such as the drama *Oshin* or animations such as *Doraemon,* as the main examples of "cross-fertilization" in Asia, in which he seems to assume that Japan occupies the central position. Hence, the argument that Japan and Asia share the common experience of "hybrid" modernization is easily developed into the assertion that Japanese experience can be a leading model for other Asians to emulate—a position which presumes that Japan is a non-Western nation that has most sincerely and successfully absorbed Western civilization and culture (e.g., Kawakatsu 1991, 244–47; 1995, 81). The transnationalization of Japanese popular culture is thought to offer a great opportunity for Japan to go beyond a hitherto too introverted and self-contained cultural formation. The era when Japan's national identity that was constructed simply in terms of its "original" and "unique" receptiveness to Western modernity is over. Japan's capacity for producing attractive cultural products and disseminating them abroad, particularly to Asia, and its leading role in creating an Asian popular cultural sphere, it is asserted, should feature in fostering the newly articulated modern Asian common.

This point is made explicit by Kumamoto Shin'ichi, a journalist working for the same newspaper as Funabashi: "In the age of the global village, we should think seriously of how 'Asian wisdom' can contribute to the hitherto Western-dominated global TV culture. Numerous possibilities are open for Japan, as the most 'Westernized' country in Asia, to internationally play a significant role in mediating Western and Eastern cultures" (Kumamoto 1993a, 218). Kumamoto's view of Japan's role as a mediator between Asia and the West is shared by a media scholar, Kawatake Kazuo (1995). He argues that the significance of the export of Japanese TV programs to Asian markets lies in countering the massive advance of Western media in those markets, a phenomenon that calls to mind the high point in Hollywood's conquest of the world. The advance of Japanese TV programs, Kawatake (1995) expects, would lead to the creation of a shared TV culture in Asia. As an Asian nation, Japan could lead the globalization of Asian media markets.

A more clear-cut remark concerning Japan's leading role in the creation of Asian modern civilization was uttered by a bureaucrat of the Ministry of Foreign Affairs in a conversational article on how Japan should present itself to the world. The article was featured in *Gaiko Forum,* a monthly journal about diplomacy published by the ministry. Referring to *Doraemon* as a made-in-Japan universal character and to the popularity of TV dramas in Asia, as well as to the fact that Tokyo Disneyland is a favorite destination for Asian youth, the author argues that Japan embodies a new, modern civilization for Asia: "We are now observing the birth of Asian modern civilization which is different from American modern civilization. In this process, Japan not only plays a leading role but, I think, the creation of a new Asian civilization is becoming a constitutive part of Japanese national identity" (Ansart et al. 1994, 54).

Articulating Mukokuseki as distinctively "Japanese"

Thus, Japanese popular culture has clearly come to feature in the Japanese department store of civilization. What has been left to answer is how Asian and American modern civilizations are different and how Japanese popular cultural formations articulate Japan's role in creating an Asian modern civilization. Tsunoyama (1995) attempts to answer the question by interpreting the spread of Japanese popular culture in Asia in terms of Japan's civilizational role in indigenizing Western material culture/civilization to suit Asian conditions. The notion of material culture is deployed as an analytical tool by Kawakatsu (1991; 1995) to explore the history of a distinctive Japanese civilization. Kawakatsu argues that every nation or ethnic group (*minzoku*) has a unique "product mix" (*bussan fukugō*) which produces a distinctive cultural ethos or values which he calls a "cultural complex" (*bunka fukugō*). Tsunoyama (1995) extends Kawakatsu's argument on "product mix" by distinguishing products and commodities in terms of their international reach. Tsunoyama (Tsunoyama and Kawakatsu 1995) argues that products as discussed by Kawakatsu were those of the premodern form of trade; they embodied the culture of a particular country or region but did not much circulate outside that region's boundaries. Culture embodied in a particular product was elevated to the status of a universal civilization, he maintains, only after products were transformed into internationally circulating capitalist commodities, and that this took place with the advent of a modern materialist civilization in nineteenth-century Europe. Commodities do not distinguish consumers in terms of race, culture, or nation. With money, commodities can be obtained and consumed by anyone in any part of the world.

It is in this sense, Tsunoyama (1995, 98–114) contends, that Japanese consumer commodities offer a clue in understanding the distinctive features of Japanese civilization. The significant role played by Japanese civilization is evident in its diffusion of Western material civilization through the production of affordable commodities for Asian markets. In his view, Japan has acted as a "transformer sub-station" which successfully refashions original Western commodities to suit the tastes and material conditions of consumers in Asia. Tsunoyama (102–4) further argues that the capacity of Japanese indigenization of things Western has elevated Japan to a new "power plant" in the world, a major exporter of many kinds of commodities, even to Western markets. These are disseminated internationally due to the universal appeal of their functional convenience in everyday life. Nevertheless, in articulating Japan's civilizational role, he puts particular emphasis on the Asian context, where Japanese civilization has consequently become a model for other parts of Asia to follow: "Western countries might see Japanese civilization as a cheap imitation or a mere extension of Western civilization. However, it is people in Asia who are now enthusiastically looking up to Japan as a familiar but yearned for nation. A rapid industrialization of postwar Japan . . . is a familiar model for other Asians to emulate" (189).

Japan, in Tsunoyama's view, does not simply present itself as a prototype of industrialization to Asia. Tsunoyama (189–92) applies his metaphor of Japanese civilization as a substation and a new power plant for Asia to the spread of Japanese popular culture in Asia:

> It is obvious that the origin of Japanese popular culture can be found in American popular culture. The Japanese indigenized American popular culture into something that suited Japanese tastes. Filtration through a Japanese prism has made American popular culture something more familiar to people in Asia. The Japanese sub-station has made American popular culture more universal, acceptable even for East Asian youths. . . . The universal appeal of Japanese popular culture in Asia is based upon its erasure of any nationality [mukokuseki] from popular culture of American origin. (191)

The term *mukokuseki* is widely used in Japan in two different, though not mutually exclusive, ways: to suggest the mixing of elements of multiple cultural origins, and to imply the erasure of visible ethnic and cultural characteristics. As I have discussed in chapter 1, while the latter meaning is closely associated with animation and computer games, it is basically via the former meaning that Tsunoyama explains the spread of Japanese popular culture to Asian regions. Tsunoyama (1995, 191) stresses that Japanese popular culture is not appreciated in Asia for its "authentic" cultural appeal. Rather, referring to the positive reception in East and Southeast Asia of Japanese TV dramas that portray romance, friendship, and the lifestyle of young people in urban settings, and of Japanese popular music that has subtly incorporated a wide range of American popular music styles (though he never refers to concrete media texts), Tsunoyama contends that it is Japan's skill of indigenizing Western culture in Asian contexts that articulates the transnational appeal of Japanese popular culture. Here, Tsunoyama does not simply assert that Japanized American popular culture is naturally appealing to Asian audiences. More significantly, he argues that Japan's subtle indigenization of American popular/consumer culture has elevated Japan to "the object of yearning for young people in other Asian countries again" (189–90).

A main problem with Tsunoyama's argument, typical of other hybridism discourses, is his failure to appreciate the existence of other modes of cultural mixing. Conferring a distinctive "Japaneseness" on mukokuseki Japanese cultural products, Tsunoyama assumes that Japan is the first and final stop in the indigenization process in global cultural flows. Hybridism discourse can hold good only so far as it can defer acknowledgment and appreciation of the multifarious and contradictory ways of endless indigenization, appropriation, and mixing all over the world. Also suppressed in hybridism discourse is the undeniable fact that Japanese culture itself, arguably the fruit of skillful hybridization, is in turn destined to be contradictorily consumed, appropriated, and indigenized in the process of transnational consumption. Tsunoyama's argument does not address the question of whether and how distinctive Japaneseness, other than the act of cultural indigenization and mixing, is concretely embodied in mukokuseki popular culture or perceived by audiences/consumers in other parts of Asia. If Japanese popular culture is well received in Asian regions, because it lacks perceptible "Japaneseness," as Tsunoyama argues, how could "Japan" become the object of yearning? I will return to this point shortly.

These questions might not concern civilization theorists who refer to the spread of Japanese popular culture as merely a convenient example of Japan's genius for cross-fertilization. However, once we closely look at how things happen in the real world, the tenacity of such a straightforward claim of Japan's central positioning in the endless transnational indigenization process of West-dominated cultural flows becomes apparent. As I will discuss in great detail in the subsequent chapters, the assumption about Japan's leading role in Asia in terms of hybridizing West and East was overtly or covertly incorporated into the strategies adopted by Japanese media industries for entering Asian markets in the 1990s. However, it did not well fit the reality and proved to be only partially successful in practice. Likewise, audience identification of cultural similarity through the consumption of Japanese popular culture in other parts of Asia is a more complex and dynamic process which does not directly generate a sense of Japanese superiority among Asian audiences. These empirical studies will thus illuminate the ambivalence and contradiction embraced in the Japanese discursive articulation of its superiority to and commonality with other parts of East and Southeast Asia.

Popular cultural diplomacy in Asia

Nationalistic employment of the meaning of the mukokuseki-ness of Japanese popular culture that highlights disregard for the complexity of transnational cultural flows is not only found in the condescending view of the "Asia yearning for Japan." The form of trans/nationalism also manifests itself differently in the discussions by Japanese journalists, industry people, government officials, and academics, who excitedly regard the export of Japanese popular culture as primarily serving the national interest of enhancing Japan's cultural diplomacy in the region.

As discussed in chapter 1, some Japanese intellectuals express objections and hesitations to the assertion of the "Japanization of Asia" thesis, due to the difficulty of demonstrating Japanese cultural influence as separate from Japanese economic power. This kind of materialist interpretation of the spread of Japanese popular culture in East and Southeast Asia tends to underestimate its symbolic appeal (which I will analyze in chapter 4). However, such disapproval of the "Japanization of Asia" thesis that put an emphasis on economic aspects cannot be lightly dismissed, because it critically draws our attention to Japan's historically constituted asymmetrical relation with other Asian countries (Murai 1993; Igarashi 1997). The historical legacy of Japanese imperialism and colonialism, as well as its lingering asymmetrical economic relation with other Asian countries, are important reminders that prevent a straightforward nationalist view of the spread of Japanese popular culture from being accepted without reservation in Japan.

As early as the mid-1980s Japan's dominant economic and cultural presence in Southeast Asia was documented in Yoshioka Hiroshi's acclaimed nonfiction work, *Nihonjingokko* (Playing at being Japanese) (1993 [1989]). The book deals with a fourteen-year-old Thai girl who deceived the Thai people in the mid-1980s by pretending to be a daughter of the Japanese ambassador. The protagonist called herself "Yūko"—which was the name of the Japanese actress who performed the role of the heroine of *Oshin*. In his investigation in Thailand, Yoshioka discovered with surprise that the real Yūko's knowledge about Japan was actually quite limited—even incorrect— and that she was not very fluent in the Japanese language either. He wondered why many Thai people could not see that Yūko was an imposter. Yoshioka found a clue when he witnessed a massive influx of foreign (particularly Japanese) cultures and commodities dominating the country, a situation Japan had never experienced. However, unlike in the 1970s when Japanese economic domination in Thailand caused anti-Japanese demonstrations, he observed in the 1980s that a number of Thai people who were eager to consume products either "made-in-Japan" or the flood of consumer commodities and popular culture that imitated its Japanese counterpart. These observations made Yoshioka sense that it was not the real Yūko's skillful performance but the Thai people's blind acclamation for Japanese material affluence that was the key to understanding the incident. When Yoshioka finally met Yūko in Bangkok, his guess turned to conviction, as she told him that no one doubted that fact of her being Japanese as long as she confidently preached to the Thai people that Thailand should emulate Japanese economic success: "Yūko surely played at being Japanese. But what her hundred-day-long performance really suggests is deceived Thai people playing at being Japanese more eagerly. Yūko at least knew that she was playing at being Japanese, but what about the deceived Thai people? Are they not still unconsciously playing at being Japanese?" (Yoshioka 1993, 293). The spectacle of the Thai people's cheerful consumption and imitation of "Japan" evoked an unease in him, as it elucidated the widening unequal relationship between Japan and Thailand, as well as the Thai's identity crisis, a serious problem precisely because most people did not perceive it as such.

Needless to say, the history of Japan's invasion and exploitation of other Asian countries is not just inscribed in the Japanese discourse on Japan's cultural export to the region.[10] The threat of cultural Japanization is still felt among Asian peoples, who have not forgotten the brutal legacy of Japanese imperialism. An Indonesian journalist, for example, called Japan the "America of Asia," suggesting that "with its growing influences, Japan has become increasingly condescending towards others" again (quoted in Choi 1994, 148).[11] No matter how difficult it might be to place Japanese cultural influence in Asian countries on a par with America's, the spread of Japanese cultural export to other Asian countries nevertheless articulates the indelibility of Japan's imperial history, unresolved issues of Japanese war responsibility, and its lingering economic exploitation of the region.

Nevertheless, the increase in the export of Japanese popular culture to Asian markets has demonstrated that Japan's colonial past does not prevent Japanese TV programs and pop idols from being accepted in East and Southeast Asia. Accordingly, a strong interest has emerged within Japan in the potential for Japanese popular culture to improve Japan's reputation and soothe—even suppress—the bitter memory of the Japanese invasion of Asia through the dissemination of an enjoyable Japanese contemporary culture throughout Asian countries, particularly among younger people who did not experience Japanese imperialism in the first half of this century.

In this context, the Japanese government has become interested in promoting the export of TV programs and popular culture in order to improve international understanding of Japan, particularly in Asian countries.[12] The Japanese soap opera, *Oshin,* is a case in point. First exported to Singapore in 1984, *Oshin* has been well received in forty-six countries throughout the world. Its ratings in many non-Western countries were much better than those of American TV dramas such as *Dallas* or *Dynasty* (Singhal and Udornpim 1997; Lull 1991). The main recipient countries are those of East, Southeast, and South Asia, the Middle East, and South America, where the series has been in most cases distributed for free under the cultural exchange program of the Japan Foundation, an extradepartmental organization of the Ministry of Foreign Affairs. In a special issue, the Japan Foundation's monthly journal explored the possibility of Japanese cultural interchange with Asia through electronic media programs, in which *Oshin* was the main focus (*Kokusai Kōryū* 1994). The international popularity of *Oshin* also encouraged the distributor of the program, NHK International, to organize an international conference on the program in Japan and to subsequently publish its proceedings in 1991. The main purpose of the publication and the conference was to discuss the transnational appeal of *Oshin* and Japanese TV programs in general, and to explore the further possibility of exporting Japanese TV dramas, with the aim of disseminating a "humane" image of Japan in the world.

If, as pointed out above, Japanese cultural export to Asia cannot be construed entirely in terms of the disappearance of visible Japanese cultural presence, it is also because the products exported to Asia include non-animated TV programs and popular music whose textual appeal is embodied in *actual* Japanese actors and musicians. Some commentators thus stress that the popularity of *Oshin* in other Asian countries is important because it gives those people an opportunity to see the "real" lives of Japanese people rather than to know about Japan only through the cars and other consumer goods they purchase (e.g., NHK International 1991; Kobayashi 1994). Itō Yōichi, a media scholar, argues: "As animation is mostly mukokuseki and therefore has little to do with Japanese ethnicity (*minzokusei*), the increase in the export of animation does not mean that Japan exports its culture. However, popular songs and *Oshin* embody Japanese culture and this is why the export of these products is unique and deserves serious analysis" (NHK International 1991, 99). For those who see the possibility of enhancing the image of Japan through the export of TV programs, animation and computer games are simply not effective in conveying the state of contemporary Japanese society and culture because they do not represent any realistic image of Japan.

Needless to say, the questions of what constitutes the "real" Japan, whether it is possible to represent the "real" faces Japan, and in what manner such images of Japan are (in contradictory ways) consumed and received by audiences, are highly contested. These questions are not taken seriously by those who stress the importance of exporting Japanese TV programs. What concerns them is the belief and the fact that a Japanese TV program, *Oshin*, has improved the image of Japan in other Asian countries. The usefulness of the TV program in this respect conversely determines what are the real and humane faces of Japan in the eyes of those observers.

Particularly significant in this respect is the fact that *Oshin* cultivates among Asian viewers a sense of commonality between Japan and other Asian nations. It is argued that the representation of common values such as perseverance, diligence, and familialism in *Oshin* is responsible for the popularity of the program in other Asian countries and has engendered a positive change in the image of Japan in Asian countries (e.g., on Indonesia, see Takahashi 1991, 1994; on China, see Kumamoto 1993a). No less significant is the sense of a common "non-Westernness"—the common harsh experience of non-Western modernization. As scriptwriter Imamura Yōichi

(1995, 15) argues, "Japan should show itself more clearly to others, particularly to Asians who are now facing similar social problems to those Japan once experienced. The popularity of *Oshin* lies in its successful representation of the social contradictions produced in the process of modernization and democratization, the interaction between tradition and modernity."

In order to overcome the distrust of Japan held by other Asian countries, Imamura (1995) suggests that Japan should stress the fact that it shares with other Asian countries the agony and suffering that are inherent in the course of modernization. However, it should be noted here that *Oshin* narrates the modern history of Japan from a woman's perspective. Japan's past is represented mostly in terms of a pacifist woman's experience of overcoming suffering caused by the war (Morris-Suzuki 1998b, 134–35; see also Harvey 1995). This representation of Japan's gendered past proves to be useful for the purpose of rendering more troublesome aspects of Japanese modern history irrelevant.

The beneficial aspects of Japanese popular culture in the country's reconciliation with its neighbors are not simply found in the common historical experience of the non-West and in traditional values. TV dramas and popular music that feature contemporary urban culture in Japan are also thought to present a new possibility of promoting cultural dialogue between young Japanese and other Asians. While this kind of optimistic use of youth popular culture for cultural diplomacy has recently been becoming even more conspicuous in terms of Japan's historical reconciliation with South Korea as the two countries co-hosted the 2002 soccer World Cup (see Fukamaru kōryū 2000), as early as 1994 *Gaiko Forum* had featured articles about the spread of Japanese popular culture among Asian youth. The September 1994 issue contained an articles written from the Japanese perspective; and in November three responses, from Thailand, Singapore, and Hong Kong, appeared (see Honda 1994a; English translation 1994b). The September article, while mentioning the importance of bilateral cultural flow and the increasing number of personal, face-to-face, contacts between people in Japan and those in other Asian nations, emphasized that the transnational attraction of Japanese popular culture in Asia offered a new possibility of Japanese cultural exchange with other Asian countries. Here, as is not the case for dramas (like *Oshin*) that stress traditional cultural values, it is the hybrid nature of Japanese popular culture that is stressed.

According to the author of the article, there are two related points in testifying to the potential of Japanese popular culture to facilitate Asian dialogue. First is the fact that Japan has had "no hand" in the dissemination of Japanese popular music and TV programs in Asian regions. The spread of Japanese popular culture "has occurred with virtually no effort on the Japanese side: the East Asian middle class took note of Japanese popular culture and chose to embrace it of its own accord" (Honda 1994b, 78). This might be reminiscent of Ishihara's view, discussed earlier, but Honda considers the "spontaneous" reception by Asian audiences to be important, if Japanese cultural exports are to overcome the historical legacy of Japanese imperialism.[13] And this is related to Honda's other point that the universal appeal of Japanese popular culture lies in its non-self-assertive mukokuseki nature.

Honda refers to mukokuseki, in the same sense as Tsunoyama's (1995) usage mentioned earlier, that is, that it is "a country-neutral quality" due to the massive influence of the American original (76). Such mukokuseki Japanese popular culture, Honda argues, unlike traditional images of Japanese culture and society, have a cosmopolitan appeal that articulates "a sharp break from the traditional, prewar image," and they will lead to "[erasing] the old, oppressive image of the country—especially among the younger generation" (78).[14] Referring to the rise of the middle classes, who are the main audiences for Japanese popular culture and who are primarily urban, Honda argued that "the link that Japanese popular culture now provides for ordinary young people from Tokyo to Singapore could foster dialogue on a scale and closeness never before achieved" (77). This is because "Japanese comics, dramas, and pop music not only provide a common topic for discussion among East Asians but also portray Japan's modern, liberated face" (78).[15]

Honda does not refer to the mukokuseki-ness of Japanese popular culture in order to illustrate Japan's civilizational excellence of cultural indigenization. Nevertheless, the crucial questions left unanswered in Honda's hopeful view are, again, what sort of dialogue can be facilitated through the transnational mass-mediated consumption of popular culture? And how might the dialogue be shaped by continuing unequal power relations between Japan and the rest of Asia? What sorts of images of "Asia" are being imagined and where is "Japan" positioned in them? All of these issues are not given due attention, as the mukokuseki-ness of Japanese popular culture is apprehended predominantly as something useful for the Japanese national interest.

Ambivalence elucidated in the "Japanization" of Asia

I have shown various ways in which the complexities and contradictions imbricated in disjunctive transnational flows of culture are discounted in Japanese nationalist discourses on its export of popular culture. Such trans/nationalism discourses in Japan, I suggest, can be seen as symptomatic of the growing difficulty of claiming the significance of Japanese cultural export in the face of the contradictory and unforeseeable consumption and indigenization process in every corner of the world. Trans/nationalism desperately attempts to resolve, though temporarily, the ambivalence that results from the international circulation of Japanese culture and cultural products in a time when the dynamics of local cultural indigenization, while deeply implicated in cultural asymmetry, tends to downplay the straightforward view of cultural power of any country of origin over another (see e.g., Miller 1995; Appadurai 1996). In the following chapters, I will try to disentangle, through empirical analysis, how these contradictions are articulated in the production and consumption of Japanese popular culture in Asian markets and the Japanese consumption of Asian popular culture. I would now like to analyze the text of the 1993 film *Sotsugyō Ryokō: Nihon kara Kimashita* (My graduation trip: I am from Japan) in terms of the way in which the consumption of Japanese popular culture in other parts of Asia articulates the contradiction and ambivalence generated by transnational cultural flows.

The film tells the story of a male Japanese university student who, while traveling, becomes a pop star in a fictional Southeast Asian country. The country is in the midst of a phenomenal "Japan boom," and the young man is recruited by a Japanese agent, wins a star-search audition, and quickly becomes a national media star. At first glance, *Sotsugyō Ryokō* seems to claims that, just as Japan has admired Western culture, other Asian countries now worship Japan.[16] The film cheerfully depicts, through food, popular music, and use of the Japanese language, how Japanese culture is consumed and appropriated, although in a distorted manner, by other Asian people. This approach to the Japanese cultural presence in the world is reminiscent of, but in stark contrast to, Pico Iyer's 1988 travelogue, *Video Night in Kathmandu,* which deals with the creative indigenization and appropriation of dominant American popular cultures in Asia. Iyer analyzes the process of negotiating American cultural hegemony in Asia, elucidating modes of "postmodern boundary violating and syncretistic cultural intersections"

The cheerful "Japanization" of Asia? A film
pamphlet for the film *Sotsugyō Ryokō* (1993).

(Buell 1994, 5), which produce "a carnivalesque profusion of hybrid forms"
(11). By conferring agency to the receiving side, Iyer's text illuminates how
the culturally dominated actively negotiate with West–dominated global
cultural flows at the local site. It is parallel with Appadurai's (1996, 29)
remark that "if a global cultural system is emerging, it is filled with ironies
and resistances, sometimes camouflaged as passivity and a bottomless appetite in the Asian world for things Western."

However, such contradictory scenarios are apparently absent in *Sotsugyō
Ryokō*. Rather, the comical depiction of Asian imitation of Japan is marked
out by a peculiar indifference to the receiving side. The predominant issue
of the film seems to be the question of how a Japanese protagonist himself
plays at being Asia's image of Japan, and of how Japan distortedly presents
itself according to the assumed expectation of Asian audiences. In this sense,
the film represents Japanese identification with the spectator subject, who
enjoys the game of others objectifying us, "the Japanese," while believing

that it is ultimately impossible.[17] It is less the putatively imitating subject, "Asia," than the object of imitation and yearning, "Japan," that is the actual subject of the film. Japan's doubleness, which is at once the subject and object of imitation, is represented through the negation of subject positions for those who consume "Japan" in other parts of Asia. While Iyer depicted the decline of American cultural hegemony through the vivacity of local consumption, this film seems to claim the rise of Japanese cultural power through a narcissistic reference to the (grotesque) elasticity of Japanese cultural products for local consumption. The supposed impossibility of any foreign appreciation of "authentic" Japanese culture ensures that "Japanese culture" remains inviolate and intact, safe in its transculturation encounter with others. Japanese observers thus have only to indulge in watching foreign distortions and (mis)appropriations of globally circulated Japanese culture in order to affirm its symbolic power status.[18]

It also can be argued, however, that *Sotsugyō Ryokō* shows the producer's refusal to offer an easy and idealized pattern of cultural exchange and dialogue between Japan and Asia. The precariousness and fallaciousness of cultural diplomacy and dialogue through asymmetrical cultural flows is comically represented in the film through Asian cultural misunderstanding of Japan, acquired via the consumption of Japanese commodities and images. Compared to other Japanese who claim that Japan has become the object of yearning for the foreign consumer of Japanese popular culture, and those who see a possibility of a cultural dialogue between Japan and Asia through popular cultural flows, Japanese film producers seem to observe the Asian consumption of Japan in a more detached and skeptical manner. Isshiki Nobuyuki, a screenwriter for *Sotsugyō Ryokō,* remarked in a Japanese newspaper interview that he had wanted to write a comedy dealing with the gap between Japanese reality and the image other Asian people have of affluent Japan (Ajia to Nihon no zure egaku 1993). When he traveled to other Asian countries such as Thailand and Hong Kong, Isshiki found the distorted images of Japan held by Asians to be quite embarrassing, since they reminded him of a similar illusionary yearning for the United States—the illusion that everyone in California must be a stylish surfer!—which he had experienced in the early 1980s. Apart from the arrogance and self-confidence displayed in his remarks, Isshiki seems to suggest that there exists an irreducible discrepancy between the "real Japan" and the "yearned-for Japan." Here, what is problematized is not just the possibility of cultural diplomacy. As was not the case with the material domination of Japan over

Thailand, described in Yoshioka's (1993) uneasy observations mentioned earlier, cultural domination of Japan over other Asian countries is also illustrated as implausible, as the meaning signified by "Japan" is inevitably appropriated there.

Moreover, in Isshiki's statement there seems to be a sober realization of the tenuousness of Japanese cultural hegemony in Asia and evidence of Japanese self-mockery of its own past imitation of America. The interesting issues dealt with in *Sotsugyō Ryokō* are the status of American popular culture and the circulation of "Japanized" Western popular culture in other parts of Asia. The film begins with a scene in Japan in 1979 in which the hero as a child is earnestly watching a Japanese star singing a Japanized version of the song "YMCA" by the American pop group, Village People. The Japanese version, unlike the original, has no gay culture subtext. Instead, it features an "original" dance. Like the discussion of the mukokuseki nature of Japanese popular culture as shown by Tsunoyama (1995), the film seems to suggest that the subtle act of indigenizing the West is interpreted as the source of Japanese cultural and civilizational excellence. However, once the discursive is materialized into an actual product, an uneasy question left uninterrogated in the hybridism discourse comes to the surface: If "imitation of America" is a significant determinant of contemporary Japanese culture itself, is there any authentic "Japaneseness" left to be appreciated by other Asian people? The apparent phenomenon of the "Japanization of Asia" does not necessarily articulate Japanese cultural power. On the contrary, it eventually arouses the ambivalence Japanese cultural producers feel toward the nature of Japanese cultural power, an ambivalence caused by the mimetic origin of Japanese cultural formation.

This point becomes sharper when we look at the fact, which is suppressed in the film, that Japanese popular culture is not simply consumed or distortedly appropriated but directly copied in some East and Southeast Asian countries. The style of the pop singer is a case in point. It is widely observed that the song, dance, hairstyle, clothing, and even names of Japanese pop idols were imitated in Taiwan, Hong Kong, Thailand, and South Korea in the 1980s (e.g., Morieda 1988; Shinozaki 1988; Ching 1994). Unlike Bhabha's (1985) concept of "mimicry," by which he tries to illuminate the scandalous subversion of the colonizer's cultural hegemony through a grotesque appropriation of the original by the colonized, this straightforward copying of Japan by fellow nonwhite Asians, I would argue, destabilizes Japanese cultural domination by revealing that there is no such thing as a cultural hegemony which originates in Japan. A cheerful Asian second-order mimicking of Japanese imitation of American popular culture sets up the Japanese unease, an unease derived from a realization that Japan's mimetic modern experience deeply underpins the formation of Japanese popular culture. That is, Asian mimesis of Japan forces Japanese to realize that Japan, after all, embarrassingly performs "grotesque America" among other Asian nations (e.g., Shinozaki 1990a; Kōkami and Chikushi 1992). The Japanese observation of the "Japanization of Asia" leads not simply to the problematization of Japan's authority and originality through secondary Asian imitation. It also articulates a moment when Japan encounters the impossibility of retaining a master position in transnational cultural flows.

At the same time, Asian mimesis of Japan does not merely prompt Japan to realize how bizarre is its own imitation of Western popular culture. It also highlights the vivacity of local consumption, which is suppressed in the observation of a "grotesque Japan" (see, e.g., Ajia de kageki ni shōhi sareru Nippon bunka 1993). Here, Asian imitation of Japanese popular culture offers Japan a common ground with other Asian nations in terms of the ongoing process of cultural hybridization/indigenization. This posture is discerned in the above-mentioned Yoshioka text too. While documenting Japanese economic and cultural dominance in Thailand, Yoshioka nevertheless realized that there is nothing different between the way that Thai companies copied Japanese clothes and the way that Japan copied Western consumer technologies: "I suddenly felt Thailand was very intimate. I can clearly see ourselves in Thais' keenness to copy Japan, the past which we forgot after Japan became an affluent economic superpower" (1993, 246). Here, awareness of the way in which Japanese popular culture is multifariously simulated and copied by other Asians destabilizes the Japanese belief that while any country can Westernize, others cannot successfully indigenize the West like "us" (i.e., like the Japanese). Asian imitation of Japan displaces Japan's hybridism in its construction of an essential national identity by exposing the fact that skillful hybridization is not unique to Japan. Rather, it is quite common to all subordinated nations (see e.g., Appadurai 1990; Hannerz 1991).

Nevertheless, the common experience of cultural hybridization can also be the source of a Japanese condescending view toward a "behind-the-time" Asia. As I will argue in chapters 4 and 5, an analysis of the two-way flows of popular culture between East Asian nations and Japan displays the unevenness in terms of the perception of temporality that Asian neighbors inhabit. "Japanization" of Asia may not signify a straightforward economic or cultural domination of Asia by Japan, but this does not mean that there is no power asymmetry between Japan and other Asian nations. This asymmetry consistently overshadows any optimism about a dialogue on equal terms. Before exploring this asymmetry, however, we must first explore how the contradiction and ambivalence articulated in Japan's trans/nationalist discourses are reflected in the corporate strategies and practices of the Japanese media industries as they try to enter Asian markets.

3

Localizing "Japan" in

the booming Asian media markets

In this chapter I shall turn to the empirical study of the strategies used by the Japanese music and TV industries for entry into the booming Asian audio-visual markets in the 1990s. The economic power of Asian countries and the proliferation of media space in the region have increased the export opportunity for Japanese popular culture. Lured by the potential of the booming Asian audiovisual markets, Japanese media industries also became keen to promote the circulation of Japanese popular music and TV programs to East and Southeast Asia. Nonetheless, Japanese media industries were at first concerned mainly with ridding cultural products of "Japanese odor" and with making "local" products in Asian markets, as well as with direct export of Japanese cultural products.

Localization strategies deployed by Japanese media industries included selling their "know-how" for indigenizing foreign (Western) popular culture in Asian markets. This strategy indicates a conviction widely held by the Japanese media industries that, no matter how Japanese TV programs become popular in Asia, other Asian countries will sooner or later follow the Japanese experience of absorbing and localizing the American media influence. Apparently, behind the localization strategy exists the same assumption of Japanese excellence and superiority in handling transnational cultural flows, as articulated in the discourse on hybridism discussed in chapter 2. Such an assumption reveals its operational limitations when put into practice. The localization of Japanese "know-how" in cultural production has been inconsistent and only partly successful. By contrast, the direct spread of Japanese popular music and TV programs in Asian markets has become conspicuous, thanks to another localization strategy deployed by local industries in East Asia. The meaning of "localization" is shifting, from the export of Japanese know-how, to the local promotion of Japanese cultural products that synchronizes with trends in the domestic Japanese market. This testifies to the increasing affiliation and integration between Japanese and other East Asian media industries and markets, which has resulted in highlighting the transnational appeal of Japanese popular culture.

The difficulty of engaging in Asian media wars

Although the export of Japanese TV programs and popular music has drastically increased in the 1990s with the expansion of Asian audiovisual markets, this development has not proceeded smoothly or straightforwardly. While there were certain efforts to export Japanese TV programs and popular music to Asian markets,[1] the Japanese TV and music industries overall were not as active as other Asian and Western counterparts in exporting cultural products to Asian markets in the early 1990s. There has even been some discussion on how Japan had fallen behind Asian countries, not to mention the West, in the development of transnational broadcasting (e.g., Shima 1994; Nihon hatsu no bangumi Ajia kakeru? 1994; Osaki ni hōsō senshinkoku 1997).

Several factors tend to discourage Japanese media industries in their efforts to export products to other Asian countries. First of all, the reluctance of the Japanese TV industry to enter Asian markets was partly due to the obstacle posed by the historical legacy of Japanese imperialism and the existence of a profitable and wealthy domestic market in Japan. As mentioned earlier, in the former colonies of Taiwan and Korea, Japanese films, TV programs, and music had been totally banned until recently. The legacy of Japanese imperialism has prevented Japan from actively exporting its "culture" to Asian countries. The South Korean government may have preferred American to Japanese products, because they were thought to be less culturally damaging and dangerous to South Korea than the products of "the Japanese Empire." Accordingly, even Japanese companies operating in Asian markets had come to think that the suppression of Japanese cultural visibility was a desirable strategy for enabling Japanese economic expansion into Asia. Kawatake (1995) found that many Japanese companies were in favor of removing any signs of "Japaneseness" from their international advertising material. Likewise, when the Japanese government amended its policy on transnational satellite broadcasting in 1994, NHK quickly announced the launch of a satellite service to Europe, but it hesitated to broadcast to Asian regions because of a fear of being accused of cultural imperialism (Kokusai hōsō Ajia de hibana 1994; TV kaigai hōsō mienu tenbō 1994).

This fear of condemnation was reinforced by the hard-line criticism made by several East and Southeast Asian governments of the Western "cultural invasion" from the sky (e.g., Atkins 1995; Lee and Wang 1995). However, at an ABU (Asia-Pacific Broadcasting Union) meeting, held in Kyoto in November 1994, this anxiety was to some extent dispelled and NHK seemed finally prepared to launch its service in Asian regions. Japanese media industries realized with surprise during the meeting that a gradual shift in other Asian countries' policies, from rigid protection to promotion of local and regional industries, was aimed at countering the Western "cultural invasion" (Nihon hatsu no bangumi Ajia kakeru? 1994). As Wang (1996, 14) has observed concerning the policies of Asian governments, these policy decisions matched an overall trend in the 1990s: "What we see in the mid-1990s, is a change in the role of communication policy, especially in third world nations, from that of a protective guardian against 'harmful, alien information' to one of a supportive sponsor for cultural production." This policy shift was based upon a realization by Asian governments that the best way to counter U.S.-driven media globalization is less to persist in the (impossible) guarding of national borders from transnational satellite broadcasts than it is to promote local entertainment industries which produce products more attractive to local audiences than those from Western countries. This shift ironically displays that, no matter how vehemently some Asian governments denounce the influx of decadent Western consumerism through media products, "Asian" cultural values can only be protected by the development of the capitalist mode of cultural production (see Dirlik 1994). The threat of cultural imperialism has been dispelled by the advent of global capitalism.

Yet, there are two additional structural and financial impediments for the Japanese TV industry in seriously entering Asian media markets (Tsuda 1996; Odagiri 1996). One is the difficulty of making profits in Asian markets. American media corporations entered Asian markets quickly as an extension of their existing global business. Almost all the satellite and cable channels, including STAR TV, have failed to make a profit in Asia, but these deficits are compensated for by their profits in affluent Western markets. However, Japan, with no presence in the Western markets, would not be able to make a profit in Asia until the price of TV programs became as high as those paid by Western markets. As a Japanese TV international sales division manager expressed it, "We are not actively selling our programs in Asian markets, as there would be no profit no matter how earnest we become" (quoted in Tsuda 1996, 53). According to a survey by the Ministry of Post and Telecommunication, 6,800 hours of programming, worth 48.1 billion yen, were imported to Japan during 1992. As for exports, 16,471 hours were sold, which were valued just at 2.1 billion yen (Nakazora 1994). Japan, then, exported about two-and-a-half times as much programming as it imported, but the industry's earnings were no more than a twenty-third of the amount paid for importing foreign (mainly American) programs. While we should remember that expensive Hollywood films account for large part of Japan's media imports, this means that the unit price of programs (cost per hour of programming) was almost fifty-five times less than their import value (based on an import price of 7 million yen and an export value of 127 thousand yen). The average production budget for a one-hour drama in Japan was about 25–45 million yen in the mid-1990s, but the same drama could be sold in Asia for only 200,000–300,000 yen (Nishi 1997, 187).

Another reason for the low export of Japanese products to Asia concerns copyright and royalties. In Japan, the production of TV programs had been primarily for a domestic market and there had been no incentives to develop copyright contracts for secondary and tertiary broadcasts in an international market. Since the early 1990s, as Japanese TV programs were increasingly exported to Asia, Japanese TV stations came to realize that copyright issues were an obstacle to selling their programs overseas. To sell a drama overseas, for example, Japanese TV stations have to get permission from the cast and music composers for each series. It takes at least six months to clarify all the copyright issues for the secondary broadcast. Some talent management offices demand fees, which are more expensive than the TV stations can afford (Tsuda 1996, 53–54; Odagiri 1996, 18–19). For this reason, an international sales division manager of Fuji TV told me in an interview in 1996 that the company could not sell even one-third of the twelve drama series it produced annually.

According to my interviews with Japanese TV station managers, in 1997 the wholesale price for programs in Asian markets was three times higher than it had been during the early 1990s but it still constituted less than 1 percent of the total sales figures of Japanese TV stations.[2] Given the low price of the programs, the cost of copying and packaging, and the extremely small percentage of total profits, it is no surprise that Japanese TV stations have not been active in exporting their programs to Asian markets.

Localization strategies in Asian audiovisual markets

Furthermore, in the mid-1990s, in addition to the historical and structural obstacles, Japanese media industries also realized the significance of localizing strategies in Asian markets. The development of these Asian audiovisual markets has shown the need for producing and distributing cultural products that are more sensitive to the diversity and tastes of local markets, as opposed to the simple distribution of the seemingly almighty American TV programs. In this respect, a joke told by a Japanese TV news reporter covering an ASEAN meeting in Kuala Lumpur in July 1997 is suggestive of the increasing significance of articulating locality with the global spread of capitalist modernities. The reporter joked that there were three requirements for becoming a member of ASEAN. First, one must play golf; second, one must love karaoke. But, unlike these first two cultural practices, which do not particularly originate in Southeast Asian but are common in male-dominated business circles and among the middle class in many parts of Asia (thanks to Japanese influence), the last requirement is very much "Southeast Asian." The reporter continued with a faint smile, saying that, last but not the least, one must be fond of *durian*, the delicious but pungent fruit of Southeast Asia. This joke suggests the rise of economic power and the emergence of a affluent middle class in Southeast Asian countries, but the punch line of the joke reminds us that the common signifiers of middle-class capitalist modernity in the region, such as karaoke and golf, are not enough to articulate distinct local identities. It is not these internationally spread cultural activities, but the local fruit with an insuppressible odor, that ultimately confers the Southeast Asian-ness of ASEAN.

This emphasis on local specificity has become the key to the global marketing of consumer goods in the last decade. In a book on global marketing and advertising strategies, Mooij (1998) argues the inappropriateness of the slogan "Think globally, act locally," because, she says, any "global" thinking must be colored by one's cultural background. According to Mooij, the imperative for transnational companies is to "Think locally, act globally," that is, to distribute products globally and market them locally. What is increasingly apparent is that Theodore Levitt's formula of "global standardization" (1983), advocated in the 1980s, actually promotes a "mythology of globalization" (Ferguson 1992) implemented by global company executives. As Mooij argues, "In reality, few successful global brands are fully standardized. The wish for global brands is in the mind of the producer, not in the mind of the consumer. Consumers don't care if the brand is global, and they increasingly prefer local brands or what they perceive as local brands" (1998, 39). More attention to local differences is called for, because global corporations "only thrive on respect for and exploitation of local cultural values" (299).

The strategy of global localization, or "glocalization" (Robertson 1995), most eloquently explains the significance of the exploitation of the locality by transnational corporations. This is a strategy for penetrating many different local markets at once. Global companies try to "transcend vestigial national differences and to create standardized global markets, whilst remaining sensitive to the peculiarities of local markets and differentiated consumer segments" (Aksoy and Robins 1992, 18). "We are not a multinational, we are a multi-local" (du Gay et al. 1997; Watson 1997), insist such transnational corporations as Sony, Coca-Cola, and McDonald's. The strategy of global localization aims to blur the distinction between the foreign and the local, making it irrelevant: such companies feature local staff, local decision-making, and locally tailored products in their efforts to manage the tension between "economic imperatives (achieving economies of scale) and cultural imperatives (responding to diverse consumer preferences)" (Robins 1997, 36).

This same realization of the significance of locality is also the main challenge faced by transnational media industries which are attracted by the potential of huge Asian markets. Apart from protectionist government regulation policies, one of the difficulties in entering Asian markets is the considerable diversity of culture, religion, language, race, and ethnicity in the region. Moreover, there is a tendency for audiences to prefer local and regional programs to their foreign (mostly American) counterparts, even though such programs may entirely imitate products of foreign origin (e.g., Straubhaar 1991; Sinclair, Jacka, and Cunningham 1996b). It is precisely the irreducible cultural difference and preference for "local" programs with which Western transnational media corporations have been struggling and which has validated, at least in part, the above-mentioned policy shift from rigid protectionism to the encouragement of domestic cultural production.

It is in this sense that local media in some Asian countries, such as Hong

Kong (which has a long-established, powerful media industry whose products have won the hearts of their people), more subtly exploit local specificities in expanding their reach to other parts of Asia: "Local TV takes on the satellite giants" (Asia strikes back 1996). In the early 1990s, Hong Kong's leading television station, TVB, began actively entering Asian markets with a capacity of 5,000 hours of programming a year (Cast of thousands 1994). TVB not only exported its programs and launched TVBI, its satellite channel service, mainly to Taiwan in 1995, but it also started to co-produce locally tailor-made programs. Apart from its production capacity, the strength of TVB lies in its presumed cultural "Chineseness," which may be more or less shared by a vast number of ethnic Chinese in the Asian region. This co-production strategy enabled TVB to penetrate the Mandarin-language market of China and Taiwan, and in cooperation with a Chinese-Indonesian partner it was extended to the Malay-language market (Honkon TVB no chōsen 1994).

Likewise, transnational media industries in Asian markets have striven to make programming "localized," as was reported in a cover story for *Asian Business Review* (Satellite TV sees gold in local content 1996): "The battle for a share of Asia's huge television audience is in full swing, with international broadcasters pouring in vast amounts of cash. But it's the players who provide local programming content that look likely to succeed." The shift in STAR TV's programming strategy is a case in point. By assuming the omnipotence of American cultural products, STAR TV conflated the centralization of distribution with that of transmission and neglected the existence of multiple local cultures at the point of consumption. The lesson STAR TV has learned is that exporting English-language programs produced in Hollywood is no longer enough. As Rupert Murdoch remarked, "We've committed ourselves to learning the nuance of the region's diverse cultures" (Satellite TV is way off beam 1994). Rather than pursuing the old-fashioned "communication-as-transmission view" of broadcasting pan-Asian programs in only one language, the strategy of STAR TV has changed to one of ensuring the availability of local programs by finding local partners (Cast of thousands 1994; TV's new battles 1994). Driven also by political reasons, STAR TV replaced the BBC World News and American MTV with drama and music programs that were more Chinese-sensitive (STAR drops MTV to help it capture China 1994). And MTV Asia has struck back with much more localized programming produced in a variety of local languages, such as Mandarin and Hindi.

The localization strategies of transnational media corporations are reminiscent of the academic critique of the "cultural imperialism thesis." As discussed in chapter 1, the cultural imperialism thesis has been criticized for implying there was a "more or less straightforward and deliberate imposition of dominant culture and ideology," and for its reliance on the "center–periphery model," which connoted a one-way flow of cultural products and meanings from the (Western) producer to the (non-Western) consumer (Ang 1994, 196). However, in the "real" world, foreign products are often locally domesticated in terms of their meanings as well as in their forms and content (Miller 1992). Moreover, non-Western regional centers such as Brazil, Hong Kong, and India export a significant volume of cultural products to regional and global markets, and in many cases these overwhelm American products in terms of their popularity (Straubhaar 1991; McNeely and Soysal 1989). However, as Maxwell (1997, 198) argues, "Along with cultural studies professors, marketers share an interest in the popular rejection and playful re-interpretations of the transnational message." Transnational media corporations are quick to incorporate the decentered media flows into their own strategies; as a manager of STAR TV commented, "There is no money to be made in cultural imperialism" (Gautier, quoted in Sinclair 1997, 144). While capital still operates on the instrumentalist logic of transmission and dissemination of messages, global media giants, by "absorbing local differences of value and taste into the global sales effort" (Maxwell 1997, 193), exploit such logic by emphasizing the sharing of symbols and aesthetic experiences among consumers in a particular niche markets.

The way we were: Marketing the experience of cultural indigenization

In the mid-1990s Japanese media industries also clearly recognized the significance of deploying localization strategies in Asian markets. In 1994, Dentsū, the largest advertising agency in Japan, organized a committee to promote the export of Japanese audiovisual products and submitted a report to the Ministry of International Trade and Industry (Dentsū and Dentsū Sōken 1994). The report's authors clearly saw the great possibility of Japanese products being further accepted in Asian markets and suggested the necessity of developing more export-oriented production systems, including market research and language-dubbing of TV programs and films. At the same time, however, many members of the committee were not optimistic about the future of Japanese cultural exports to Asia. Interestingly, they pointed to the strong likelihood that Japanese cultural products would soon be superseded by local ones. This view corresponds with my own research. In November 1994 and February 1996, I interviewed more than twenty people working for the TV and music industries in Japan concerning the popularity of Japanese products in Asia. Almost every producer thought that Japanese products would not be well received in Asian markets for long. One program sales director of a Japanese TV station whose TV dramas had been well received in many Asian countries clearly stated that the popularity of these dramas would not last to the end of the twentieth century. As a long-term strategy, Japanese media industries were not as keen to export Japanese products as to be somehow involved, and to take the initiative, in the (co)production of "local" media products in various Asian markets.

The stress on involvement in the local production process indicates that Japanese media industries have tried to engage with global-local dynamics differently from Western and other Asian local media industries. This posture is hinted at by the fact that a Japanese transnational corporation, Sony, has had a strong policy of becoming a global company from the outset and, as mentioned in chapter 1, is considered to be the primary developer of the marketing strategy of "global localization." As we saw earlier, global localization today is not exclusively a Sony practice, but a marketing buzzword of the global business world. Nevertheless, as Robertson (1995) points out, the *Oxford Dictionary of New Words* (1991, 134) clearly acknowledges that *global localization* and the new word *glocal* originate in Japan and that global marketing strategy is another of Japan's significant contributions to consumer society: "In business jargon: simultaneously global and local; taking a global view of the market, but adjusted to local considerations. . . . Formed by telescoping global and local to make a blend; the idea is modeled on Japanese *dochakuka* (derived from *dochaku* 'living on one's own land'), originally the agricultural principle of adapting one's farming techniques to local conditions, but also adopted in Japanese business for global localization, a global outlook adapted to local conditions."

It is indeed an intriguing question why the term *glocal* was originally used by Japanese companies,[3] but we should not regard the act of dochakuka (indigenization) as uniquely Japanese. As I discussed in chapter 2, cultural borrowing, appropriation, hybridization and indigenization are common practices in the global cultural flow. A more relevant question to be addressed regarding any distinct Japanese engagement with glocalization is how Japanese companies are imagining Japan's position in the global cultural flow when they develop strategies of glocalization.

Behind the development of the Japanese localization strategy, we can see the intertwining of Japanese media industries' negative and positive self-appreciation of their capacity for popular cultural production. On the one hand, there is apparently distrust widely held by Japanese media industries concerning the appeal of visible "Japaneseness" embodied in cultural products in a global context. In chapter 1, I argued that the major cultural products which Japan exports are characterized as "culturally odorless." Yet, it is no accident that Japan has become a major exporter of culturally odorless products. Japanese media industries seem to think that the suppression of Japanese cultural odor is imperative if they are to make inroads into international markets. The producers and creators of game software intentionally make computer-game characters look non-Japanese because they are clearly conscious that the market is global (Akurosu Henshūshitsu 1995). Mario, the principal character of the popular computer game, Super Mario Brothers, for example, does not invoke the image of Japan. Both his name and appearance are designed to be "Italian." Even if Japanese animators do not consciously draw mukokuseki characters with export considerations in mind, the Japanese animation industry always has the global market in mind and is aware that the non-Japaneseness of characters works to its advantage in the export market (Akurosu Henshūshitsu 1995, 36–97). Since the advent of Tezuka Osamu's *Astro Boy* in the early 1960s, Japanese animation has long been consumed internationally. Japan routinely exports animated films, which made up 56 percent of its TV exports in 1980–81 (Stronach 1989) and 58 percent in 1992–93 (Kawatake and Hara 1994). While other film genres are mostly exported in Japanese, only 1 percent of animated films are in Japanese. This implies that animation is routinely intended for export (Stronach 1989, 144). Japanese producers are even more determined to localize (or Americanize) its Pokémon characters in various international markets to hide their "Japaneseness" as a part of their global promotion strategy (Hatakeyama and Kubo 2000; Invasion of the Pocket Monsters 1999, 68–69). For example, the local renaming of 151 Pokémon characters (with the exception of Pikachu) helped make the individual characteristics of each Pokémon monster understandable and familiar in differing global markets. As a consequence, Pokémon game software is translated into five other languages (English, French, German, Spanish, and Portuguese) and animations and trading-cards into ten (Italian, Mandarin, Cantonese, Korean, and Greek, in addition to the previous five).

As the negative side of these developments, the Japanese TV industry speculated in the early 1990s that Japanese TV programs, other than animation, would not attract Asian audiences, due to Japanese cultural and language differences (Nihon hatsu no bangumi Ajia kakeru? 1994). The Japanese TV industry itself seems to assume that its product would suffer a high "cultural discount" (Hoskins and Mirus 1988) in international markets, since, unlike "culturally odorless" products, the imagery of TV programs and popular music is inescapably represented through living Japanese bodies.

On the other hand, and more importantly, the Japanese invention of glocalization, I would argue, points to the way in which the localization strategies of Japanese media in Asian markets is informed by the industries' convinced reflection on Japan's own experience of successful indigenization of American popular culture. As the organizer of the above-mentioned Dentsū committee told me, Japanese cultural producers believed, from their own experiences, that "foreign popular culture such as TV programs and popular music will sooner or later be superseded by domestically produced ones, particularly as local media industries absorb foreign influence." Japanese cultural export to Asia is no exception to this rule of transnational cultural flows. While Japanese media industries are not very much convinced of the exportability of Japanese audiovisual products other than animation, from experience the industries are convinced that other Asian countries will take the same path as Japan in terms of the rapid indigenization of foreign (American) popular culture. And it is in this process that Japanese media industries have tried to take the initiative.

Since World War II, Japanese popular culture has been deeply influenced by American media. Rather than being dominated by American products and "colonized" by America, Japan quickly localized these influences by imitating and partly appropriating the originals. At the inception of Japanese TV history (in 1953), Japanese TV programming relied enormously on imports from Hollywood in the 1950s and early 1960s. However, this imbalance has drastically diminished since the mid-1960s. As early as 1980, Japan imported only 5 percent of all programs, and this trend has continued (Kawatake and Hara 1994). There were several reasons for this rapid transformation. First, two national events around 1960 contributed to the ascendancy of TV popularity. One was the crown prince's wedding in 1959, and the other was the Tokyo Olympics in 1964. These two events created a nationwide boom in television sales. Second, the maturity of feature-film production lent itself to the quick ascendancy of the TV industry, ironically, at the cost of its own decline. The popularity of TV decreased Japanese movie attendance, which declined drastically from 1.1 billion theater admissions in 1958 to 373 million in 1965 (Stronach 1989, 136). The number of feature films produced fell from more than five hundred in 1960 to just fifty-eight in 1990 (Buck 1992, 126). Accordingly, capable filmmakers turned to television, and this led to the maturity of the TV industry. In the end, Japan's economic miracle and the large size of the domestic market made this rapid transformation possible. The Japanese population of more than 120 million people and its economic wealth make the Japanese audiovisual market, along with that of the United States, one of the only two self-sufficient markets in the world.

This is not to say that foreign popular culture is no longer consumed in Japan. In fact, American popular culture has continued to strongly influence Japan. People in Japan have been saturated with American popular culture. Japan is one of the most important buyers of Hollywood movies (O'Regan 1992, 330). Many Japanese TV formats and concepts are also deeply influenced by and borrowed from American programs, and information about the American way of life appears in the mass media frequently. However, directly imported TV programs have not been truly popular, particularly since the 1980s with occasional exceptions such as *The X-Files,* which became popular in 1997. In Japan, people can watch many popular American TV series such as *Dallas, Dynasty,* or *The Simpsons,* but these programs have never received high ratings (concerning the failure of *Dallas* in Japan, see Liebes and Katz 1993). Popularity does not depend upon whether the product is originally Japanese or not, but rather upon how Japan localizes the original. Who knows or cares, for example, whether the Japanese version of the globally popular quiz show, *Who Wants To Be a Millionaire?,* is of Japanese origin or not? What the Japanese audience cares about is whether the program contains a "Japanese odor" through localization.

These experiences, as I show below, seem to drive Japanese media industries to believe that if there is anything about Japan which attracts Asian people, it is the hyperactive indigenization and domestication of "the West." Put differently, behind the localizing strategies of Japanese media industries in Asian markets there is a firm conviction that the localness to be exploited in Asian markets is in the process of indigenization rather than in the product per se. Japanese localization strategies attempt to create local zones by gauging the practices of local media centers and their dynamic indigenization processes. These are strategies that incorporate the viewpoint of the dominated, who long ago learned to negotiate Western culture in their consumption of media products imported from the West. "What was marked as foreign and exotic yesterday can become familiar today and traditionally Japanese tomorrow" (Tobin 1992a, 26). This dynamic is exactly what Japanese media industries have tried to produce in Asian markets and what they believe are the commonality between other Asian nations and Japan.

Here, we can nevertheless see how Japanese localization in Asian markets is imbued with a condescending posture toward other Asian nations. It is an unambiguous presupposition that as in Japanese civilization theories discussed in chapter 2, Japan's successful indigenization of foreign (Western) cultural influences presents a developmental model for other Asian countries to follow. A newly articulated "Asia" embedded in the localizing strategies of Japanese media industries thus illuminates the asymmetrical relationships between Japan and other Asian nations in the context of globalized production of indigenous modernities.

Finding local pop stars: The Japanese music industry in Asian markets

One of the popular localizing strategies of the Japanese TV industry entering Asian markets in the early 1990s was "format trade" (Bangumi urimasu 1993; Eisei 1995). Japan would sell program concepts rather than the programs themselves to other countries, thereby ensuring that video materials would contain hardly any "Japanese odor." Concept trade is a widespread business practice throughout the world.[4] Japanese exports of concepts are not restricted to Asian markets. For example, NTV, a Japanese commercial TV station, has sold the format and visual material for the quiz show, *Show-by-Show-by*, to Spain, Italy, Thailand, and Hong Kong. The original concept of *America's Funniest Home Videos* can be found in a Japanese variety show.

In the early 1990s "format trade" in Asia was promoted by the largest advertising company in Japan, Dentsū.[5] Dentsū's main purpose was to promote "syndication" so that it could sell commercial time to Japanese sponsors in several Asian countries as well as selling the program concepts. Syndication sales compensated for the low trading price of TV programs in

Asian markets ("Eisei" 1995, 32–33).[6] Like Hong Kong's TVB, Dentsū sells the program concepts of chat shows and game shows which have been well-accepted in Japan, together with video material, the supervision of production, and Japanese program sponsors to Asian TV stations (Thought of in Japan 1994). All local TV stations have to do is provide local celebrities and audiences, and to learn the know-how of TV production from Japanese producers.

However, the most active exploitation of localization has been forged by the music industry. Although some Japanese pop idols and singers such as Sakai Noriko and Chage & Aska were popular in Asian countries, especially in Hong Kong, Taiwan, and Singapore in the early 1990s (e.g., Manga mo aidoru mo NIEs sei 1990; Taiwan ga Nippon ni koi o shita 1996), the Japanese music industry aimed less to promote those Japanese musicians in East and Southeast Asian markets than to seek out "indigenous" pop stars who could be sold to pan-Asian markets with Japanese pop production know-how (see Ongaku sangyō wa Ajia mejā o mezasu 1992). The Japanese project of finding pan-Asian pop singers is thus motivated by a chimera of producing trans-Asian popular music through cross-fertilization of a Japanese initiative.

I argued in the previous chapter that a 1993 Japanese film about the Japanization of Asia is suggestive of how Japanese film producers imagine the global cultural flow. The premise of the film is that the basic model of Japanese popular culture is American, and that Japan can provide a model for localizing efforts. What the film does not show is the endless simulation of American pop in Asia through the second-generation simulation of "home grown" Japanese pop music, which unquestionably owes a debt to American trends. A Japanese version of the song "YMCA" was covered in Canto pop, which became popular in Hong Kong and Singapore. Another popular song, "Rouge," was covered at least in Hong Kong, Singapore, Indonesia, Thailand, Burma, Vietnam, and Turkey (Hara 1996, 144–51). Japanese popular music, much of which is deeply influenced by American popular music, has been well received in East and Southeast Asia, but there is little local awareness of this because most of the songs are sung by local singers in local languages (Hara 1996, 144–57). For example, Chinese audiences listening to Hong Kong pop are unaware when the songs they are hearing are actually cover versions of Japanese songs because they do not know the Japanese originals (cover songs might well constitute, along with consumer technologies, computer games, and comics/animation, a fourth

"C" of Japanese culturally odorless products). In a 1994 Japanese news report on the Japanese music industry in China, both the owner of a record shop and a customer admitted that local people knew very few Japanese songs (Hatsunetsu Ajia, 1994). They also noted that Japanese songs were not popular in China and that Japanese record companies should develop more subtle marketing strategies. But this was followed by a Japanese narration observing that people listen to many Japanese songs in China without realizing their origin, because the songs have come to Shanghai via Hong Kong or Taiwan.

These examples suggest the way in which Japanese popular music is influential as a mediating element in the chain of transnationalization of America-dominated popular culture: Japanese popular music, which is arguably the product of Japanese indigenization of American and other, mostly Western, popular music, tends to be further localized and differently appropriated in other Asian markets. It is through this cultural role that the Japanese music industry has attempted to make inroads into the music business in the region (see e.g., Akurosu Henshūshitsu 1995, 98–131; Ichikawa 1994). As the director of Epic Sony told me in an interview in 1994: "The Japaneseness of Japanese popular music production can be found in its capacity for cultural mixing, which makes the original source irrelevant. I think we are good at appropriating quality aspects from American popular music and reconstructing our own music. . . . In the same vein, if we produce something stunning, trendy, and newly stylish in local languages by local singers, I am sure that it can sell in Asian markets. The base [of the stunning style] is American popular culture."

In this venture of boosting cultural indigenization of American popular culture in Asian markets through a Japanese filter, the Japanese music industries, at least from a marketing perspective, seems to realize that Japan is not the final stop of transnational cultural flows in Asian regions. However, the localization strategy of the Japanese music industry in Asian markets posits an evolutionary temporal lag between Japan and other Asian nations. Japan's past is found in the present of other East and Southeast Asian countries, as the director of an influential Japanese music-ranking magazine commented: "The Japanese know-how of producing pop idols is applicable to other Asian countries, as the present situation in Asia looks like that of Japan about sixteen or seventeen years ago" (Aidoru sangyō nimo kūdōka no nami? 1994). That is to say, there is a certain degree of economic growth which enables (particularly younger) people to consume cultural products such as cassette tapes, CDs, concert tickets, and magazines; there is also the development of commercial TV, which is the major vehicle for promoting popular songs and idols (Inamasu 1993; Ogawa 1988). The rise of economic power in East and Southeast Asia and the rapid growth of commercialized TV markets in the region has not only reminded the Japanese music industry of the high times of the Japanese idol boom of the late 1970s and early 1980s, but has also pushed the industry to apply the well-worn techniques of manufacturing pop idols in other Asian markets.

The value of idols does not necessarily lie in any distinctive singing ability. The main feature of what is called the Japanese *aidoru* (idol) system is the production of an intimacy between stars and audiences and the blurring of the distance between professionals and amateurs, which is different from the Hollywood star system (see Inamasu 1993; Ogawa 1988; Ching 1994). This explains why, while the medium for Hollywood stars is film, intimate pop idols are better produced using TV as a medium. The frequent exposure of a pop idol through commercial films and other TV programs makes him or her appear to be like someone living next door or studying in the same classroom. Once again, the film *Sotsugyō Ryokō* illustrates this method of finding and developing a pop star. The protagonist achieves fame through an audition and through subsequent frequent appearances on TV programs and commercials, which gives audiences the feeling that anyone in Asia can be tomorrow's star. In the 1970s and 1980s a televised star-search audition became the basis for the development of the Japanese pop idol system—the process by which media industries manufactured pop idols.

In the early 1990s Japanese media industries adapted the strategy for the booming East and Southeast Asian markets. A Japanese TV station, Fuji TV, began producing a talent-quest program in 1992 jointly with Singapore, Malaysia, Indonesia, Taiwan, and South Korea.[7] The title of the program, *Asia Bagus!,* means "Asia is terrific!" in Malay/Indonesian. The program has three presenters, one Japanese woman and two Singaporean men. All presenters speak English and in addition each speaks, respectively, Japanese, Malay/Indonesian, and Mandarin Chinese. This program has been broadcast almost simultaneously in five countries since April 1992; in Singapore on TCS-5, in Malaysia on TV3 (since 1997 on NTV-9), in Indonesia on TVRI (since 1996 on RCTI), and since 1994 in Taiwan, on TTV (since 1996 on TVBS). While the Japanese original was scheduled at midnight in Japan, most of the other countries broadcast *Asia Bagus!* in prime time—in Singapore and Malaysia, for example, it was broadcast at 7:30 p.m. on Sunday night, which is a significant time for TV programming—and it constantly gets high ratings in those countries (Nihon no bangumi 1994); the rating in Malaysia, for example, has been as high as 70 percent of total viewers in this time slot (*Chiki wo musubu kakenhashi* 1994). Although *Asia Bagus!* was directed and produced mainly by Japanese staff, its production was done in close cooperation with other Asian TV stations. It was filmed in Singapore, in order to make the program more "Asian." My field research in Singapore suggests that about half of the studio audiences did not associate *Asia Bagus!* with Japanese production. Most responded that the attractiveness of the program had much to do with its "Asian" flavor, which cannot be limited to the influence of a single country.

The program had obviously borrowed its concept from a Japanese popular star-search program from the 1970s, *Sutā Tanjō* (A star is born). The distinctive feature of the earlier program lay in the fact that it was not merely an amateur singing contest. Recording companies and talent agencies were closely involved in the program. The same is true with *Asia Bagus!* Each week, four amateur singers from among five countries compete with one another, and the winner is guaranteed to make a professional debut and a recording contract with Pony Canyon, a company that belongs to the same media conglomerate group as Fuji TV, the producer of *Asia Bagus!* Pony Canyon has established branches in Hong Kong, Taipei, Singapore, and Kuala Lumpur. Unlike the global corporation Sony, Pony Canyon set out to become an Asian industry operator in order to activate intraregional flows in Asia (Ongaku sangyō wa Ajia mejā wo mezasu 1992). Pony Canyon's Asian market strategy has benefited from the popularity of *Asia Bagus!* The program introduced a trans-Asian audition system in East and Southeast Asian countries where to that point there had been no established system of opportunity for young people whose dreams were to become a pop singer (Kanemitsu 1993).

Likewise, Japanese recording companies and talent agencies actively invested in the potential of Asian markets by avidly seeking pan-Asian pop stars through organizing auditions in the early 1990s. Sony and Sony Music Entertainment implemented a series of music auditions called the "Voice of Asia" in eight Southeast Asian countries, for example, in the hopes of finding a new pan-Asian pop star in 1991. About four thousand groups and singers competed and the winner was a female Filipino singer, Maribeth (Kyūseichō Ajia nerau ongaku sangyō 1994). It was the huge size of the Chinese population in Asia that most enticed Japanese media industries in its search for pan-Asian pop idols. A Japanese producer stressed in my interview in 1994 that "while the Japanese market consists of a Japanese-speaking tribe of merely 120 million people; we can sell Chinese popular songs to a global Chinese population of 1.5 billion" (see also "Eisei" 1995; "Mezase"! 1993; Chūgoku māketto no neraime 1994). Lured by the potential of the Chinese cultural market, in 1994 Sony Music Entertainment and Yoshimoto Entertainment, the biggest agency representing comedy artists in Japan, also held auditions in Shanghai, with the aim of producing a pop group to be called "Shanghai Performance Doll" (Utatte odoreru aidoru shūdan 1994). The group took its name from Tokyo Performance Doll, a popular female group in Japan. According to my interview with the director of Epic Sony, Sony wanted to exploit the up-tempo dance music of Tokyo Performance Doll by exporting the group's style, in the guise of Shanghai Performance Doll, to China and other Asian countries; for their part, Yoshimoto aimed to produce a variety TV show featuring the new group (Ongaku to owarai 1994; Warai no Yoshimoto 1995). Japanese talent agencies have also actively tried to find and develop Chinese pop stars. One of the biggest agencies in Japan, HoriPro Entertainment Group, established branches in Hong Kong and Beijing in 1993. Although it also organized an audition in Vietnam in August 1995, HoriPro's main target is the Mandarin-speaking market. In 1993 HoriPro held auditions all over China to find Chinese pop stars, and the final competition was broadcast by STAR TV. Five winners were selected from more than 400,000 contestants and made their debuts in 1994. Another big talent agency, Amuse, held auditions in Shanghai in 1993. Their goal, similar to HoriPro's, is to produce a Chinese pop star, using Japanese capital, management know-how, and marketing strategies, who can be sold in the potentially huge Chinese market in Asia (see Chūgoku tairiku de yūbō tarento 1993).

Music is an attractive export to the Japanese industry, not only because of its low cultural discount, but also because of the sale of associated consumer commodities such as CDs and CD players. The target market encompasses those countries in East and Southeast Asia whose economic growth has enabled their populations to enjoy the consumption of such cultural products, both hardware and software. These countries include China, South Korea, Taiwan, Hong Kong, the Philippines, Thailand, Singapore, Malaysia, and Indonesia. Moreover, in order to participate in auditions, people practice by themselves and repeatedly listen to their own favorite songs to become a star, as well as being fans and consumers. In this way, consumer technologies such as karaoke, the Sony Walkman, and CDs find new sources of revenue. Pioneer, a Japanese producer of audiovisual equipment, had held amateur karaoke contests in seven Asian countries since 1991 in order to promote sales for laser-disc players and discs. In 1993 more than 10,000 people joined the contest and Pioneer shipped 600,000 laser-disc players to the East and Southeast Asian region, more than double the number that were shipped in 1992 (Kyūseichō Ajia nerau ongaku sangyō 1994).

Japanese media industries assume that Asian audiences are willing consumers, just as the Japanese people have been since the late 1950s. With the development and diffusion of TV in Japan, the American middle-class way of life, as represented in some American drama serials, has had a tremendous influence upon the Japanese people. It is a life abounding in electrical appliances. The Japanese electronics industry has subtly exploited the desires of the people by using the catchphrase, "the three treasures," which associates the acquisition of electrical appliances with a happy middle-class lifestyle (see, e.g., Kelly 1993; Ivy 1993). In the late 1950s the three treasures were the "three S's"—senpūki, sentakuki, and suihanki (the electric fan, the washing machine, and the electric rice cooker); in the 1960s, the "three C's" were a car, a cooler (air conditioner), and a color television. The strategy of the audition-based star system, combined with consumer technologies, was also the vehicle for promoting consumerism in Japan, especially in the 1970s and early 1980s. In the 1990s the same strategy has been deployed in the Asian market. The industry tries to exploit and produce desire among the people to be members of the middle class in a modern capitalist society.

Thus, Japanese capital and transnational manufacturing companies have supported Japanese media efforts with the aim of marketing consumer commodities in Asian. According to a 1995 survey of the most well-known companies and product names in China, Japanese companies occupy six of the top ten positions, as follows: Honda, no. 10; Suzuki, no. 9; Marlboro, no. 8; Mickey Mouse, no. 7; Toyota, no. 6; Tchingtao, no. 5; Toshiba, no. 4; Panasonic, no. 3; Coca-Cola, no. 2; and Hitachi, no. 1 (Nihon burando 1995). These companies all look for an "image character" to sell their products in the local markets in Asia. Thus, Sony pushed Asian singers in those markets in order to promote sales not only of CDs but also of CD players. The Filipina singer, Maribeth, is a case in point. Maribeth's first album sold more than 350,000 CDs and cassette tapes in Indonesia in just four months, which is close to Michael Jackson's best-selling record of 400,000 cassettes and CDs sold for *Alone Against the World* (Kyūseichō Ajia nerau ongaku sangyō 1994). The main reason for Maribeth's success in Indonesia was the use of her hit song in a TV advertisement for Sony CD players. Maribeth's single was titled "Denpasar Moon." Sony created an advertisement for a CD player that featured Maribeth singing the song in Bali, which contributed to sales of both CD players and CDs (Ichikawa 1995, 336). According to what a director of Sony Music Japan told me in 1994, Maribeth's next song would be a duet, and Sony planned to promote the song along with its karaoke machines which have a dueting facility. This is a common strategy in Japan, called a "tie-up," and the strategy has obviously worked well—in the case of Maribeth, in Indonesia. Likewise, Panasonic has changed their "image girl" for the Asian market, from a Japanese idol who is quite popular in Taiwan and China, to a Chinese singer, the winner of the audition held by HoriPro Entertainment Group in Beijing in 1995 (Eisei 1995). Yaohan, a big retail chain store in Asia, used Shanghai Performance Doll to disseminate Yaohan's good image when it introduced its stores in Shanghai (Ongaku to owarai 1994). Indeed, the export of Japanese popular culture to other parts of Asia is interlinked with that of Japanese consumer commodities and department stores (Igarashi et al. 1995).

It is in this Japanese capitalist exploitation of "the new rich" in Asia (Robinson and Goodman 1996) that the featuring of local pop stars for diverse local markets was supposed to work better than the direct export of Japanese musicians. In order for the Japanese music industry to profit from multimedia strategies, these pop icons need not necessarily be "indigenous," strictly speaking. The Filipino singer Maribeth, for example, is popular in Indonesia, where she evokes the common experiences and dreams of Indonesians, dreams of an affluent, commodity-saturated lifestyle.[8] The clothing, hairstyles, and attitudes of highly "Westernized" Asian celebrities are much more stimulating to Asian viewers than those of American stars. It is much easier and more "realistic" for them to identify with Asian stars. One producer of *Asia Bagus!* told me that one of the most important things Japan does in producing the program is the use of a first-rate Japanese makeup artist and fashion stylist to make an ordinary person into a star on the TV screen.

It can be argued that Japanese media industries do not try to offer, much less impose, "authentically Japanese" concepts or pop stars through TV. Likewise, neither are Asian pop stars (including Japanese stars) presented as representative of "traditional national cultures" or as "authentically Asian."

Panasonic Electronics product pamphlet
for Asian markets featuring a Chinese
"image girl."

Rather, they represent a variety of "Asiannesses" that intensely indigenizes
"Westernness" or "Americanness." The Japanese music industry attempts to
produce Asian pop idols who are skillful at "domesticating the West" in
Asia.[9] Each singer from different locales appropriates Western culture in his
or her own way, to the extent that hierarchical relationships cannot be
discerned between the original and the indigenized, at least not by Asian
audiences. What Asian pop idols embody is neither "American" nor "traditional Asian," but something new and hybridized. People no longer consume "the West" or a "Westernized Asia" but an "indigenized (Asianized)
West"; they are fascinated neither with "originality" nor with "tradition,"
but are actively constructing their own images and meanings at the receiving end. The specificities, or "authenticity," if you like, of local cultures are

to be found "a posteriori not a priori, according to local consequences not local origins" (Miller 1992, 181).

Yet the active construction of meanings takes place under the system of global capitalism in which Japan has a major role. The flow of cultural products and of profits is unquestionably one-sided and asymmetrical. People's freedom of negotiation at the receiving end of the global cultural flow coexists with the unambiguously centralized control of the production and distribution system. No matter how production processes are localized, they are financially at the mercy of giant corporations. It is this contradiction between the privatized negotiation of meanings and the centralization of production and distribution which not only characterizes but also reinforces the strategy of "global localization." In other words, the strength of "global localization" lies in the simultaneous mustering of "local consequences" and global structural constraint, which are closely interconnected and inter-penetrated. While most people do not personally feel the global forces that structure their everyday lives, these forces are nonetheless structurally and analytically real.

It is also naive to generalize about urban middle-class culture in Asia, as the term still excludes too many peoples and regions across Asia. This point has been particularly highlighted as the recent economic crisis in Asia has deprived many people of the material base for middle-class status. The danger, as Sreberny-Mohammadi (1991) argues, is that "global players" are still confined to "the affluent few" and the local tends to be equated with the national, which neglects various unprofitable "locals" based upon class, gender, and ethnic inequalities within each nation. In marketing consumer culture, Japanese media industries imagine a particular kind of Asian audience without considering any sublocal specificity and how actual people live their everyday lives in their locales. This is not to say that Japanese media industries fails to recognize the existence of multiple social and cultural differences across the region. *Asia Bagus!* encountered many problems in the production process, caused by such irreducible cultural differences among participating nations as fashion, religion, language, and the frequent changes of broadcasters and participating countries.[10] The Japanese producer of *Asia Bagus!* clearly recognized the irreducible diversity of Asian cultural markets (Kanemitsu 1993). The point is, however, that while the localization strategy is meant to be attentive, from a marketing point of view, to regional and national differences in East and Southeast Asia, "Asia" is nevertheless reconstructed by the Japanese media industries, which are enchanted with the idea of the Japanese orchestration of a pan-Asian entertainment project as a bounded capitalist space of ardent consumer aspiration for indigenizing Western modern culture. In this space, Japan does not simply share the aspiration with other Asian nations, but it is also qualified to guide them in how to develop local forms of vernacular consumer and popular culture.

The limits of glocalization

Because of economic difficulties encountered by the Japanese media industries, however, Japanese ventures for cultivating pan-Asian pop idols have only been, at best, partially successful. In entering Asian markets with these localizing strategies, Japanese recording companies and talent agencies did not expect immediate returns on their investment in the Asian entertainment business, but they gambled on the potential of flourishing Asian, and particularly Chinese, markets (Eisei 1995; Wasei poppusu wa Ajia wo mezasu 1994).[11] In spite of their original intentions, many Japanese music companies could not continue to bear their accumulating losses, and so they retreated from their projects to find local pop idols in Asia. When I returned to Tokyo in January 1997, to meet media industry people whom I had interviewed in October 1994, their earlier passionate and optimistic comments about localizing projects in Asian markets had been replaced by more sober and exhausted voices. The prolonged economic recession in Japan and other Asian countries had made it difficult for Japanese media industries to sustain their low profits in Asian markets in comparison with the rich domestic market. A manager at Dentsū who had promoted the concept trade of Japanese TV variety shows had been transferred to a different section. He told me that he still saw possibilities in the idea of concept trade, but that Dentsū could not currently sustain his endeavor. Beyond advertising agencies, the economic crisis in Japan and Asia had also cast a dark shadow on the activities of Japanese media industries. Pony Canyon had actually retreated from the Asian markets in late 1997. After its radio station (an affiliate) was listed on the Japanese stock market, most of its offices in Asian cities, except those in Malaysia and Hong Kong, had been closed and liquidated. Yaohan, which had attempted to use Shanghai Performance Doll for its marketing campaign, also went bankrupt in 1996.

The despondency in the media industries also has much to do with the more general limitations of localization strategies that have come to light through actual operations in Asian markets. A music producer for HoriPro

Entertainment Group told me that there was gap between ideals and reality. In many cases, the different media system in China and strict control of the media by the Chinese government presented difficult obstacles for the Japanese media industries. The producer pointed out, for example, that in China, unlike Japan, a song is not necessarily guaranteed widespread popularity if it is chosen to be the theme song for a TV commercial or a TV program. The most powerful medium for the promotion of popular music in China according to him, is FM radio, and the way in which deejays broadcast a song is a key to its success. However, the Chinese government has imposed a cultural policy that gives top priority in airplay to songs composed and recorded by Chinese performers. Second priority is given to songs that originate in Hong Kong and Taiwan. Other, internationally "corrupted" songs, either composed or performed by non-Chinese, face difficulties in reaching an audience. The situation is much worse in Vietnam, where HoriPro Entertainment Group also organized an audition in 1995. The Vietnamese government allows foreign capital to establish joint companies in Vietnam. However, the government is quite nervous about the prospects of a Western-style entertainment industry, which would have a "bad" cultural influence on the populace. HoriPro Entertainment Group could not obtain permission from the Vietnamese government to establish an entertainment company. Without a local office, HoriPro could not promote their music in Vietnam. As a Chinese staff member of HoriPro's International Department told me in January 1997: "I think the Asia boom is cooling down. Each new album accumulates not profit but deficit. Maybe we are moving from 'Let's do something in Asia' to a sober confrontation with the reality."

A director of Epic Sony also lamented the difficulties of working with the Chinese media system. Shanghai Performance Doll made its debut in 1996 both in China and in Japan. The group quickly sold 80,000 copies of its cassette tape recordings in China. But the Chinese publisher of the tape refused to repress additional copies. No matter how much Sony pushed the Chinese publisher to repress the album, according to the Sony director, the company was reluctant to follow through, insisting that they were following the Chinese way of business. In 1994, the director told me passionately, he had wanted to produce many versions of Performance Doll in various Asian countries, but two years later he seemed to have recognized the difficulties of doing business in China, and he had lost interest in exporting the Japanese system to other Asian countries as well. By February 1997, his thinking had changed. He now told me that the "Japanese music industry should not impose a Japanese way on other Asian markets" and that "we should not attempt to forcibly develop local music industries." His comments might sound ethical, but they were derived from his unsuccessful try to break into the Chinese market.

Another related issue is the way that Japanese media industries do business in foreign countries. In my research, I often heard that Japanese companies imposed their own way of doing business without considering local differences in terms of business culture and market structures. The Chinese staff who worked for HoriPro Entertainment Group related in an interview that the frequent conflicts between the Japanese and the local (Chinese) staff over promotional strategies and the selection of songs for CDs were always resolved at the company's Japanese headquarters and that this had led the local Chinese to distrust the headquarters group. A Singaporean music producer also complained that Japanese music companies were too vigorous in imposing their thinking, leaving few decisions to the local staff, even though the Japanese did not fully understand the local market. This sounds like a contradiction when one considers the way that Japanese companies are celebrated for their glocalization strategies. Japanese media tend to stress that they hire local staff and leave everything to them (see Akurosu Henshūshitsu 1995, 100–19), but there is a significant gap between what they say and what they do. The structure remains highly centralized and final decisions tend to be made in Tokyo.

The then managing director of the Taiwan office of a Japanese recording company described in an interview with me in 1997 the difficulty he had encountered in trying to convince the Tokyo office of the necessity of spending money on publicity to sell CDs in the Taiwanese market: "Japanese companies naively assume that Japanese know-how is completely transferable to other Asian markets, but they do not understand how media environments vary and systems work differently. In Taiwan, TV is a medium that just sells spot commercial time, and recording companies have to pay for using it, even when the record is the theme song from a TV drama. This is common practice throughout the world, as far as I know, but [the head office] does not realize this." These comments show some of the impediments the Japanese music industry faced in exporting Japanese know-how to Asian markets.[12] The Japanese media naively assumed that they could localize Japanese experiences by themselves, but in fact they either knew too little about the specificity of the local market or they left the local business decisions totally in the hands of Japanese management staff.

Japanese media industries have attempted to become translators of "the West" for "Asia." A Japanese cultural producer stressed in an interview with me in 1996 that the strength of the Japanese media industries vis-à-vis the Asian industries are their fifty years of experience and the accumulated know-how of its "American education," a view which is widely shared by other cultural producers, as discussed earlier. He, like others, seems to believe that Japan is able to perform such a cultural translation for other Asian nations because it is the most successfully Westernized non-Western country in the world. The confidence of the Japanese media industries in their own superiority at indigenizing the West is, as a Chinese staff member of a Japanese talent agency told me, not only perceived as arrogance by local staff but also often deters Japanese media industries from appreciating different ways of negotiating Western cultural influences in other parts of Asia.

This attitude was well discerned by a Japanese director of the Singapore branch office of a Japanese advertising company. In my interview with him, he deplored the fact that Singapore did not have a sophisticated advertising culture, that advertising in Singapore too straightforwardly promotes commodities in terms of competitive price and quality, to effectively foster a Japanese-style consumer culture (*mono bunka*). This perception of the cultural role of advertising companies is based upon his own experiences in Japan. For example, he was involved in promoting an advertisement for a Japanese department store in the 1980s. The advertisement featured an image of Woody Allen with a depressed expression, over which was superimposed the Japanese phrase "*Oishii seikatsu*" (literally, "Delicious life"). This ironical and paradoxical appropriation of an American cultural icon for the Japanese cultural scene was more than a straightforward advertising message (Wark 1991). What the Japanese advertising manager wanted to export to Singapore was a highly image-oriented advertising culture, which he believed would be more culturally significant: "Singapore so easily and directly imports things from outside. They never try to indigenize it in a Singaporean way. This is because there are no cultural producers who can work as cultural filters that indigenize the foreign to the local."

He wanted to be such a cultural filter for Singapore, but in vain. As a result, he tended to denigrate Singapore's consumer culture as backward compared with that of Japan and Western countries. Singapore's alleged incapacity for absorbing foreign influences through "local" filters was not the issue, but rather the Japanese inability to recognize a different mode of negotiating Western cultural influences. The specificity of the Singaporean situation is elucidated by Wee (1997, 44), who argues concerning the spread of Japanese popular and consumer culture in Singapore that "it would appear that people seem to feel that there is no need for a Japanese mediation between them and the images/representations of the West. . . . With regard to Japanese products, why consume what could be construed as a second-hand modernity?" For many Singaporeans, the direct consumption of Western popular culture might be experienced as much more exciting and desirable.

These cases propel us to reconsider the emphasis placed by Japanese media industries on their sophisticated capacity for indigenizing "America" as symptomatic of a growing disquiet generated by the globalization of indigenized modernities. Behind the confidence of Japanese music producers in their know-how concerning indigenizing the West, I would argue, there is also an anxiety that "the Japanese system is too self-contained to extend its power overseas" (as the Japanese manager of the Taipei office of a recording company put it in an interview with me). As transnational cultural flows and cultural indigenization are ever more intensifying and accelerating in the world, the Japanese claim to an unmatched Japanese experience in the formation of non-Western indigenized modernity has been dismantled. And what is more disturbing is the fact that other Asian countries, particularly the Chinese, are now bypassing Japan and are now indigenizing the West directly and possibly more subtly.

Some Japanese media producers clearly recognize this dark picture and share with other economic sectors a pessimistic view of the country's standing vis-à-vis the rise of other Asian economic powers. It seems that the world has shifted, from Japan-bashing, which loomed large in trading between Japan and the United States in the late 1980s, to Japan-passing, and now to Japan-nothing (E. Saitō 1997; McCormack 1998).[13] Although the Japanese director of the advertising agency in Singapore whom I interviewed saw Singapore's direct import of the West as somewhat unsophisticated, some cultural producers have increasingly come to realize that in the 1990s other Asian countries are more eagerly and creatively indigenizing Western popular culture. The producer of *Asia Bagus!* emphasized this point in an interview with me when he suggested that the direct consumption of popular cultures all over the world, and particularly those of the West, makes the pop culture scene in other Asian countries more creative and exciting than it is in Japan.

Another cultural producer elaborated on this point: "Japanese media industries have a misconception that Japan is more advanced than any other Asian country in terms of popular cultural production, but what is happening is that other Asian countries are also rapidly absorbing American culture in their own ways. I think an Americanization of Asia cannot be avoided. Japan has to be involved in this process in order not to be left out of the prosperous Asian markets. I would propose the acronym 'USA' to stand for the United States of Asia. Like the United States of America where many different cultures are fused, our USA should fuse different cultures so something new emerges in Asia." He was stressing that Japan must be fused with other parts of Asia, particularly with the Greater China cultural bloc. The speaker's production house, Amuse, has been the most active in promoting the coproduction of films in East Asia. In 1995, for example, it coproduced with Shanghai TV twenty-five one-hour episodes of a drama series, *Shanghai People in Tokyo*. The drama concerns the lives of overseas students from Shanghai in Tokyo.[14] Amuse is also very active in coproducing films with Hong Kong production houses. Since 1994, it has coproduced three films, *Nankin no Kirisuto, Hong Kong Daiyasōkai,* and *Kitchen* (Higashi Ajia konketsu eiga 1997). In 1997 Amuse established a joint production company with Golden Harvest Hong Kong to produce a string of love stories (Amyūzu 1997) and also set up a branch in Seoul soon after the South Korean government decided in late 1998 to phase out restrictions on importing Japanese popular culture.

If Amuse sustains an accumulating loss in its ventures in Asian markets,[15] this is because, as the manager of Amuse suspects, it is the only way for Japan not to be left out of transnational popular culture markets in the Chinese cultural bloc (see also Mizukoshi and Baeg 1993). The company is struggling with the question of how to be involved in the rise of cultural markets in the Chinese cultural sphere before it is too late, before the deconstructive forces of cultural globalization render Japan's know-how not simply irrelevant and unappreciated by other Asian nations, but also completely isolate Japan from the increasingly Chinese-dominated market in East and Southeast Asia.

"Real time" local promotion of Japanese popular culture

Another consideration in the analysis of Japanese localization strategies in Asian markets is that they are deployed mainly in relatively immature markets, such as China, and not in mature markets like Taiwan and Hong Kong, where Japanese popular culture has long had an influence (see, e.g., Morieda 1988; Shinozaki 1988; Ching 1994). The producer of *Asia Bagus!* has made it clear that Hong Kong has not been included in the program because its market and media are too mature to penetrate (Kanemitsu 1993). Such countries have imitated and indigenized American popular culture, as well as the Japanese idol system, on their own accord and there is not much need for Japanese media industries to teach them the techniques of cultural indigenization in the 1990s.

The Taiwanese music industry conscientiously copied the Japanese idol system during the 1980s, particularly in terms of the performers' appearance, clothing, and music. Imitating the Japanese model was an easy and safe way to for the then not-so-mature Taiwanese music industry to promote its own pop idols; producers thought that the success of the Japanese system would guarantee their own success (see Ching 1994). However, that imitation stage is over. By the early 1990s, local idols had begun to create their own styles. The chief editor of a Taiwanese version of the Japanese idol magazine, *Up to Boy,* told me in 1997 that "Taiwanese idols used to be quite conscious of which Japanese idols to copy, but this is no longer the case. They are now emphasizing their own styles and are considering the international market as well. There is no time lag between Japan and Taiwan any longer." The move toward local maturity is also seen in the composition of music hits. As mentioned earlier, Japanese popular songs had been "covered" extensively by Taiwanese and Hong Kong singers. Now, local composers have brushed up their capabilities and the local industry has quite consciously striven to improve its expertise. For example, Hong Kong's influential radio station, Commercial Radio, banned the broadcasting Japanese cover songs in 1994. Seen as a protectionist measure, this decision can also be interpreted as a reflection of the increasing confidence of the Hong Kong music industry in its own production capacity and in the maturity of the music market.

This is not to say that Japan no longer has any cultural influence in these areas, however. On the contrary, it is precisely in such mature East Asian markets that Japanese popular music and TV programs are most keenly imported and consumed. An emerging trend since the mid-1990s is that while the export of the Japanese idol system has proved to be sporadic, the dissemination of Japanese popular music has become more constant and synchronous (Honkon, Taiwan, Nihon wa poppu kyōeiken 1997; Ajia mo watashi no ikiru michi! 1997). Although there are no reliable figures available, according to executives in the Taiwanese recording companies, in 1997 Japanese popular music was estimated to occupy only a 2–4 percent share of the Taiwanese market in terms of CDs sold (the estimates for China were 75–80 percent of the market, and for the international market, 15–20 percent). However, Japanese popular music has been gradually increasing its presence in Taiwan throughout the 1990s. According to the International Federation of Phonogram and Videogram Producers (IFPI), for the week 25–31 March 1997, five Japanese songs were in the top-10 for single-CD sales—two songs by the Japanese artist Amuro Namie (one of which held the No. 1 slot), two songs by the group Globe, and one song by Dreams Come True. This is an astonishing phenomenon, even if we consider that Taiwanese and Hong Kong artists generally do not issue single-CDs and thus Japanese pop music single-CDs do not compete with the most popular local (Taiwan and Hong Kong) pop music there.

In a feature article in the monthly popular magazine *Bart,* the "real time" popularity of Japanese pop songs in Taiwan, Hong Kong, and Singapore was described as "unassuming" (*shizentai*), as distinguished from the gambling spirit required to penetrate booming Asian markets and the rhetoric of cultural diplomacy that called for "bridging Japan and Asia" (Ajia mo watashi no ikiru michi! 1997). Referring to the increasing cooperation and coproduction among Asian cultural producers and musicians, the article implied that the emerging trend toward regional synchronization of popular culture in Asia, which has been promoted by media globalization processes, is seen somehow as an organic development among East Asian nations. Behind this development, however, there are massive promotional efforts and money invested by the media industries. "Real time" and similar expressions, like "simultaneity" or "no time lag," are terms I frequently heard in my interviews with Japanese as well as Taiwanese and Hong Kong music producers. These terms are not simply the expression of an increasing confidence in the Hong Kong and Taiwanese industries, as noted above; they are also uttered as part of a key marketing strategy for promoting Japanese popular music in East Asia. As the Japanese managing director of a recording company in Taiwan told me in 1997: "Taiwan used to be a place where Japanese idols on the wane could still sell, but nowadays they must be popular simultaneously in Japan in order to succeed in Taiwan because the information and images circulate in real time. The popularity of Japanese artists/idols in Taiwan is closely influenced by daily Taiwanese media coverage of how many records they have sold and how much fame they have attained in Japan."[16]

What should be noted here is that in this synchronous circulation of Japanese popular music in Taiwan and Hong Kong, the ascendancy of Japanese popular music is not a result of successful promotion by Japanese media industries. Rather, it is the local media and the local music industry that have been earnestly marketing Japanese products. As I will elaborate for Japanese TV programs in the next chapter, along with political and economic liberalization, the development of communication technologies and the expansion of the entertainment market in Taiwan has been important in facilitating the influx of Japanese popular culture in Taiwan since the late 1980s. These developments have exposed the audience in Taiwan to more information about Japanese pop icons, through newspapers, magazines, television, and the Internet, and they have given the locals an incentive for exploiting the commercial potential of Japanese popular music by encouraging them to invest a large amount of money in promoting it in Taiwan. The disappearance of time lag thus operates in a double sense—by erasing the developmental lag in popular music production capacity and market development, and by facilitating the transnationalization of fame through the instantaneous circulation of imagery and information. Both factors have been responsible for and have generated the local promotion of Japanese popular music in Taiwan and Hong Kong.

During the time of my field research in Taipei in 1997, two local companies, Magic Stone and Sony Music Taiwan, were particularly keen to sell Japanese artists in Taiwan. Interestingly, neither company is controlled by a Japanese company. Magic Stone distributes Japanese popular songs through Avex Japan, a company which has no established branches in Asian capitals but which promotes its CDs through licensing agreements. The manager of Avex Hong Kong who was in charge of exporting their CDs to Asian markets told me that licensing allows this small independent company to avoid the high cost of maintaining an office and employees. For Japanese popular musicians, Japan itself is no doubt the most important market and they cannot afford to sacrifice it so as to visit other, less profitable markets. The group Chage & Aska, which has toured Asia twice, were exceptional in this regard and were also exceptional in the extent of their popularity overseas. The Japanese music industry and pop musicians are hesitant to invest huge sums of money in other Asian markets where profits may not seem very likely. The result is that Japanese companies avoid investing much of their own money, and Japanese artists do not tour frequently outside of Japan to promote their music. One disadvantage of the system is that the artists whom Avex wants to sell do not necessarily attract licensing partners, and the amount of money to be spent on publicity is at the total discretion of the licensing partner. Nevertheless, this licensing strategy has been successful in Taiwan.[17] The promotional strategy taken by Magic Stone has paved the way for the Japanese dance music of Komuro Tetsuya (the then most popular and influential artist and producer in Japan), which has become "cool" in Taiwan. Taiwanese record companies usually spend a lot on publicity for the new albums of local artists but relatively little for international artists. The managing director of Magic Stone boasted to me that, for the first time, Magic Stone had invested the same amount of money in promoting Japanese artists in Taiwan as it historically had done for local artists.

A similar arrangement can be seen in Sony Music Taiwan's promotion of the trio Dreams Come True. It was Sony Music Taiwan, not Sony Music Japan, which took the initiative in deciding which Japanese artists to sell in the Taiwanese market. Sony Music Taiwan had cautiously made plans to promote Dreams Come True in Taiwan over a two-year period and had finally succeeded in inviting the group to Taiwan in 1996. According to the vice-president of Sony Music Taiwan, the company spent a considerable amount of money on promotion in Taiwan, almost ten times the average for international artists, and the result was sales of over 200,000 copies of the latest CD for the group, a phenomenal success for a foreign artist.

The increasing popularity of Japanese popular music in Hong Kong has caused the Hong Kong–based STAR TV to more actively forge transnational alliances with the Japanese music industry. For example, Komuro Tetsuya made inroads into Asian markets by establishing a joint company with News Corp.'s TK NEWS in 1996 (Mādokku to kunde Komuro Tetsuya 1996; Sekai tenkai senryaku Komuro Tetsuya 1997). The purpose of the new company was not simply to promote Komuro's music in Hong Kong, but also to popularize the Komuro Family as performers throughout East Asia. The strength of TK NEWS is that it is closely connected with STAR TV's music channel, Channel [V], on which Komuro and his family now appear frequently. In January 1997 Amuro Namie (she is part of the Komuro family) was selected as Channel [V]'s "artist of the month," the first time that designation has been given to a Japanese artist. Her single went to number-one on the channel's Asian Top-20.

In May 1997 the Komuro Family's two scheduled concerts in Taipei surprisingly attracted more media attention than did global pop star Whitney Houston, who happened to be giving a concert two days before the Komuro Family and who was staying at the same hotel. TK NEWS also produced a star-search TV program, *TK Magic,* to discover new Taiwanese artists; the result was that a thirteen-year-old Taiwanese female singer called Ring made her debut with the Komuro Family in April 1998. This sounds like the familiar strategy of finding a local star, but the crucial difference is that Komuro is not only an artist but also a capable producer. Komuro announced his willingness to learn from News Corp.'s localizing marketing strategies developed for Asia (Sekai tenkai senryaku Komuro Tetsuya 1997); however, for TK NEWS, it was Komuro's fame that was important, not localizing his sound—though localizing his lyrics was considered important. The selling point for Ring was that she *was* a local artist whose producer was the best producer in Japan. As a result, Ring's first single went to the top of the IFPI Taiwan single-CD chart immediately after its release in 1998.

Behind this promotion of Japanese popular music there is a strong conviction among industry people in Taiwan and Hong Kong concerning the unambiguous attractiveness of Japanese popular music for East Asian audiences. The director of Channel [V], Jeff Murray, who was also the intermediary between Komuro and News Corp., expressed that opinion to me. According to Murray, in terms of the subtle absorption and indigenization of a variety of Western pop styles, Japanese music production is definitely more sophisticated than its counterpart elsewhere in Asia, and Japanese music, though a new taste for the Taiwanese audience, is more similar to Taiwanese pop and easier to relate to than Western pop. The recognition of an "Asianness" in Japanese popular music is significant for Channel [V]'s strategy of differentiating itself from MTV Asia. Murray stressed to me that the strength of Channel [V] is that its content is more local than that of MTV Asia: "If MTV can be compared to McDonald's, Channel [V] is dim sum [Chinese snack food]." When I asked whether Japanese popular culture and music are also dim sum, he answered "yes." However, he noted that it is not simply one dim sum among others. As well as suggesting a primordial cultural commonality among Asian nations, Murray predicted that "being Japanese will be fashionable in the twenty-first century" (Honkon, Taiwan, Nihon wa poppu kyōeiken 1997). This view was shared by the Taiwanese managing director of Magic Stone, who told me: "Japan should be confident of its own popular culture. . . . The 1990s are a turning point in which

Japanese popular culture is taking over the symbolic role of American popular culture in Asia." By this he meant that Japanese popular culture is becoming another object of desire for young people in Asia.

To what extent these scenarios, which locate Japan at the center of intra-Asian cultural flows and transnational regional modernity in Asia, will come to pass remains to be seen. Since the predictions were made by people in managerial positions, they strongly reflect the desire and will of those managers to turn their predictions into self-fulfilling prophecies. As the managing director of Magic Stone asserted during our conversation, the promotion of Japanese popular music in Asian markets can only be done effectively in conjunction with the marketing strategies of the local industry. In sum, the meaning of localization for Japanese popular culture in Asian markets has gradually shifted its emphasis from the export of Japanese know-how in localizing Western popular culture to the synchronous promotion of Japanese popular culture by local industries in Taiwan and Hong Kong, which ardently attempt to turn the attention of audiences to the "fragrance" of Japanese popular culture.

The sweet scent of Asian modernity?

It should be noted, however, that Japanese popular culture has not prevailed in Taiwan to the extent that the local odor no longer matters. The desire to become at once modern and different is one which globalization processes generate (Hannerz 1996, 55). It is this desire that lets the durian articulate the "modern" local identity of Southeast Asia; and the glocalization strategy of transnational corporations, including Japanese companies, increasingly attempts to exploit this same desire by re-demarcating the boundaries of a larger cultural/civilizational formation such as the Chinese cultural bloc, which indiscriminately includes all people of Chinese descent in Asia. The Japanese market is not immune to transnational media industries' strategies of glocalization. Yoshida Miwa, the female vocalist with the pop group Dreams Come True, appeared on the cover of the 14 October 1996 issue of *Time Asia*; the cover story was entitled "The Divas of Pop." Yoshida was one of these divas, along with Celine Dion, Gloria Estefan, Whitney Houston, Mariah Carey, Alanis Morissette, Tina Arena, and Faye Wong. In Japan this story was reported in major newspapers and sales for the issue almost tripled (according to my phone interview with *Time Japan*). But Yoshida only appeared on the cover of the Japanese version of *Time Asia*. In other Asian countries, including Taiwan, the cover carried a picture of Faye Wong, a Beijing-born Hong Kong singer. No matter how well received it is in other parts of Asia, it will not be easy for the sweet scent of Japanese popular culture to fully overpower the deodorant of transnational media industries, which are the main forces for organizing cultural diversity and selling cultural odor to local markets.

On the other hand, as I have shown, there is an emerging trend for the synchronous interpenetration and interconnection of East Asian cultural markets that feature Japanese cultural products seen as embodying a transnational regional modernity in East Asia. The rise of Japanese popular music in East Asian markets indicates that media globalization is not only promoting global homogenization and local heterogenization, but also (supra-national) regionalization (e.g., Straubhaar 1991; Sinclair, Jacka, and Cunningham 1996b; Hawkins 1997). The development of communication technologies, the acceleration of information flow, and the maturity of local audiovisual markets and industries in East Asia, all of these globalizing forces have increased the cooperative contact between various local industries and intensified the real-time, intraregional cultural flow within Asia, in which Japanese popular music and TV programs are becoming alluring commodities. As Hall (1991, 28) argues, transnational capital attempts to "rule through other local capitals, rule alongside and in partnership with other economic and political elites." Hall's argument is concerned with American global cultural power, but this logic is equally applicable to the transnationalization of Japanese popular culture. While the global promotion of Japanese animation is carried out by American and British distribution companies such as Disney, even intraregional coproduction in Asia cannot escape the shadow of the global corporations. Komuro Tetsuya's inroads into transnational markets have been facilitated by the global media conglomerate News Corp.[18] Even in concept trade, *Oshin,* a globally popular Japanese melodrama, has been remade in Indonesia by the Australian production house Beckers Group, which exports TV programs internationally (Indonesia ban de Oshin 1997). These examples clearly testify to the fact that the operation of Japanese media industries and the transnational marketing of Japanese media products in regional Asian markets cannot be conducted effectively without partners at each level.[19]

However, we cannot explain why Japanese popular music and TV programs other than animation are well accepted in Asian countries solely in terms of the logic of capital and marketing strategies, no matter how effective and powerful they are. Apart from the self-congratulatory comments made by representatives of the Taiwanese, Hong Kong, and Japanese media industries concerning the scent of Japanese popular culture, there is something culturally embedded in the spread of Japanese popular culture and hence in the rise of Japanese transnational cultural power in East Asia. We have seen that the capitalist logic of transnationalization finds a boundary— however porous and fluctuating—to the transnational reach of Japanese popular cultural appeal in East Asian regions. But it is also important to direct our attention to "Japanese odor," to the textual and symbolic appeal embodied in Japanese popular culture without falling into the trap of assuming that the media industries' manipulative techniques are omnipotent or that some preexisting cultural commonality is at work in spreading Japanese popular culture in Asian markets.

We have seen that the image of Japan as a translator of Western popular culture does not match the actual market situations throughout East and Southeast Asia, yet the increasing outflow of Japanese popular culture suggests that the "Japaneseness" with which resonates for some people in modernized Asian countries might have more to do with a distinctively Japanese cultural modernity, something which is not simply a response to Western modernity. The textual appeal of that popular culture is closely associated with the lifestyles and social relationships of present-day Japan, as embodied in living Japanese actors, not animated or digitalized characters. Unlike traditional culture, in which the irreducible difference of one culture from others tends to be shaped, contemporary popular culture, though highly commercialized, reminds Japan and Asia alike that they share a common temporality and a common experience of a certain regional (post)modernity which American popular culture cannot represent well. If Japanese popular culture tastes and smells like dim sum to the media industries and consumers in Hong Kong and Taiwan—and tastes like kimchi to South Koreans (Cute power! 1999)—it might be because it embodies a sophisticated co-mingling of the "global" and "local" within an East Asian context. It is this transnational appeal of Japanese popular culture, and the newly produced asymmetry of cultural flows in East Asia that accompanies it, that will be analyzed in the next chapter by looking at the reception of Japanese TV dramas in Taiwan.

4

Becoming culturally proximate:

Japanese TV dramas in Taiwan

In the previous chapter I argued that intraregional cultural flows and industry connections are becoming more intensive and regular, particularly among East Asian nations whose popular cultural markets are relatively mature. These developments have helped increase the prominence of Japanese popular culture in the region. In this chapter and the next, I examine the sorts of cultural resonances that are experienced by audiences in this context. I explore how cultural similarity and distance are favorably but differently perceived by audiences in East Asia in their consumption of media texts from neighboring countries. This approach will elucidate how the asymmetrical cultural flows and power relations between Japan and other East Asian countries are articulated at the site of consumption.

This chapter discusses the reception of Japanese TV dramas (with particular attention to the popular drama series *Tokyo Love Story*) in Taiwan. In examining the consumption of Japanese popular culture in East Asia, I focus on Taiwan for two reasons. First, Taiwan has become, at least quantitatively, the most receptive market for Japanese popular cultural products, particularly TV dramas, which, unlike animation, are in most cases not exportable to Western countries and are popular only in Asian markets. Second, the rapid commercialization and promotion of Japanese TV programs in Taiwan highlights the necessity to understand the popularization of Japanese TV programs in that country within the wider dynamic context of political liberalization, economic development and media globalization, as well as the history of Japanese colonization. As a former colony of Japan, Taiwan has long had to deal with a Japanese cultural presence. However, it was after the Taiwanese government officially abandoned its ban on the broadcasting of Japanese language programs in late 1993 that Japanese products gained wide favor among young people. As well, it should be noted that Japanese cultural exports to Taiwan dramatically increased in tandem with the rise of

Taiwan's cable TV industry. This development was the result of the country's strong economic growth and the forces of market liberalization that had taken place since the late 1980s, factors that prompted the influx of foreign media products into Taiwan.

What the Taiwanese case study illustrates is that by configuring the analysis of audience reception of Japanese TV drama in this wider context, we can better grasp the intertwined relation between the cultural distance perceived by other Asian audiences and the rise of Japanese transnational cultural power in the looming intraregional cultural flow in East Asia in the 1990s. It is often observed that the spread of Japanese popular culture in Asia owes much to the "cultural proximity" (Straubhaar 1991) between Japan and other Asian nations. The notion of "cultural proximity" tends to connote the seemingly natural—and thus, power neutral—recognition by audiences of primordial cultural similarities. This chapter challenges what is an essentialist view of such similarities and addresses the questions of how and under what conditions the "cultural proximity" of Japanese TV dramas is experienced and perceived by Taiwanese audiences. The emphasis is on how multilayered forces and factors intersected in the 1990s through the popularity of Japanese TV dramas to articulate audiences' expression of "cultural proximity." By examining "cultural proximity" in a new light, as a dynamic process, I argue that in the case of Taiwanese consumption of Japanese TV dramas, such an apprehension is due in part to an emerging sense among the Taiwanese of coevalness (Fabian 1983) with the Japanese, that is, the feeling that Taiwanese share a modern temporality with Japan. And it is through the production of these understandings of "cultural proximity" and coevalness, I suggest, that Japanese transnational cultural power manifests itself in Taiwan.

Waning affection for "Japan"?

In the 1990s, in spite of the pessimism of Japanese media industries, the spread of Japanese popular culture among Asian audiences became ever more conspicuous and arresting. In a feature article in *Asiaweek*, for example it was reported that Japanese TV programs, particularly animation, were more appealing than their American counterparts in Asia (Asia says Japan is top of the pops 1996). Similarly, *Asian Business Review* reported on the increasing Japanese export of TV programs to Asian markets, stating that "Japan's entertainment exports to Asia are on a roll" (Satellite TV sees gold in local content 1996). This phenomenon has been described dramatically by a Taiwanese-American scholar, Leo Ching (1994, 199), who notes that "throughout Asia, Japan is in vogue."

The steady rise of Japanese TV programs in Asian markets has finally encouraged the normally cautious Japanese TV industry to invest in the transnational broadcast of such programs. Because of the positive reception of Japanese TV programs, particularly dramas, in Taiwan and Hong Kong, the Japanese TV industry has been convinced that they do have the potential to sell in Asia. Hence, their interest in exporting their programs directly to Asian markets. The manager of Dentsū, a company which promotes the Japanese quiz-show format in Asia (see chapter 3), alluded to this new approach in a personal interview in October 1997: "What has been made clear is that Japanese TV programs have gained a certain transnational appeal. The next step is to produce programs that target international, particularly, Asian markets." The Japanese TV industry began setting up a royalty structure for the second and third use of programs. In 1997, a further step was taken when Sumitomo Trading Co., Ltd. launched the first transnational Japanese pay-TV channel, JET (Japan Entertainment Television), in partnership with TBS, a commercial TV station whose profits from selling programs overseas are the highest in Japan. Dubbing Japanese into three languages—English, Mandarin, and Thai—the JET channel broadcasts by satellite link-up from Singapore to seven Asian countries (Taiwan, Hong Kong, Thailand, Singapore, Malaysia, Indonesia, and the Philippines) and is devoted exclusively to Japanese programming—dramas, cartoons, and variety shows. In its advertising, JET declares: "People with an eye for trends have their eyes on Japan. On its fashions, celebrities, and hit products— anything that's new and fun. Today, trend-conscious viewers throughout Asia can enjoy up-to-date programs from Japan twenty-four hours a day: on JET–TV." The explicit emphasis on "Japaneseness" and the attractiveness of Japanese popular culture has clearly become a key to the export strategies of the Japanese TV industry in Asian markets.

This is not to say that the spread of Japanese popular culture in East Asia is an entirely new trend. On the contrary, comics and animation aside, as Ching (1994) suggests, Japanese popular culture has been influential in the region since at least the late 1970s or early 1980s. Japanese TV program formats have been exported and massively copied (pirated). As several Taiwanese TV producers told me, it is not overstating the matter to say that in Taiwan, most variety shows are at least partly copied from popular Japanese programs. Japanese popular music has also been widely covered in Hong Kong and Taiwan, and there have been frenzies for several Japanese TV dramas and idols since the 1970s. However, the recent popularity of Japanese programming in Asia rests on a much broader consumer base than before. In the 1980s, when Japanese idols were famous in East Asia, audiences were limited to a minority of Japanophiles. A woman in her mid-twenties told me in Taiwan, at that time, those who liked such artists were somewhat marginal. In the 1990s, though, it has become common for young Taiwanese to chat about Japanese idols and TV dramas.

At the same time, it was often observed that in the 1990s the widespread interest in Japanese popular culture in Asia has paradoxically been accompanied by a waning of the region's affection for "Japan." It is even claimed that the zenith of the craze for "Japan" in Asia occurred in the early 1980s and that "Japan" is now in decline. In 1996, the *Honkon Tsūshin,* a Japanese-language magazine in Hong Kong ran a feature on Hong Kong Japanophiles from the late 1970s and 1980s, when Hong Kong was importing more Japanese TV programs and there emerged enthusiastic fans of Japanese pop idols there (Nihon otaku to yobitai hitobito 1996). The Japanophiles, now in their late 30s, reported that they still enjoyed the good old Japanese popular culture and continued to follow the careers of their old Japanese idols. When I interviewed him, the magazine's chief editor told me that by the mid-1980s the boom in things Japanese had run its course. He remarked that although the audience for Japanese popular culture in Hong Kong was increasing, the engaged affinity with "Japan" had drastically waned. I heard similar comments in Singapore. When I traveled there in late 1996, the chief editor of a Singaporean TV weekly told me that he clearly remembered how passionately Japanese pop idols were received there in the early 1980s. However, he added, while Singapore's import of Japanese popular culture, such as TV programs and pop music, seemed to be increasing, the craze for Japan had faded away (replaced by one for Hong Kong in the late 1980s, and by local, Mandarin pop culture in the 1990s).

In Taiwan, which has eagerly imported and promoted Japanese popular culture in the 1990s, the situation is more complicated because of the history of Japanese colonial rule. The recent surge of Japanese cultural influence is inevitably discussed there in relation to that rule. In 1997 a leading weekly news magazine in Taiwan featured an article on Japanese popular culture and introduced a new Taiwanese word, roughly translated as "(young) people who adore things Japanese" (Watch out! Your children are becoming

Japanese 1997). While Japan was not strongly condemned for its "cultural invasion" in the article, the spread of Japanese popular culture was associated with the colonial habit of mimicking, which has percolated deeply into Taiwanese society. The issue revealed here is how the historical legacy of Japanese colonization has overdetermined the recent influx of Japanese popular culture. From food and housing to language, examples can easily be found of a lingering Japanese cultural influence in Taiwan. Besides Korea, the number of people who speak Japanese in Taiwan is by far the largest outside Japan itself, and many Japanese words and cultural meanings have become indigenized. Older people who were educated during the Japanese occupation still speak fluent Japanese and enjoy Japanese-language books, songs, and TV programs. No small number of them also regard their former colonizers in a relatively positive light, the bitter memories of their rule having diminished, especially when contrasted to the repressive and authoritarian rule of the Kuomintang (KMT) government which moved from mainland China to the island after World War II (see Liao 1996). These conditions surely make Japanese TV programs much more accessible than in other parts of Asia, particularly in stark contrast to South Korea.

However, those who were educated after World War II hold quite different views of Japan. This generational divide and the grim, violent process of decolonization are elucidated in Wu Nianzhen's film, *Dosan: A Borrowed Life* (1994). The film deals with the nostalgia of older Taiwanese for the Japanese period. In brief, the film narrates the story of a Taiwanese man who has long harbored a dream to visit Japan. His dream can be seen as a wish on his part to affirm an identity and history which were forged under Japanese colonial rule but which he was later forced to deny or repress under the KMT government, in conjunction with Japanese indifference to the aftermath of its colonization policies. Wu, the director of the film, has recollected how, as a student who was taught negatively about the Japanese occupation at school, he hated his father's longing for that period—a longing which was betrayed by the unresponsiveness Japan displayed to Taiwan after the War (Taiwan ga Nippon ni koi o shita 1996, 40–42).[1]

This generational divide has been exacerbated by the emergence of avid young consumers of Japanese popular culture. In May 1997 I witnessed two incidents in Taiwan that nicely illustrate that country's complicated relationship with Japan. The first was an anti-Japanese demonstration over the issue of Japan's possession of the Diaoyu Islands. The other was a rock concert featuring such popular Japanese artists as Globe and Amuro Namie,

Cover of a special issue of *The Journalist,* which featured articles on the Taiwanese youth craze for Japanese popular culture. Reprinted with permission.

which attracted much media attention as well as young audiences. This juxtaposition of "anti-" and "pro-" Japanese sentiment articulates the new generational divide (see also Pro-Japan vs. anti-Japan in Taiwan 1997). The positive meaning "Japan" possesses for young Taiwanese, most of whom do not understand Japanese language, is undoubtedly different from that which it holds for their forebears. Wu has also commented on the recent popularity of Japanese culture among the younger generation in Taiwan, "My generation and my father's generation have a deep love-and-hate feeling towards Japan, though in quite different ways. But the younger generations have no special affection for Japanese culture, as there is no difference between Japan, America, and Europe for them. Japan is just one option among many. I think the relationship between Taiwan and Japan will be more superficial in terms of affective feelings while deepened materially" (quoted in Taiwan ga Nippon ni koi o shita 1996, 42). As is the case for other Asian nations, Wu suggests that the symbolic meaning of "Japan," articulated through Japanese popular culture, is marked in Taiwan by a waning affection.

These observations of the shift in the Asian reception of Japanese popular culture, from an enthusiastic embrace to a more detached, superficial consumption, are reminiscent of a general feature of the postmodern consumption of global culture. Postmodern theories discuss the domination of the sign-value of a commodity over its materiality (e.g., Lash and Urry 1994; Featherstone 1991; Baudrillard 1981, 1983). As the production and circulation of signs and images proliferate, "objects are emptied out of both of meaning (and are postmodern) and of material content (and are thus postindustrial)" (Lash and Urry 1994, 15). Of particular importance to my discussion here is that, as discussed in chapter 1, the proliferation of signs and images has also been accompanied by the promotion of a "peculiar form of homogenization" of the world by American transnational power, since the development of a "global mass culture" dominated by television and film, as well as by the imagery and styles of mass advertising, is predominantly "American" (Hall 1991, 27–28). In this context, it can be argued that Japanese popular culture is losing its symbolic idiosyncrasy, its essential "Japaneseness," and thus it has simply become one among many consumer options available from different parts of the world. In other words, Japanese cultural products have been sucked into the maw of the American-dominated global cultural system, which relentlessly reproduces commercialized cultural signs and images for fugitive and depthless consumption through endless pastiche and simulation (Jameson 1983; Baudrillard 1983). Such products are "here and now and everywhere, and for its purposes the past [and, I would add, other cultures] only serves to offer some decontextualized example or element for its cosmopolitan patchwork" (Smith 1990, 177).

Chō (1998), a Chinese scholar living in Japan, makes a similar point about the consumption of Japanese popular culture in China. He notes the increasing circulation of Japanese cultural commodities, as well as general information about Japan, in Shanghai, and he argues that these events are paradoxically accompanied by a decrease in Japanese cultural influence in China. Recalling how passionately the Chinese consumed Japanese popular

This two-page editorial spread from *The Journalist* depicts the pros and cons of the Japanese cultural influence in Taiwan. Pro: Youth are excited about a Japanese pop concert. Con: A protest against Japanese possession of the Diaoyu Islands. Reprinted with permission.

保釣運動已經不是新鮮的話題，但激情仍舊存在。不過，當哈日族對著小室家族張開樂拜雙手的同時，日本的警察卻以鎮暴裝，對著台港的保釣人士張牙舞爪。

政府要求你
退出日本領海

小室家族演唱會現場幾乎沒有成年人，很多日僑或是說日文的東方臉孔進場。到目前為止，祇有支持陳水扁的人潮，曾經將這個足球場擠得水洩不通。顯然支持小室的人還抵不過我們的阿扁市長。由此也可以看出，在媒體上大紅特紅的安室現象，與現實存在一段明顯差距。

literature, films, and TV dramas in the 1970s, he claims that in the 1990s Japanese culture is being consumed simply as transient information and signs by a fragmented youth audience. Although his analysis is literature-oriented and tends to romanticize the past, when Japanese popular culture was more seriously received and absorbed into Chinese culture, his argument hits the point about the postmodern condition, in which local audiences can enjoy many kinds of local and international cultural products as fickle consumers. In the 1970s and 1980s Japanese TV programs were viewed in the context of a scarcity of local software due to the low production capacity of the Asian media industries. With the proliferation of satellite and cable TV channels, as well as the development of production capabilities in many Asian countries, Japanese TV programs are now broadcast as one way to fill the abundant media space. In this context, they are popular in the countries where they are seen, Chō argues, primarily because they are seen as repositories of information about trendy fashion, interior decoration, and hair styles, commodities that contain few marked "Japanese" features.

The question of "cultural proximity"

Although it hints at a significant change in the transnational consumption of Japanese popular culture, a "postmodern" perspective like Chō's does not sufficiently address the issue of why Japanese culture is preferred over other world cultures. If disaffection with "Japan" has paradoxically generated a profusion of Japanese popular culture in East Asia, this might be because it newly provides something appealing that Asian audiences do not find in their local culture or in American culture. The question then becomes: In an age of global mass culture, what cultural resonances are evoked for East Asians by Japanese popular culture? Is the ascent of Japanese popular culture closely associated with the scent of transnational regional modernity in Asia that Japanese popular culture articulates?

In media studies, the notion of "cultural proximity" has been used to account for such regional resonances. It explains the audience preference for products from countries with which their consumers allegedly share cultural ties. Against the characterization of globalization as the spread of and response to Western (American) popular culture, the emphasis here is on regionalization of media and the dynamics of media export within particular geo-cultural regions (Straubhaar 1991; Sinclair, Jacka, and Cunningham 1996b). Straubhaar (1991) has argued that national and regional markets have developed in the periphery despite the dominance of the United States in the world TV program trade. By indigenizing American influences, some non-Western countries, such as Brazil or Mexico, have developed local industries which can produce their own programs and export them to regional markets. Audience preference, as well as the maturity of the local TV industries, plays a significant role in the development of local and regional TV markets. In his research in Latin America, Straubhaar (1991, 56) found that the audience's search for "cultural proximity" in television programs reveals "a preference first for national material, and, when that cannot be filled in certain genres, a tendency to look next to regional Latin American productions, which are relatively more culturally proximate or similar than are those of the United States." Language is the most important factor in cultural proximity, but there are other cultural elements such as religion, dress, music, nonverbal codes, humor, story pacing, and ethnic types.

No one would deny the empirical validity of the "cultural proximity" thesis. The existence of geo-linguistic and geo-cultural TV markets has been proven, and not only in the Latin American context. Other studies (e.g., Sinclair, Jacka, and Cunningham 1996b; Lee 1991) have also shown that local TV programs tend to be the most popular in any country and region. However, precisely because of its apparent empirical validity, the notion of cultural proximity resists further theorizing. The significance of cultural similarity, as an influence on a TV viewer's preferences, appears too obvious to merit investigation. Yet, it is precisely the seeming naturalness of this idea that deserves interrogation.

The studies of intraregional media flows suggest the significant role played by cultural-linguistic regional centers such Brazil, Mexico, Hong Kong, India, and Egypt in the transnational flow of film/television. Such a grouping of cultural-linguistic regional markets, perhaps not surprisingly, tends to correspond to the "civilizations" of Samuel Huntington's clash-of-civilization thesis (1993), even though Japanese, African, and Slavic-Orthodox "civilizations" are in most cases omitted from the analysis (e.g., Sinclair, Jacka, and Cunningham 1996b). Nothing is intrinsically wrong with such groupings, but if the notion of cultural proximity is used only to explain the tendency of audiences to prefer local programs and programs imported from countries of a similar cultural makeup, the study of its role in the consumption of foreign media products runs the risk of representing culture in an ahistorical and totalizing way. Such an approach tends to be based on the assumption that there are given cultural commonalities which spontaneously direct an audience's interest toward media texts from culturally similar regions, but it ignores the diverse historical contexts and internal differences which exist within cultural formations.

Likewise, the prevalence of Japanese popular culture in East Asia tends to be (easily) accounted for in terms of the presupposed salient cultural and racial similarities (e.g., Yoshioka 1992; Ishii and Watanabe 1998; Nihon no terebi dorama Tōnan Ajia de torendī 1998). Such accounts are deployed from various points of view. A journalist quotes a young Chinese mother on a Japanese TV drama, for example, to evoke Japan's close ties to Asia, hitherto hindered by Japan's imperialist past: "It does not sound strange if the Japanese speak Mandarin, because we have the same skin color. Moreover the urban lifestyle of Tokyo, particularly fashion, is very appealing to us [Chinese]" (Kumamoto 1993b, 215). As discussed in chapter 2, this kind of view is readily absorbed into the Japanese nationalistic assertion that other Asian nations essentially yearn for Japan while at the same time claiming the commonality between them. However, the belief is also promoted by its critics who, employing the same premise, reach quite different conclusions. As discussed in chapter 2, Murai (1993) dismissively accounts for the spread of Japanese popular culture in Asia in terms of its closeness and readiness to be copied and imitated by other Asian peoples, in comparison with Western products. Yet, the underlying assumption of the existence of cultural and racial similarities between Asians and Japanese as the self-evident cause of the reception of Japanese popular culture in Asia remains uninterrogated.

As I show below, in my field research in Taipei I also discovered that most Taiwanese viewers tend to account for the appeal of Japanese TV dramas, if not completely, at least in part, in terms of their perceived cultural proximity. This tendency is even more pronounced when the Taiwanese compare such programs with their American equivalents. However, the critical consideration of this belief shows that "cultural proximity" is never as self-evident as it appears to be. Most obviously, Japan does not share with other parts of Asia the most important factor of cultural proximity, namely, linguistic commonality. Unlike most South American nations, which, at the very least, possess a common language and history of Spanish colonization, Asia is marked by enormous social, cultural, and historical diversity. Even Huntington separates Japan from his grouping of Asian nations.

This is not to say that the notion of "cultural proximity" is entirely fallacious and irrelevant to the analysis of the popularity of Japanese TV dramas in Asia. Rather, I would suggest that the questioning of the obviousness of the notion directs us to rethink the dynamics of transnational regional cultural power. The appreciation of foreign media texts in terms of a favorable cultural distance is never power-free, given that the producing countries of such media texts are still limited to a small number of regional centers. Transnational cultural power does not necessarily mean the straightforward embodiment and recognition of one culture's superiority over another but can be defined as the capacity of a culture to produce symbolic images and meanings which "appeal to the senses, emotions, and thoughts of the self and others" (Lull 1995, 71; see also Thompson 1995). It can be argued, then, that Japanese cultural power in East Asia is distinguished by its ability to produce media products through which Asian audiences are encouraged to experience cultural resonance and immediacy, expressed in the form of "cultural proximity."

What I am proposing here is that by examining the notion of "cultural proximity" in a wider context and as a dynamic process, we can expose the nature and workings of Japanese transnational cultural power in the 1990s, which is inextricably intertwined with the audience's perception of it. For this purpose, we can utilize Stuart Hall's concept of "articulation" (1996b, ch. 6). As developed by Ernesto Laclau, the concept was originally intended to explain how particular ideological elements become dominant in a specific historical and social conjuncture. The concept is based upon the dual meanings of the term *articulate,* which means both "to utter clearly" and "to form a joint." It is the latter meaning that Hall (1996b, 141) emphasizes: "An articulation is thus the form of the connection that can make a unity of two different elements, under certain conditions. It is a linkage which is not necessary, determined, absolute and essential for all time. You have to ask, under what circumstances can a connection be forged or made?"

It is the sense of historical contingency that tends to be suppressed in the notion of cultural proximity, but taking it into account can help us understand the context of the ascendancy of Japan's intimate cultural power. The experience of cultural similarity perceived as such by audiences through the consumption of a particular program is not a given but depends upon specific historical and social conditions. We should ask under which historical conjuncture does the idea of cultural similarity become associated with the pleasure of a text. In Taiwan, this has occurred with the development of media industries, especially cable TV, under the forces of media globalization, which has enabled Japanese dramas to be constantly shown. These structural factors can, in turn, be situated within a wider historical context:

the traces of Japanese colonial rule; the democratic and liberal movements that have grown up in Taiwan since the 1980s; the emergence of a pro-Japanese leader in 1988; and the advance of consumer culture brought about by the rapid economic growth of the 1980s. The last factor is of particular relevance to this chapter, as it could be the case that the rise of Japanese cultural exports to Taiwan is facilitated by the perception, generated by Taiwan's material affluence and the diffusion of "global mass culture," of a diminishing spatio-temporal distance between Japan and Taiwan. All these circumstances must be considered in any attempt to make sense of how cultural proximity is articulated in Taiwan.

We should also carefully examine the ways in which audiences identify with different texts. What is lacking in the study of cultural proximity is a sense of the agency of the audience. Cultural proximity should not be regarded as a predetermined attribute of the text. Such a belief reduces the viewer's active input in constructing the pleasure of the text. Following Miller's discussion of "a posteriori authenticity" (1992), I argue that cultural proximity does not exist a priori but occurs a posteriori. Cultural proximity is not something "out there." It is articulated when audiences subjectively identify it in a specific program and context. One of the problems for the study of the regional flow of TV programs is the relative absence of audience research. As Sinclair, Jacka, and Cunningham (1996a, 19) argue, audience research has concentrated on the reception of American programs, and that "far more than for the USA, the success or otherwise of peripheral nations' export is contingent on factors other than those captured by established modes of audience study. This explains why so little audience reception research has been able to be conducted on their products in international markets, and why we need instead middle range analysis to do so." I agree with Sinclair, Jacka, and Cunningham that middle-range analysis, which addresses issues of acquisition, time-scheduling, and publicity, is important in understanding the global and intraregional flow of TV programs. Nevertheless, so as not to conceive of cultural proximity in a deterministic way, I would argue that it is also imperative to examine how and why certain programs become popular and others do not, and what sort of pleasure, if any, audiences experience when identifying cultural similarities in specific programs.

A familiar cultural value does not necessarily offer pleasure in watching programs. In some cases, audience might reject a program precisely because of the negative appeal of their society's cultural values. There is also a possibility that the sense of cultural proximity is expressed as a result of a positive identification with foreign media texts that represent alternative ideas, values, and forms of life that look desirable and reachable (thus "proximate"). Such expression might reflect audiences' cognizance that the media texts are from a supposedly culturally proximate country, but cannot be regarded as a straightforward recognition of "real" cultural commonalities. To attend all these complexities, we need to analyze the audience's enunciation of cultural proximity, not by taking it at face value, but by scrutinizing the way in which audiences in Taiwan associate the attractiveness of Japanese TV dramas with the perception of cultural similarity. In sum, the reconfiguration of Japanese cultural power, in terms of its capacity to produce media artifacts that allegedly are culturally proximate to Asian audiences, can only be grasped if we consider the broad context in which such media artifacts have circulated and the textual pleasure experienced by audiences at a specific historical time, as well as the middle-range factors that have led to the routine consumption of them in Taiwan.

Markets conditions: Singapore, Hong Kong, and Taiwan

What has become noticeable in the mid-1990s is that, among the many genres of popular culture available, Japanese TV dramas have been well received in many Asian countries. According to a 1997 communications white paper published by the Japanese Ministry of Posts and Telecommunication, Asian markets in 1995 represented 47 percent of total TV program exports; and TV dramas occupied 53 percent of exports to Asia.

The popularity of Japanese TV dramas varies from country to country. Although some dramas such as *Oshin, Tokyo Love Story,* and *101st Proposal* have been hits in such Southeast Asian countries as Thailand, Indonesia, and Singapore, Japanese TV dramas have been received most favorably in East Asian countries such as Taiwan, Hong Kong, and (to a lesser extent) China (on China, see Chō 1998; on Indonesia, Kurasawa 1998; see also Iwabuchi forthcoming). While differences in the popularity of Japanese TV dramas cannot be explained entirely by local TV markets, a comparative inquiry into the structural factors that regulate circulation and promotion of these shows in some Asian markets is in order here.

In 1996 international programs made up half of the programming on TCS−8, the most popular Chinese channel in Singapore. Almost 50 percent of them were from Hong Kong, 35 percent from Taiwan, and 15 percent from Japan. According to the programming manager of TCS—8, there had been a strong trend toward Japanese popular culture in the early 1990s when the dramas *Tokyo Love Story* and *101st Proposal* first became popular. He conceded, however, that this trend did not last long, and noted that the reason why Japanese TV dramas have not been consistently popular in Singapore is because Japanese stars receive far less exposure in the local media than their American counterparts. His claim was supported by the chief editor of *8 Days,* a well-known local TV magazine, who blamed the lack of promotion of Japanese media stars for the comparatively low ratings of Japanese TV dramas. The importance of such exposure, he argued, is demonstrated by the success of the Japanese pop duo Chage & Aska, who sing the theme song for *101st Proposal.*

The programming manager of TCS—8 characterized the penetration of Japanese TV programs in this way: "The presence of Japanese TV programs is increasing slowly. It was very little ten years ago. But it is still not quite visible or consistent. I think there is a potential but not enough time and money to put energy in promoting them in Singapore." This structural restriction, he stated, renders relatively insignificant the influence of Japanese TV culture in Singapore. Western culture has always been the mainstream in Singapore, he commented, whereas its Asian (Japanese, Hong Kong, and Taiwanese) equivalents have been only seasonal.

In Hong Kong the situation is different in one respect, but similar in another. Japanese cultural influences are much more profound in Hong Kong. TVB—Jade is the most popular Chinese channel in Hong Kong; according to my interview with a programming officer, in the week of 10—16 February 1997, 19.5 percent of all programs broadcast on the channel were of foreign origin, and about three-quarters of these were Japanese. Most were animations, but dramas and game shows were also regularly broadcast. The officer also told me that the height of the popularity of Japanese TV programs has been, as was the case in Singapore, in the 1970s and early 1980s, when about 30 percent of TV programming on the channel was occupied by Japanese productions. Between the mid-1980s and early 1990s, the share of Japanese TV programs had significantly declined, but since the early 1990s it had been slowly increasing again, as some Japanese dramas became popular. The TVB officer told me that American dramas were the most popular foreign programs in the 1980s, but that in the 1990s their Japanese equivalents had been in the ascendancy.

However, even Japanese dramas are not popular enough to compete with local dramas. The officer remarked that while TVB had tried to promote the Japanese detective drama *Kindaichi Shōnen no Jikenbo,* which features famous young Japanese idols, its ratings were less than 20 (the average for a local popular show is 30). This is because the audience for contemporary Japanese dramas is limited to young people between in their mid-teens and early twenties. In Hong Kong and Singapore, where two TV channels dominate the local market, the main target audience is not younger people but children and housewives over 40, who comprise the most avid viewers. For this reason, any popular drama must deal with such issues as love and the family, according to the TVB officer. The same point was made by the programming officer of another station, ATV, who told me in his 1997 interview that even *Tokyo Love Story,* the most famous and well-received Japanese drama in various Asian countries, had not been very successful in Hong Kong. It did not appeal to this target audience, he said: "The response was good, but the ratings were not good." He added that whereas Japanese TV dramas were popular among all generations in the 1970s, they are now only well known among the younger generation.

Nevertheless, the existence of an "open" black markets for pirate videos and VCDs (video CDs) works in favor of the spread of Japanese TV programs in Hong Kong.[2] Even if Japanese TV dramas are not available for viewing on free-to-air TV channels, Hong Kong youth can watch most of them on pirated VCDs. In the Sino Center Building, where many shops sell such VCDs, the latest Japanese dramas are generally available with Cantonese dubbing just a few days after their initial broadcast in Japan. Also, information about Japanese TV idols regularly circulates in daily newspapers and weekly entertainment magazines. These factors distinguish Hong Kong from Singapore in terms of the popularity of Japanese TV dramas.

It is in Taiwan that the media market structure works most favorably, however, for the exposure of Japanese TV dramas. There, too, VCDs are an important medium through which the youth gain access to Japanese TV dramas. But in Taiwan, young people have more channel choices via satellite and cable TV services, so that free-to-air channels have been relatively unpopular among them, which is not the case in Singapore and Hong Kong. The satellite network, STAR TV, has been the pioneer in the dissemination of Japanese TV dramas throughout Asia since its inception in 1991. Although STAR TV has attracted much academic attention for its pan-Asian satellite broadcasts and its possible penetration into the Chinese market, from the outset the Taiwanese market has been a main target, too. This is particularly the case for the STAR Chinese channel and music channel [V], which replaced MTV in 1994. Moreover, since STAR TV launched its new Chinese channel, Phoenix, aimed at the mainland Chinese market, in 1997, the STAR Chinese channel is now broadcast mostly in Taiwan, and the channel has made extensive use of Japanese programs, especially dramas, in prime time to attract a large Taiwanese audience. The manager of the STAR TV Chinese channel told me that Japanese TV dramas are particularly important to the network's programming. It has devoted of an hour of prime time to Japanese drama since June 1992, and according to the manager, Japanese programs are indispensable to STAR TV's strategy of localization for the Taiwan market.[3]

It is the Taiwanese cable-TV market, however, that has made the strongest initiative in promoting Japanese TV dramas (STAR TV is also watched on cable). The rapid development of cable TV has been responsible for the nearly constant influx of Japanese TV dramas in Taiwan. While such programs are generally not popular enough for the free-to-air channels, the cable channels, whose target audiences are more narrowly focused, have given them a new pattern of TV popularity. Given that the Taiwanese cable market has taken the strongest initiative in promoting Japanese TV dramas, before elaborating on their popularity in Taiwan, I should provide a brief outline of the history of cable TV in Taiwan.

In Taiwan, there are four free-to-air commercial TV stations: Taiwan Television Enterprise (TTV), the China Television Company (CTV), and the China Television Service (CTS), and Formosa Television (FTV). TTV was established in 1962; CTV, in 1969 by the Kuomintang (KMT); and CTS, in 1971 by the Ministry of Defense; and FTV, in 1997 by the Democratic Progressive Party (DPP). Although all are privately owned, their programming is not free from state control. There is a restriction on the amount of foreign programming (30 percent or less), and by regulation at least 50 percent of programs must be non-entertainment offerings. Cable TV started in Taiwan in the 1960s as a way to make the three free-to-air channels available to those who could not receive their on-air signals, but it was the illegal cable channels, whose programming consisted of foreign entertainment—Hollywood films, Hong Kong dramas, and Japanese programs—that became popular with subscribers. The development of illegal cable TV in Taiwan (which was called the Fourth Channel) occurred rapidly after the late 1970s, as the service expanded to satisfy the audience's hunger for the entertainment programs the three free-to-air stations could not offer.

Government attempts to exercise strict control over these illegal cable channels by cutting the cable were in vain; cable operators would quickly reconnect. From its inception, the popularity of the Fourth Channel has never flagged. The diffusion rate of the cable channels rapidly increased when the democratic and liberal movements gained currency after the end of martial law in 1987. Even the then-opposition party, the DPP, used the Fourth Channel for political broadcasts. Given this new situation, the government changed its policy from one of banning to one of regulating the Fourth Channel. In 1993 the new Cable TV Law was finally passed, and in the preceding year a new copyright law had been passed; this legislation made it possible for foreign channels and program suppliers to broadcast their programs through the cable (Hattori and Hara 1997). Even before the legislation, about 50 percent of households watched cable channels. The number increased after the legislation. In 1998, nearly 80 percent of households were enjoying cable television (Republic of China Yearbook 1999), and Taiwan currently has one of the most developed cable television systems in Asia.

Japanese cable channels in Taiwan

The Cable TV Law requires at least 20 percent of the programs on a cable channel to be locally produced, but many cable channels obviously do not abide by this rule. Most channels buy all their programming from overseas sources, mainly the United States, Hong Kong, and Japan. Lewis et al. (1994) argue that the development of cable TV facilitated the "re-Americanization" of Taiwan after the period in the 1970s and 1980s when the people's preference for local programs decreased the number of American programs (see also Lee 1980). The inroads of ESPN, HBO, the Discovery Channel, and CNN International can be said to be representative of this process. It should be noted, in this respect, that the United States had applied strong pressure on the Taiwanese government to legalize the cable channels so as to protect American film and TV industries from piracy and to enable them to operate legally in Taiwan (Lewis et al. 1994).

An increase in Japanese programming in Taiwan has also been a significant trend since the early 1990s, however. After the Japanese government officially reestablished diplomatic relations with China in 1972, the Taiwanese government banned the broadcast of Japanese-language programs. Although Japanese programs continued to be widely watched through pirate videos and illegal cable channels in Taiwan, they became even more accessible after the Taiwan government removed the ban at the end of 1993. With this policy change, the colonial connection between the two countries resurfaced, particularly in terms of business links. Typically, it is those who lived under the Japanese occupation and who speak fluent Japanese who have utilized their old connections in Japanese business circles to become the owners and managers of Japanese cable channels in Taiwan. For example, according to my interview with its manager, the launch of the Po-shin Channel, a pioneering Japanese cable channel in Taiwan, would not have been possible except for the old friendship between the Channel's former managing director and the president of Tōei Movie Japan (see also Sekai-ichi no yūsen rasshu 1995). In this sense, the Japanese cultural presence in Taiwan continues to be shaped by the legacy of Japanese colonization.

In 1997 there were five Japanese cable channels in Taiwan. Apart from NHK Asia, which simultaneously broadcasts most programs from Japan by satellite, four other channels—Video Land Japanese, Gold Sun, Po-shin Japanese, and JET (Japan Entertainment Network)—buy their programming from Japanese commercial TV stations.[4] These channels broadcast exclusively Japanese programming twenty-four hours a day (with many repeat showings, since basic daily original programming ranges from 6 to 10 hours a day). In addition, other cable and free-to-air channels also regularly broadcast such programs. As a result, the number of Japanese TV programs imported into Taiwan has greatly increased since 1994. In 1992 a total of about 600 hours of programming was exported from Japan to Taiwan (Kawatake and Hara 1994). There are no exact figures available for Japanese program exports to Taiwan after 1993. However, according to my interview with TBS, in 1996 that commercial TV station alone exported 1,000 hours of programming to Taiwan.

Before the new Cable TV Law, there had been as many as 600 cable operators; immediately after its introduction, their numbers were reduced to 126.[5] There are about 100 suppliers of programming, and since most operators can afford to broadcast at most 60 to 70 channels, it is crucial for program vendors to secure a place in the allocations of the cable operators so as to maximize the penetration of their programming into a large number of households. According to one survey conducted in 1996, local general channels such as SUPER–TV, TVBS, and Sanli–2, as well as global/transnational channels such as HBO, ESPN, and STAR TV Chinese, have the highest penetration rates in terms of subscriptions with cable operators. Among the eighty-one cable channels, those that broadcast Japanese programming tend to be ranked around the 20th place—Gold Sun was in 19th place, NHK Asia was 21st, and Videoland Japan was 26th—and all of them were ranked above such channels as CNN, MTV, TNT, the Cartoon Channel, and the Discovery Channel (Redwood Research Service 1996).

The penetration rate, of course, does not necessarily reflect the popularity of a channel. Another significant quantitative measure of popularity is ratings. One survey conducted by Ishii, Watanabe, and Su (1996) showed that Videoland Japanese was the sixth most commonly watched channel and Gold Sun was fifteenth, but it is also true that local and Western (mainly American) cable TV channels are more popular in Taiwan in terms of their cumulative reach (Hattori and Hara 1997; Ishii, Watanabe, and Su 1996). However, if one looks closely at specific genres and sections of the audience, this is not always the case. As far as TV dramas are concerned, Japanese programs attract greater audiences in Taiwan than Western/American ones and are even more popular than Hong Kong and Taiwan dramas (Hattori and Hara 1997; Ishii, Watanabe, and Su 1996). This is particularly true for young audiences (age 13–25) and for female (age 26–35) audiences. As Hattori and Yumiko (1997) suggest, young women in general like TV dramas, but not American ones, while young males do not rate dramas highly, except Japanese ones. When they asked viewers to grade each genre on a scale of 1 to 10, Hattori and Yumiko discovered that, overall, Japanese dramas scored highest with 6.8. In contrast, Western (American) dramas scored 6.6, Hong Kong dramas 6.2, and Taiwanese dramas 6.7. For both male and female audiences in the age groups 13–15 and 16–25, Japanese dramas scored significantly higher. The preference of young audiences for dramas shows an interesting contrast between Japanese and American programs. While drama constitutes the strongest genre of Japanese TV programs, TV dramas are the least appreciated American genre in Taiwan.

Japanese idol dramas: Something to talk about

The appreciation for Japanese TV dramas by young people in Taiwan does not mean that they have become mainstream there. Ratings for cable TV channels are still low compared to those for free-to-air channels. The TV programs with the highest ratings continue to be those that have been domestically produced, as was the case in the 1970s (Lee 1980). However, the popularity of Japanese TV dramas is best measured not by ratings but by their central role in the daily gossip of young people (particularly women). Given the scarcity of publicity about such dramas in the Taiwanese media, their renown owed much to word of mouth. A reporter who writes about Japanese dramas for a local newspaper told me: "Most high school and university students who watch Japanese dramas discuss the story line with their friends. It is the most common topic for them, just as Taiwan prime-time dramas [those broadcast as 8 P.M.] used to be." My informant's employer, the *China Times*, is one of the most popular dailies in Taiwan and it inaugurated an interactive column on Japanese TV dramas in February 1996.[6] Apparently the column was targeted to teenage readers of the newspaper's Saturday edition.

The Japanese dramas give audiences lots to talk about. Not surprisingly, one of their main drawing cards for young Taiwanese is the good-looking actors who perform on these series. This is apparent from the common name that has been given to the genre—"Japanese Idol Drama,"—which was coined by STAR TV. It is clear that STAR TV thought that these young Japanese idols would be the principal attraction of such dramas for the Taiwanese. Many people in Taiwan confirmed for me that this was indeed the case.

People also remark that they enjoy viewing the food, fashion, consumer goods, and music that are presented in these programs. This is not for the first time such items have been introduced to the Taiwanese through Japanese TV dramas. Even before the advent of such programs, they had already gained a certain renown in Taiwan through Japanese magazines. For instance, a popular fashion magazine for teenage girls is *non-no*, a biweekly Japanese magazine. Most Taiwanese do not understand Japanese; they purchase such magazines predominantly for their pictures. *Non-no* was first imported into Taiwan in the late 1970s and became popular during the 1980s. Approximately 100,000 copies are imported monthly (two issues) from Japan. According to Nippan IPC, the Japanese firm that exports *non-no*, export figures for the magazine increased in the 1990s (particularly in 1993–94), which was roughly the period when Japanese TV dramas in Taiwan became phenomenally popular. The magazines, combined with the TV dramas, serve to keep the Taiwanese current, not only on what they should consume to improve their lifestyles, but on how they should consume—that is, how they should wear their clothes, or how they should arrange their furniture in a room to make it look stylish (e.g., Ichikawa 1994; Ueda 1996; Chō 1998).

There is more to watching Japanese dramas, however, than admiring the latest in Japanese commodities and fashion. More importantly, it is their story lines and characters that Taiwanese audiences find appealing and that they eagerly discuss with their friends and colleagues. Their plots, settings, and subgenres, ranging from urban love stories and family dramas to detective series, are diverse, but the most popular programs are those that deal with the lives and loves of younger people in an urban setting. In most cases, the dramas are filmed in Tokyo and thus depict modern urban life in Japan. In contrast, Taiwanese TV dramas are more family-oriented and are aimed primarily at housewives. Rarely do they engage with the experiences of young Taiwanese in a modern urban setting. Hence, it is the greater relevance of Japanese dramas that seems to account in part for their popularity among young Taiwanese viewers.

Watching *Tokyo Love Story*

It was the drama *Tokyo Love Story* that ignited interest in Japanese dramas and prompted a recognition of their quality in Taiwan and other East Asian countries. Originally broadcast in Japan between January and March 1991, it was shown for the first time in Taiwan in 1992 by the STAR Chinese channel in eleven, one-hour-long episodes. Briefly, the drama is a love story about five young men and women in their early twenties. The heroine, Akana Rika, who has spent some time in the United States, is an unusually expressive and positive Japanese woman. She falls in love with Nagao Kanji ("Kanchi" to her), a gentle but rather wavering young man. Kanji, in turn, loves an old high-school classmate, Sekiguchi Satomi, but she does not return his affections, preferring instead to have an affair with another old classmate, Mikami Kenichi. Although perplexed by Rika's straightforwardness in expressing her love for him—on one occasion she famously exclaims, "Kanchi, let's have sex!"—Kanji nevertheless becomes attracted to her and enters into a relationship with her. Gradually, though, he becomes exhausted with their relationship and again attempts to link up with Satomi, whose relationship with Mikami has meanwhile broken up. Rika keeps it up despite the odds, but ultimately Kanji and Satomi marry, and Rika moves to the United States for work. The drama ends with their unexpected reunion in Tokyo several years later, where Rika proves to be as forward-looking as ever, with no regrets about the past.

Tokyo Love Story was an epoch-making drama series in Japan in terms of subtlety of production styles and the way in which the youth's lives in urban setting is represented. The drama's innovativeness was appreciated with much sympathy by young viewers in Taiwan as well as in Japan. STAR TV has broadcast *Tokyo Love Story* several times since 1992, and TTV, the most popular free-to-air channel, screened it twice in 1995. The success of the program encouraged a group of university students to conduct research into its popularity (Li et al. 1995).[7] In their survey of sixty-one university students, they found that about 83 percent had enjoyed watching the drama and roughly 65 percent had watched it more than twice. A crucial issue not dealt with in this quantitative survey is a more qualitative exploration of how viewers perceived *Tokyo Love Story*. As Ien Ang (1985, 20) argues, "Popular pleasure is first and foremost a pleasure of recognition." What matters, then, is whether and in what ways the audience can identify with the drama.

The popularity of *Tokyo Love Story* had much to do with the identification of its female audience with its attractive heroine, Rika. Her single-minded pursuit of love and her frankness, unbeaten by hardship, are seen as admirable traits worthy of emulation. Her resolute and independent attitude represent a desirable image of the "modern" or "new age" woman. My interviewees often expressed two seemingly contradictory statements about her. On the one hand, they might say, "I have a strong feeling that she is exactly what I want to be," on the other hand, they might also remark, "I would not be able to become as brave and open as Rika." It is thus Rika's role as an ideal model that many women consider particularly appealing: she is what one wants to be but can never quite become. Satomi, in contrast, serves as Rika's foil. She is the embodiment of a more traditional woman—dependent, submissive, domestic, and passive. It may be the case that audiences find Satomi more empirically realistic in the Taiwanese context. As such, she was an object of aversion for all of my interviewees. The juxtaposition of Rika and Satomi brings Rika's attractiveness into sharp relief.

This sort of identification with the desirable is similar to what Richard Dyer calls utopianism: "Entertainment offers the image of 'something better' to escape into, or something we want deeply that our day-to-day lives don't provide. Alternatives, hopes, wishes—these are the stuff of utopia, the sense that things could be better, that something other than what is can be

東京愛情故事

TOKYO LOVE STORY

主演：織田裕二 / 鈴木保奈美

The Taiwanese VCD cover for *Tokyo Love Story*.

imagined and maybe realized" (1992, 18). Dyer argues that entertainment does not offer "models of the utopian world" but provides its consumers with the possibility of experiencing "what utopia would feel like rather than how it would be organized" (18). Referring, in particular, to the musical form, Dyer points out the importance of non–representational means such as music and colors, and the simplification and intensification of people's relationships in entertainment's articulation of utopianism.

Though Dyer's argument is about musicals, these points well fit the structure of many Japanese idol dramas, including *Tokyo Love Story*. Apart from the comparatively large budget and the sophistication of the production techniques, two structural and technical factors make Japanese dramas attractive for their Taiwan audiences. First, Japanese dramas are not soap operas; they always end within ten to twelve episodes (each episode being an hour long). By contrast, Taiwanese and American dramas seemingly never end. Most of my Taiwanese respondents commented that they felt such programs were unnecessarily protracted. Because Japanese dramas finish in a comparatively short time and their plots are usually less complicated than those of traditional soap operas, my respondents found it easier to focus on these dramas and enjoy the progress of their narratives. In addition, Japanese dramas, like movies, use orchestral music and theme songs repeatedly and effectively. The use of a theme song in a drama is particularly important. Each week, the theme functions not just as background music but as a constitutive part of the climactic scene. The theme song works in these instances to encourage the emotional involvement of the audience. It thus serves to evoke "romance," helping the audience to enjoy a "romantic, beautiful love story," as one of my interviewees put it.

However, there is a crucial difference between Dyer's utopianism of musicals and the realism of Japanese dramas. The attractiveness of *Tokyo Love Story* does not reside simply in making audiences feel that "something other than what is can be imagined and maybe realized." Emotional involvement in the drama is facilitated by its depiction of something which the audience thinks and feels desirable and not unrealistic. It is not just a dream of tomorrow but a (possible) picture of today. The things that happen in *Tokyo Love Story* also seem to be realistic, or at least accessible to most of its young audience. The same things could happen in their own everyday lives. On his Web site, a young Hong Kong man explained why he likes the drama in these terms: "The twenty-something urban professionals of the series face a tightrope of coping that young people in many Asian cities have faced, but rarely more sympathetically. The major attraction of *Tokyo Love Story* to me is that it is not a story about somebody else. It is a story about our generation, about us, about myself. I can easily identify shadows of Rika or Kanchi among my peer group, even in myself" ("Kevin's Home," http://home.ust.hk/~kwtse).

This sense of the series being a "story about us" was strongly shared by the Taiwanese fans. More than 60 percent of those surveyed by Li et al. (1995)— and 75 percent of the female subjects—replied that love affairs such as those portrayed in *Tokyo Love Story* could happen around them. However, as was the case for the realism of Rika's character, discussed earlier, this should not be straightforwardly read as evidence of the objective, empirical realism of *Tokyo Love Story*. As Ang (1985, 44–45) argues concerning audiences' identification with *Dallas*, "The concrete situations and complications are rather regarded as symbolic representations of more general experiences: rows, intrigues, problems, happiness and misery. And it is precisely in this sense that these letter-writers find *Dallas* realistic. In other words, at a connotative level they ascribe mainly emotional meanings to *Dallas*." What audiences find "realistic" in viewing *Tokyo Love Story* is thus not that an identical love affair would actually happen or that anyone could become like Rika. Li et al. (1995) suggest that one of the attractions of *Tokyo Love Story* for university students in Taiwan is its new style of portraying love, work, and women's role and position in society. These are all issues which young people are actually facing in urban areas in Taiwan, but which American or Taiwanese TV dramas have never sympathetically dealt with. It is in at this more generalized level of meaning concerning love affairs and human relations represented in *Tokyo Love Story* that audiences in Taiwan perceive it as "our" story.

Audience preference and the perception of "cultural proximity"

The question of particular importance here is whether and how the "realism" of Japanese programs, the Taiwanese sense that they dramatize "our" stories, is encouraged by a perceived similarity between Japan and Taiwan: whether the perception of cultural proximity facilitates the sense of immediacy. I asked Taiwanese audiences comparative questions about Japanese dramas, Taiwanese dramas, and American dramas. Most of my interviewees in Taipei noted that emotionally they engaged more with Japanese dramas than they did with Western or Taiwanese dramas. Of course, insofar as Japanese dramas are broadcast in Japanese with Chinese subtitles, the Taiwanese cannot help but regard them as foreign; but for all that, they do not regard such dramas in quite the same way as they do the American programs. This is because Taiwanese audiences tend to remark that, racially and culturally, they have more in common with the Japanese than they do with the Americans. "Japan is not quite but much like us," another woman in her early twenties said. "Yeah, Japan is a foreign county and this (foreignness) makes Japanese programs look gorgeous and appealing. But the distance we feel to Japan is comfortable. Americans are complete strangers." Another female fan of Japanese drama in her mid-twenties also mentions the relative cultural distances between Taiwan, Japan, and the West: "I do not think that Japanese dramas are a totally new genre, something I've never seen before, but rather I've never seen such dramas which perfectly express my feeling. . . . The West is so far away from us, so I cannot relate to American dramas." She opined as well that the likeness between family and romantic relationships in Japan and Taiwan made it easier for her to relate to Japanese dramas.

The above point can be illustrated further through a comparison of Taiwanese perceptions of *Tokyo Love Story* and an American drama, *Beverly Hills, 90210*. For instance, one informant, a woman in her early twenties who had just started working for a Japanese cable TV channel and was an admitted fan of Japanese dramas, informed me that while she enjoyed watching the lifestyles and romances presented in *Beverly Hills, 90210,* she found Japanese love stories to be more accessible and resonant with Taiwanese situations. Moreover, some interviewees stated that, for all the program's color and excitement, they could not imagine experiencing life as it was lived in *Beverly Hills, 90210*. A seventeen-year-old high school student declared: "Japanese dramas better reflect our reality. Yeah, *Beverly Hills, 90210* is too exciting [to be realistic]. Boy always meets girl. But it is neither our reality nor dream." When I suggested that some Japanese dramas were not empirically realistic either, she replied, "Well, maybe not, but it might happen. Or at least I want to have it." Whereas the attractiveness of *Tokyo Love Story* stems from its mixture of alleged empiricist and emotional realism, *Beverly Hills, 90210* appears to many Taiwanese fans of Japanese TV dramas "realistic" in neither sense.

These comments suggest that Taiwanese audiences' emotional involvement in Japanese dramas is fostered by a perceived cultural similarity between Japan and Taiwan. However, such an explanation for audience preference solely in terms of cultural similarity is too simplistic. The differing responses of Taiwanese to *Tokyo Love Story* and *Beverly Hills, 90210* may be the result not only of the sense of cultural proximity or distance these shows establish, but also of the degree of their textual emphasis on intimacy and ordinariness. The rich lifestyles depicted in *Beverly Hills, 90210* deter some Taiwanese audiences from identifying with the series. As a female university student told me in an interview, *Beverly Hills, 90210* is not a story about ordinary people and thus has little to do with her everyday life.

It can be argued that some Taiwanese audiences' discontent with the unrealistic affluent lifestyle depicted in *Beverly Hills, 90210* actually reflects their disapproval of the drama's narrative. Their failure to emotionally identify with the characters and human relationships in the drama might have secondarily generated their detachment from the material lavishness of the series (see Ang 1985; McKinley 1997).[8] Nevertheless, at the least, we cannot discount the possibility that the emphasis of Japanese dramas on the quotidian strengthens the sense of cultural proximity felt by Taiwanese audiences. Most Japanese dramas depict the mundane lives of ordinary people rather than the glamorous dream-worlds of the rich that are often depicted in American soap operas. My *China Times* informant also told me that although the American medical drama *ER* is of high quality and well received in Taiwan, it does not get people emotionally involved with the world of medicine. On the other hand, she said, *Kagayaku Toki no Nakade,* a Japanese drama about medical students, does make many people in Taiwan feel like working as medical professionals. More recently, a Japanese version of *ER, Kyūmei Byōtō 24ji,* which was broadcast from January to March 1999, featured a female intern as the story's main character and emphasized the layperson's view of medicine. Thus, it might be that it is not only the cultural proximity between Japan and Taiwan, but also the focus on medical students rather than professional practitioners, that made this Japanese drama look more intimate and ordinary than *ER*.

Another comment I frequently heard was that love is expressed more delicately and elegantly in Japanese dramas than it is in their more crass American equivalents. Japanese dramas, I was told, are more romantic and subtle at conveying emotion than American and Taiwanese shows, in which emotions tend to be presented in an overexaggerated manner. The subtlety is associated with ways of directing as well as the story lines. A woman in her late twenties gave me an example of this nonverbal subtlety in Japanese drama: "I think Japanese dramas are very subtle in showing delicate feelings. Japanese dramas place more value on depicting feelings deep inside. When a woman cries, her emotions are skillfully expressed by the movement of the fingers. A scene of parting is also well directed by the subtle movement of the fingers between lovers." Another woman in her mid-twenties told me: "I clearly remember that a scene of *Tokyo Love Story* very subtly used the actors' backs to show the delicate sentiment of lovers parting. Such delicateness cannot be found in other [American and Taiwanese] dramas. I like Japanese dramas because I can feel and experience such delicate feelings." The *China Times* reporter gave me another example, explaining that she personally liked the romantic scene in *Tokyo Love Story* in which Rika narrates Kanji's life history while placing candles one by one on a birthday cake. She said that she had never seen such an elegant way of celebrating a lover's birthday.

In light of the fact that Japanese TV dramas are favorably received only in East Asia, it may appear that the reputed elegance of their representations holds a particular appeal for audiences of culturally proximate regions. The truth is, though, that the appreciation of the subtleties of nonverbal communication and the sensitive presentation of social relationships is not exclusively related to East Asian cultural commonalities. This Japanese skill of "wrapping" is appreciated in the West as well (see Hendry 1993). Moreover, Taiwanese seem to believe that Japanese subtlety is very different from the Taiwanese mode of cultural presentation. It was when we discussed this reputed subtlety of the Japanese programs that Taiwanese usually lamented the poor quality of their local dramas. As one interviewee stated, "Taiwanese dramas unnecessarily exaggerate their stories. In Taiwanese dramas, women always cry, cry, cry. There is no subtlety at all in expressing emotion, as in Japanese dramas." When I asked her whether Taiwanese TV could produce dramas in the same way, she said, "No, I do not think Taiwan can produce (romantic) love dramas similar to the Japanese ones. Taiwan dramas cannot present delicate emotions in the Japanese way. I think it is not a matter of learning how to produce TV dramas, but that of the cultural difference between the two countries." This indicates that the Taiwanese preference for the "delicateness" or "elegance" of Japanese dramas is not necessarily associated with any cultural proximity between Japan and Taiwan.

Even perceived common cultural values and attitudes cannot be straightforwardly regarded as the incarnations of some primordial cultural proximity. Li et al. (1995) argue that Rika's attitude to love in *Tokyo Love Story* is different from that of the female characters in American dramas like *Beverly Hills, 90210,* who are too open and not single-minded enough. Her attitude is also different from that of women depicted in Taiwan dramas, who are generally represented as more passive and submissive. In reply to my question about the difference between Rika, who spends some time in the United States and can therefore appear to be somewhat "Americanized," and American women as they are depicted in American dramas, a postgraduate student in Taiwan remarked:

> About Rika, I think it is true that people in Taiwan identify themselves with her more than with American women. My opinion is that this is because Rika is an Asian woman. She has yellow skin, black hair and speaks Japanese (or Chinese) on TV. . . . I think not many people would relate Rika to America. Her education in the United States was not often

mentioned in *Tokyo Love Story*. And I think Rika is not totally Americanized. She kept the American style of femininity only in her pursuing something directly. But she still has some traditional Asian femininity in her personality. For example, she loves a man faithfully. And that is why Asian women identify themselves with her. She is a mixture of American and Asian femininity—she represents the image of a "New Age woman" to the audience.

As this student's remarks about Rika indicate, Japan is apparently regarded as culturally proximate because of its perceived "Asianness," that is, in the similar appearance and single-mindedness of Rika in *Tokyo Love Story*.

Even in this case, however, the sense of cultural proximity perceived by the Taiwanese viewer in watching *Tokyo Love Story* should not be overgeneralized to explain the popularity of Japanese TV dramas in Taiwan. Viewers might find some shared cultural values concerning family and individualism in Japanese dramas, but the perception of such values does not necessarily lead to the favorable reception of the TV drama that represents them. For instance, Taiwanese dramas often emphasize traditional values, such as the "fidelity" in women (Chan 1996, 142), but young Taiwanese often do not positively accept or are even critical of such widely acknowledged cultural values, as we have seen with their expressed hatred for the character of Satomi. Nevertheless, it can be argued, youthful audiences respond positively to Rika's "active single-mindedness" in contrast to the "openness" depicted in American TV dramas, since this represents a "common" value in East Asia and thus can be related to. Here again, however, what is important is not fidelity or single-mindedness in general or essentialized terms but a specific kind of single-mindedness as it is represented in *Tokyo Love Story*. Which is to say, this single-mindedness has been articulated through a Japanese (at the site of production) and a Taiwanese (at the site of consumption) reworking of cultural modernity in a particular media text. Only through these dynamic processes has it come to embody an attractive single-mindedness, which is perceived to illustrate a "New Age woman" in that it is at once implicated in the global (in the sense of "American," in this instance) context yet situated in an East Asian context. In order to understand the complexity of audiences' identification with Rika's attractive character in Taiwan, we thus need to consider it in the wider sociocultural context of the 1990s in which cultural modernity is reworked in East Asia.

Becoming "culturally proximate"

The preference of some Taiwanese viewers for Japanese TV dramas over American ones and the associated experience of cultural similarity is, I argue, suggestive of the shifting nature of the symbolic power of American pop icons as well as the nature of transnational cultural consumption in general. In non-Western countries, America has long been closely associated with images of modernity. Whenever American popular culture is consumed, people vicariously satisfy a yearning for the American way of life and appropriate the images of romance, freedom, and affluence associated with it. As Featherstone (1995, 8) argues, "It is a product from a superior global center, which has long represented itself as the center. For those on the periphery it offers the possibility of the psychological benefits of identifying with the powerful. Along with the Marlboro Man, Coca-Cola, Hollywood, Sesame Street, rock music, and American football insignia, McDonald's is one of a series of icons of the American way of life. They have become associated with transposable themes which are central to consumer culture, such as youth, fitness, beauty, luxury, romance, freedom." Indeed, I clearly remember feeling that I was becoming American after I ate at Kentucky Fried Chicken in the late 1970s in Tokyo. But that stage of cultural development is over. In 1995 I saw a seven-year-old Japanese boy express his amazement at seeing Kentucky Fried Chicken in the United States on TV, "Wow, there is a Kentucky in America as well!" (see also Watson 1997). "American dreams" have been indigenized in some modernized non-Western countries. It seems that some popular American icons have also become "culturally odorless," in the sense that they may no longer be recognized as essentially "American."

Tomlinson argues that terms such as cultural domination or imposition are no longer appropriate to describe the current global cultural condition, which is not necessarily coercive. He argues that, unlike imperialism, "the idea of 'globalization' suggests interconnection and interdependency of all global areas which happens in a far less purposeful way," and that as a consequence, "the cultural coherence of *all* individual nation-states, including economically powerful ones—the 'imperialist powers' of a previous era" is undermined (1991, 175; emphasis in original). As Chen (1996, 56) rightly criticizes, there is a danger that this kind of argument on globalization, which stresses the decline of Western/American cultural hegemony, "neutralizes power relations" of the "not-yet-post-imperialist" world which we still inhabit. Yet, we cannot deny that it is becoming increasingly difficult to identify "the West" ("America") as the unambiguously dominating supplier of images of modernity for people of modernized non-Western nations that have already achieved a certain level of material affluence.

"Americanization" seems to have reached another level of signification. It operates at the level of form rather than content: Abstract concepts such as freedom, luxury, and romance have diffused so widely that there is no longer an unambiguous correlation between such concepts and American symbols. "Americanization" has become overdetermined by local practices and contingencies. Unlike the era of high Americanization, when the form of capitalist consumer culture was closely associated with the content of American dreams (Frith 1982, 46), the content and image now associated with America tend to be detached from the form. To appropriate Beilharz's (1991, 15) argument about how Althusser's concept of "overdetermination" points to the limitation of a Marxist concept of economic base, "Americanization," like the economic base, could be "a kind of bluff, a slumbering last instance never to be called upon." The process of reworking modernity by the non-West could be relatively autonomous from the base, "Americanization."

If in the modern, secular age the conception of "time" is characterized by homogeneity and emptiness (Benjamin 1973), what is now becoming homogeneous and empty in the process of globalization is the conceptual form of various images. While the concept of "homogeneous time" was the basis of the construction of "imagined communities" of the nation (Anderson 1983), the global diffusion of shared popular cultural forms is not producing a singular global imagined community. Rather, it is intensifying cultural heterogenization across the world. A globalizing hegemony, as Richard Wilk argues, involves "structures of common difference": "The new global cultural system promotes difference instead of suppressing it, but difference of a particular kind. Its hegemony is not of content, but of form. Global structures organize diversity, rather than replicating uniformity" (1995, 118). What the recent popularity of Japanese dramas in Taiwan suggests, however, is that the global diffusion of empty "forms" not only structures diversity but also (re)activates intraregional cultural flows and (a sense of) cultural proximity through the consumption of popular/consumer culture. "Content" and "image" are at once de-territorialized and re-territorialized at an intraregional level, as García Canclini (1995, 229) describes: The two processes as "the loss of the 'natural' relation of culture to geographical and social territories and, at the same time, certain relative, partial territorial relocalizations of old and new symbolic productions."

The re-territorialization of "American" images in East Asia has not brought about by the emergence of a new symbolic power. When I asked whether Japanese dramas had had any influence on her, a Taiwanese interviewee in her mid-twenties, who used to love American programs but now watches many Japanese dramas, thoughtfully replied, "Japanese dramas are more delicate than Western ones and I can relate easily to Japanese ones. They are more similar to our feelings . . . but not much influence [at a deeper level]. . . . Maybe Japan is a sort of mirror, but it is perhaps America that we always follow and try to catch up with." Even for those who delight in Japanese TV dramas, "Japan," as an object of yearning, does not enjoy the status that "America" once did. As my *China Times* informant told me, "Japan is too close to have a yearning for." The key expression here is "easy to relate to." In Taiwan, American celebrities are mainly movie stars, whereas their Japanese counterparts are TV idols who look like their fans; American movies may be glamorous and entertaining, but Japanese dramas provide topics for everyday conversation and serve as vehicles for vicarious experience; things "American" are dreams to be yearned for and conceptual forms to be pursued, whereas things "Japanese" are examples to be emulated and commodities to be acquired.[9]

As I will discuss in the next chapter, Taiwanese favorable consumption of Japanese popular culture is not matched by Japanese consumption of the Taiwanese counterpart. Nevertheless, as far as audience reception is concerned, the popularity of Japanese television dramas in Taiwan does not attest to a center-periphery relationship between the two countries, contrary to claims made by Japanese nationalists. Rather, it indicates that the Japanese cultural presence in Taiwan is sustained by a sense of coevalness. As Fabian (1983, 23) argues in his discussion of how Western refusal to recognize the sharing of the same temporality with non-Western cultural Others has been institutionalized in anthropological research, the term *coevalness* denotes two interrelated meanings: synchronicity and contemporaneity. The development of global communication technologies and networks may further the denial of "contemporaneity" of the periphery through the facilitation of "synchronicity." To illustrate, Mark Liechty (1995, 194) elucidated the Nepali experience of modernity as "the ever growing gap between imagination and reality, becoming and being." The disappearance of a time lag in the distribution of cultural products in many parts of the world has left wide political, economical and cultural gaps intact, so much so that they facilitated the feeling in non-Western countries that " 'catching up' is never really possible" (Morley and Robins 1995, 226–27).

This is no longer the case, however, with the relationship between Japan and Taiwan. An interviewee in her early twenties who has long been a fan of Japanese popular culture stressed the emerging sense of shared temporality with Japan as one reason for the rise of Japanese popular culture in Taiwan: "Taiwan used to follow Japan, always be a 'Japan' of ten years ago. But now we are living in the same age and sharing similar lifestyles. There is no time lag between Taiwan and Japan. I think this sense of living in the same age emerged three or four years ago. Since then, more people have become interested in things Japanese." A manager of a Japanese cable channel explains this shift more astutely: "When Taiwan was still a poor country, we had just a dream of a modern lifestyle. It was an American dream. But now that we have become rich, we no longer have a dream but it is time to put the dream into practice. Not the American dream, but the Japanese reality, is a good object to emulate for this practical purpose."

This posture displays that the perception of living in the same temporality is intertwined with what Thompson (1995, 175) calls "the accentuation of symbolic distancing from the spatial-temporal contexts of everyday life" in the media-saturated age. The abundance of information, ideas, and images of other cultures and nations disseminated through the media presents one with various kinds of alternative ideas and ways of living, thus urging one to take a reflexive distance from one's own life, culture, and society (see Appadurai 1996). This tendency is indicated by the reception of Japanese TV dramas in Taiwan, as we saw with the viewers' positive identification of Rika's particular kind of single-mindedness and their negative reception of Satomi's femininity. What is crucial here, as modernity for people in Taiwan, especially for the younger generations in urban regions, is no longer just dreams, images, and yearnings of influence, but a lived reality—that is, the material conditions in which they live—the mediated reference for self-transformation has changed for some Taiwanese young people from the abstract to the practical, something within reach. Japanese TV dramas offer for their fans a concrete and accessible model of what it is like to be modern in East Asia, which American popular culture could have never presented.

Seen this way, the experience of cultural proximity, if we still want to use this notion, should not be conceived in terms of a static attribute of "being" but as a dynamic process of "becoming": It is a matter of time as well as space. The emerging dialectic of comfortable distance and cultural similarity between Japan and Taiwan seems to be based upon a consciousness that Taiwan and Japan live in the same time, thanks to ever-narrowing gaps between Taiwan and Japan in terms of material conditions; the urban consumerism of an expanding middle class; the changing role of women in society; the development of communication technologies and media industries; the reworking of local cultural values; and the re-territorialization of images diffused by American popular culture. Historically overdetermined by Japanese colonization, under simultaneously homogenizing and heterogenizing forces of modernization, Americanization, and globalization, all these elements interact in a complicated dynamic to articulate the cultural resonance of Japanese TV dramas for some Taiwanese viewers who synchronously, contemporaneously, and self-reflexively experienced "Asian modernity" in late–twentieth-century East Asia.

This point should not be generalized or overemphasized, however. Western popular culture is still widely consumed in East Asia, and there are many young people in Taiwan who do not like Japanese TV dramas. Many economically deprived people are still excluded from the shared experience of modernity in the region. Neither should we engage uncritically with the transnational regional flow of highly commercialized materialistic consumer culture. The sense of contemporaneity might not be derived from objective reality but from an imagination which is fabricated by the instantaneous circulation of information and commodities in the region. This sense is oblivious of Japan's colonial legacy in the region and lends credence to the voices of many Japanese Asianists who are desperately seeking commonalities between Japan and Asia.

Moreover, the analysis of intraregional cultural flows and consumption highlights the newly articulated asymmetrical power relations in the region. While displacing the view of power as the articulation of a Taiwanese yearning for Japan, the cultural immediacy which Taiwanese audiences feel in Japanese TV dramas does not necessarily articulate cultural dialogue on equal terms. The flow among East Asian countries, and particularly between Japan, Taiwan, and Hong Kong, is gradually becoming bilateral and more young people in Japan are also sampling popular culture from other parts of Asia—Hong Kong films, Canto-pop, or Taiwan idols (Honkon, Taiwan, Nihon wa poppu kyōeiken" 1997). Still, there is no doubt that the flow of audiovisual products tends to be in one direction, from Japan to other countries. This asymmetry is evident not just in terms of quantity but, more importantly, in terms of the perception of temporality manifest in the consumption of the media products of cultural neighbors. As observed by a Taiwanese journalist, the sense of coevalness in the Taiwanese experience in their consumption of Japanese popular culture also gives them a certain sense of vanity that "We've finally caught up with Japan" (Watch out! Your children are becoming "Japanese" 1997, 70), but Taiwanese or other popular culture does not necessarily signify the same perception of coevalness for Japanese consumers. This articulation of Japanese transnational cultural power as the capacity for producing cultural products through which Taiwanese audiences experience cultural proximity would be highlighted if we looked at cultural flows in the opposite direction and then experienced transnational regional modernity through them. This is the theme of the next chapter.

5

Popular Asianism in Japan:

Nostalgia for (different) Asian modernity

In the previous chapter, I argued that the sense of resonance that some Taiwanese audiences experience when watching Japanese TV dramas is closely related to an emerging sense of coevalness, the perception of a historical synchronicity between Japan and Taiwan. In this chapter, I examine cultural flows in the opposite direction, that is, Japanese representation and consumption of Asian popular culture and the idea of "Asia." Through the analysis of what can be called "popular Asianism" in 1990s Japan, I discuss how the asymmetry in transnational cultural flows in East Asia is articulated at the site of media consumption.

Japanese interest in Asian popular culture did not start recently. In the 1970s and 1980s, for example, kung fu films from Hong Kong became quite popular, and several Hong Kong, Taiwanese, and Korean pop singers made their debuts in Japan. Although, compared with Japanese cultural exports to other parts of Asia, the flow of popular culture from these regions into Japan has been less extensive, the overall media coverage of Asian popular culture has drastically increased, and interest in Asian films and pop music captured a broad Japanese audience in the 1990s (see Ajia karuchā ryūnyū no 30 nen 1994; Tadashii Ajia no hamarikata 1997). Japanese representation and consumption of Asian popular culture has become so diverse that it is impossible to deal with all aspects of the culture in a single chapter. Hence, I have chosen to focus on two topical issues in order to show the contradictions and ambivalence articulated in the Japanese discursive construction of "Asia" through the reception of other Asian popular culture. First, some Japanese critics and intellectuals have attempted to find in Asian popular culture different modes of non-Western modernity. This view, unlike the nationalist discourses discussed in chapter 2, illustrates the attempt to reject and transcend asymmetrical conceptions of temporal and spatial difference between Japan and other Asian nations. The Japanese reception of the Singaporean pop musician Dick Lee is a case in point. In the midst of the world music boom around 1990, Lee's syncretic music prompted these analysts to challenge the, to that time, dominant view of Asia as an inferior Other and to engage with "modern" Asia on equal terms.

However, as Asian economic development stirred Japanese media and industry attention and broadened Japanese interest in Asian popular culture in the 1990s, such a reflexive posture was gradually swallowed up by Japan's historically constituted conception of a culturally and racially similar, but always "backward" Asia. Through an analysis of mainstream commercials, films, TV dramas, and publications in Japan, I will argue that the self-critical stance in the discourse on Asian popular culture has been overwhelmed by a stress on the temporal lag between Japan and other Asian nations in the mid-1990s. Now, modernizing Asian nations are nostalgically seen to embody a social vigor and optimism for the future that Japan allegedly is losing or has lost. This perception, revealing as it does Japan's refusal to accept that it shares the same temporality as other Asian nations, illustrates the asymmetrical flow of intraregional cultural consumption in East Asia.

My analysis is based on empirical research I conducted in Tokyo in 1997 and 1998. It suggests that the aforementioned ambivalences in Japan's fascination with Asia are apparent in the Japanese reception of Hong Kong popular culture. In the mid-1990s, the frequent media coverage in Japan of Hong Kong popular culture significantly increased the number of fans of Hong Kong films and pop stars. While the approval of such fans still tended to be informed by a nostalgic longing, some perceived Hong Kong to be the modern equal of Japan. In their eyes, it was Hong Kong's synchronous temporality with Japan, not its temporal distance that had brought about the differences between Japan and Hong Kong. This perception encouraged a different view of Asian cultural modernity, one through which Japan's modern experiences could be critically reconsidered.

This does not mean that the consumption of Asian popular culture in Japan shows a critical engagement with deconstructing the prevailing conception of "Asia." Rather, Asian popular culture has become a site where the continuity, rearticulation, and rupture of a historically constituted Japanese imagination of "Asia" are all complexly manifested. It is these contradictions, embodied in the Japanese consumption of Asian popular culture, that I will attend to in this chapter.

Commonality and temporal lag:
The Japanese discourse on "Asian" pop music

A significant feature of the Japanese consumption of Asian audiovisual imagery is the prevalence of writing on the subject. As an editor of a Japanese magazine on Asian popular music told me, "Publications on Asian pop sell much more than the music itself in Japan." Beginning in the 1980s, this trend had become particularly conspicuous by the 1990s with the growth in the popular literature on Asian countries (the so-called *Asia-bon*) (Maekawa and Ōno 1997). Asia-related publications in the 1990s have been distinguished by the prevalence of travelogues and personal reports, which are designed to explain daily life and popular culture in Asia to younger Japanese readers (Ōno 1996; Ajiabon no shuppan kakkyō 1994).[1] This predisposition is in contrast to the previously dominant themes of books on East and Southeast Asia, which focused on Japan's role in World War II and its lingering economic exploitation of the region suffering from poverty (e.g., Tsurumi 1980, 1982; Murai 1987; Murai, Kido, and Koshida 1983). As other Asian countries have achieved greater economic development (an achievement manifested clearly in Seoul's hosting of the Olympic Games in 1988) and with the development of tourism to Asian regions, an interest in the culture of urban Asia has become prominent. In these publications, Japanese writers attempt to understand Asia, not through "study" but through firsthand "experience" (Maekawa and Ōno 1997).

The main topics of popular Asia-related publications range from information about consumer items such as food, shopping, beauty salons, and massages to articles about the media and popular culture (TV, films, music, etc.). While their encounters with these quotidian aspects of life in Asian cities often point to irreducible cultural differences between Japan and other Asian nations, Japanese writers nevertheless perceive underlying commonalities. In her best-selling travel book, *Ajia Fumufumu Ryokō* (1994), Mure Yōko confesses that she had long been fascinated with the West and never had an interest in Asia, which for her connoted backwardness. However, when she traveled to Hong Kong, Macao, and Seoul for the first time in the early 1990s, she found these cities so modern and exciting that she became addicted to traveling across Asia. She encountered many curiously familiar scenes in Asia and realized that the region shared "something" with Japan—though just what that "something" was she does not make explicit. While traveling through the United States, she had enjoyed its sheer Otherness, but in Asia she had delighted in its "bit of difference" based on same-ness. Along with the elusive question of what Japan and other Asian nations share, what the deployment of this "familiar difference" (see Ang and Stratton 1996) between them tells us merits consideration here. If Japan's Asian identity is evoked through the perception of a familiar difference rather than as a cardinal cultural commonality, is this familiar difference overtly or covertly employed to confirm Japan's superiority? Or does it feed on the conception that Japan meets such nations on equal terms? It is Japan's often contradictory posture toward Asia, the ways in which the spatio-temporal similarities and differences between Japan and other Asian nations are articulated, that the analysis of a popular Asianism in Japan will elucidate.

In the 1990s, Asian pop music significantly stimulated Japan's awareness of its Asian identity. In this regard, an intriguing statement appears on the cover of an edited volume entitled *Poppu Eijia* (Pop Asia) (1990), "The popular music of Asia reminds us that Japanese are Asian." Judging from the content of the publication, in which more than ten Japanese music critics explore the relationship between Japanese and other Asian popular music, two elements appear to be behind this evocation of Japan's Asian identity: the common experience of a (forced) cultural hybridization and of indige-nization of foreign (mainly Western) cultural forms; and the influence of Japanese cultural production. Which perspective is employed depends on the region in focus. Some writers (Saitō 1990a; Shinozaki 1990b; Kawakami 1990) in the volume point out that as far as popular music style is concerned, Japan shares more with East Asian nations—Hong Kong, Taiwan, and South Korea—than with Southeast Asia.[2] Such cultural commonality for East Asian popular music is, according to them, articulated through the recep-tion of (Westernized) Japanese popular music. Saitō (1990a, 22) argues that "Japanese influence on Asian music industries is the key factor for the demarcation of the boundaries between East and Southeast Asia." In South-east Asia, the influence of English-language pop music has been direct, but "East Asian nations tend to prefer Japanese pop music, as it acquires somehow '[East] Asian' flavor through the absorption and indigenization of Western pop music" (Shinozaki 1990b, 105). Here, familiar difference is perceived in the way in which other East Asian nations develop their pop music production to a greater or less extent through Japanese influence. Japan's Asianness is articulated, as in hybridism discourse, in terms of its role as a translator between Western and Asian modern cultural formations.

Japan's Asian identity is differently articulated when attention is paid to popular music in Southeast Asia, where Japanese commentators (Saitō 1990a; Shinozaki 1990b) acknowledge that Japanese cultural influence is arguably much weaker. Here, as the subtitle of *Poppu Eijia* suggests—"Tingle with the excitement of cultural hybridization when listening to Asian pop"—Asian popular music illuminates the common act of producing local culture through cultural indigenization and hybridization. For one thing, the West's dominant cultural power, underlining the shared experience of cross-fertilization, articulates the similarity between Japanese and Southeast Asian pop music. As a young Japanese male commented, "I have listened mainly to Western pop music, but when I listened to Thai pop for the first time, it did not sound entirely strange to me" (Ajia myūjikku saikō! 1995). This remark suggests that the familiarity of Thai pop to Japanese is due to its incorporation of Western pop elements. At the same time, the common practice of hybridization also articulates the familiar difference of Southeast Asian pop music in a rather spectacular and exotic manner. According to Saitō (1990a, 23), unlike East Asian pop music, "most Japanese audiences are attracted to its fascinating way of cultural cross-fertilization of the local and the foreign" (see also Kubota 1990). Southeast Asian pop music thus more often than not conjures up the Japanese perception of a quite different mode of Asian cultural modernity. I will return to this point shortly.

Which of these two modes of familiar difference is emphasized—although they are sometimes commingled—in Japanese discourse on Asian popular culture and Japan's Asian identity also depends on historical context. In the 1980s, there was still a distinct gap between the cultural production capacity of Japan and other Asian nations. Japanese authors, in their search for Japan's Asian connection, tended to encounter this gap in terms of apparent Japanese cultural influence in the region. The popular essayist Morieda Takashi's *Chūkanzu de mita Ajia* (A worm's eye view of Asia) (1988) is a case in point. Morieda's perspective was also that of the urban consumer and he attempted to escape the conventional focus on some authentic, traditional Asia. He stressed the significance of introducing the popular and consumer culture of Asia to Japanese readers, as this would deepen their interest in Asia in the same way that many people in Japan became acquainted with the United States through Hollywood popular films (68). Examining popular and consumer culture in Asia, however, Morieda found a significant influence of Japanese culture in the region in terms of food, fashion, and animation, as well as popular songs. As the result, while acknowledging the asymmetry in the relations—both economic and cultural—between Japan and Asia, Morieda concluded with no more than an expression of the hope that his book would be a first step to correct this asymmetry by assisting the bilateral flow of information between Japan and Asia: "In any case, there are many people in Asian countries who are fans of Japanese pop idols. In South Korea, people eat the same pickle as in Japan. Thai people love watching *Doraemon* and *Oshin*. These facts will make Asia more familiar and intimate to Japanese readers" (235). Since the Asia he introduced to readers is one whose popular culture has been deeply influenced by Japan, Morieda's intention of evoking Japan's Asian identity by making the information traffic two-way ironically resulted in the confirmation of Japan's dominant position in Asia.

In this period, there was also a Japanese attempt to forge a more self-critical discourse on the relationship between Japan and Asia via Asian popular music. Just as world music appeals to the Western "liberal/left" as the ideological antithesis of an American-centric view of the world (Barrett 1996), Asian pop music serves for some Japanese commentators as an antidote to Japan's exploitative relationship with Asia and to claims of Japanese superiority (based on Japan's reputed closeness to American popular culture). Shinozaki Hiroshi is one such commentator. A prominent writer on Asian pop, in 1988 he published a book on the subject entitled *Kasettoshoppu e Ikeba Ajia ga Mietekuru* (Understanding Asia through pop music cassette-tape shops). In his work, Shinozaki explores the politics, economies, and societies of Asian countries through their popular music. He also examines their relations with Japan with reference to Japan's imperialist history, its economic exploitation of them, and Japan's role in the Asian sex industry. While recognizing the influence of Japanese popular music in the region, he nevertheless tries not to put Japan and other Asian countries on a linear developmental line. He confesses to being overwhelmed by a sense of déjà vu upon hearing local music in many parts of Asia, but he adds that this experience of cultural similarity is not based on his actual historical memory of Japan's past: "The historical path of one country is not necessarily followed by another country. I rather hope that other Asian countries will take different paths from that of Japan. Asia is a really tough other in that it is culturally quite similar to but simultaneously altogether different from Japan" (Shinozaki 1988, 235). While he implies that a primordial cultural similarity exists between Japan and other Asian nations, Shinozaki avoids comparing the contemporary Asian music scene with Japan's past and tries to conceive of the familiar difference of Asia on equal and coeval terms.

Is Asia still one? The Japanese appropriation and appreciation of Dick Lee

Shinozaki's (1988) caution about the Japanese Orientalist conception that "their" future is "our" past was directed against a faith in Japan's advanced capacity for producing pop music in the late 1980s. The success of Singaporean musician Dick Lee in the world music genre around 1990 dramatically displaced this perception, however, and threw Southeast Asian hybridity into high relief.[3] Dick Lee has been the most successful Asian pop singer in the Japanese market in terms of CD sales figures.[4] The attractiveness of his syncretic music for Japanese audiences lies in its playful mixing of Western pop and various adaptations of traditional Asian music. Particularly well received were Lee's two albums *The Mad Chinaman* (1989) and *Asia Major* (1990), in which he attempted to articulate his search for an impure identity as a Singaporean and an Asian, respectively, through the syncretic remaking of traditional Asian songs and instrumentals in contemporary (Western) pop music styles. As Kitanaka (1995, 34), a well-known music critic, suggests, the attraction of Lee's music resides in the combination of two factors. The first is an exoticism which derives from the incorporation of local cultural traditions, and the second is a sophisticated modern music style, backed by the use of the latest technologies. Lee's music made Japanese realize that Asian pop is not backward but represents a highly sophisticated mode of cultural hybridization (see Shinozaki 1990a; Tokyo FM Shuppan 1995, 168).

Dick Lee became a cause célèbre for Japanese critics because his music embodied a radical sense of a hybrid Asian identity that was beyond the reach of the self-contained Japanese cultural formation (e.g., Shinozaki 1990b, 107–8). All by himself, Lee had produced "a new sound by fusing West and East that Japanese musicians, who just mimic Western music style, could never do" (Yoshihara 1994, 188). His music presented a different form of cultural negotiation between Asia and the West, a more cosmopolitan mode of hybridization that Japan had yet to attain (e.g., Shinozaki 1990b; Kubota 1990). This point has been expanded by Nakazawa Shin'ichi (1990), a prominent Japanese advocate of postmodernism. He argues that Lee's music reflects the postmodernist condition of Singapore, a floating intersection of cultures which, unlike China or Japan, lacks a strong sense of communal identity. Japan can never be such an intersection because it cannot resist the pull of communal gravitation (217). In contrast, Nakazawa contends, in

Singapore no attempt is made to insert its diversity of cultures into a nationalizing melting pot that homogenizes them: "Dick Lee for the first time succeeded in making Asian pop music attain a consistent multiplex structure, so much so that his music suggests the possibility of the mingled existence of multiple different rhythms in one song. . . . Dick Lee as a Singaporean is free from a strong drawing force to the motherland and therefore has attained the freedom as well as the sorrow of a nomadic subjectivity" (217–18).

Nakazawa seems to suggest that Japanese musicians have long been endeavoring to indigenize foreign (Western) pop, but in a way that removes all traces of the original. In Lee's music, in contrast, the warp and woof of different musical traditions are highlighted. As was observed in chapter 2, the Japanese way of mixing cultures suppresses its foreign origins, thereby articulating "Japaneseness" by rendering the product mukokuseki (expressing non-nationality). Dick Lee's mixing is takokuseki (expressing multinationality/ethnicity); it subtly juxtaposes many diverse cultures without erasing their original features (Saitō 1990b).[5]

Arguably, the above views on Lee's music and Singapore fail to notice the contradictory cultural and identity politics operating in Singapore, its in-betweenness, which is not a voluntary condition but one that was forced upon Singapore by its history of Western imperialism (see Ang and Stratton 1997). Moreover, these views celebrate Singapore, through the vehicle of Lee's syncretic musical style, as an idealized postmodern city of nomads, in a rather uncritical manner. It can be claimed, for instance, that Lee's music is just a fashionable, commercialized, apolitical pastiche of Western pop and traditional Asian music; that his claim of possessing a pan-Asian identity is purely a promotional strategy; and that his claim operates, within the context of Singapore's cultural policies, to stress a multiracial, pan-Asian identity in nationalist terms (see Kong 1996; Wee 1996). However, the debate over the cultural politics of Lee's music has, on the whole, failed to have an impact on Japanese critics and audiences, who appreciate the music as they incorporate it into a Japanese context.[6] In this sense, the Japanese discourse on Dick Lee's music is reminiscent of another contentious issue of intercultural communication—the appropriation of cultural Others via media consumption. The development of communication technologies has intensified contact with cultural Others predominantly through a mediated experience (e.g., Meyrowitz 1985; Thompson 1995). Accordingly, the development of international communications has made transnational media consumption a site where an Orientalist gaze upon a dehumanized, cultural Other is invariably reproduced (Said 1978; Morley and Robins 1995, 125–46).

However, I would argue that Japanese discourses on Lee's music, although they largely ignore the debate about the music in Singapore, cannot all be dismissed simply as another attempt to domesticate something innovative by casting it as an inferior, exotic, Asian other. At the least, some display an effort to appreciate Lee's music as the embodiment of an Asian modernity whose difference articulates a telling critique of the formation of Japanese modernity and its discourse on hybridism. This is a more encouraging posture for dealing with cultural Otherness in transnational media consumption: engaging with it "in a relation of mutuality and equivalence" (Hamilton 1997, 149) in order to change one's own subjectivity.

Adopting the above perspective, Ueda (1994) contends that Lee's music, with its affirmative emphasis on the dynamic and hybrid "banana" identity of modern Asians—yellow on the outside, white on the inside—deconstructs a static, essentialist binarism of East and West that has long been prominent in Japanese conceptions of Asia. Ueda makes his point by comparing Lee with Okakura Tenshin's phrase "Asia is one," uttered at the turn of the nineteenth century. In his famous book, *The Ideal of the East with Special Reference to the Art of Japan* (1904), Okakura used a binary East–West opposition in an attempt to grasp "Asia" as a coherent space characterized by the existence of "love" underlying art and aesthetics in the region.[7] More significantly, Karatani (1994) has argued that in Okakura's essentialist construction of Asia, he does not simply attempt to articulate a cardinal Eastern value and aesthetic. Rather, Okakura's work reflects his desire that Asia be given an imaginary coherence by Japan. Here, Okakura's argument is closely in line with the Japanese discourse on hybridism. Okakura imagined not just Asian unity in diversity but a curator, "Japan," through whom this unity could be achieved in the first place.[8] Admitting Japan's deep cultural and intellectual debt to China and India, Okakura argued that many of the arts, religions, and ideas that had been lost in other parts of Asia were preserved in Japan. Okakura conceived of Japan as the museum of Asian civilizations. Okakura's famous assertion of "Asia is one" thus assigned Japan the exclusive "historical mission not only to represent, but also to speak for the highest ideal of Asia" (Ching 1998, 76).

In contrast, Ueda (1994) asserts, Dick Lee in his work does not reify the East–West opposition. Even in his album *The Mad Chinaman,* in which he expresses his ambivalence toward his position as a Singaporean between Asia and the West, tradition and modernity, Lee still tries to incorporate both sides of the binary rather than valorize one at the expense of the other. According to Ueda, Dick Lee's "One Song" succeeds in expressing an Asian aesthetic by incorporating different Asian musical traditions and languages into a new form without rejecting the West: "Dick Lee's message 'Let's sing one song' is active and dynamic while Okakura Tenshin's 'Asia is one' is static. Dick Lee does not exclude Western elements from his conception of Asia. The articulation of Asianness goes hand in hand with the keen hybridization of many elements of West and East. Okakura's conception of Asia was only derived from a binary oppositioning between East and West" (46).

Furthermore, Lee's music does not presuppose any center in the process of Asian cross-fertilization. Ueda approves of Lee's claims that many Asians share a common identity and that, in the course of indigenizing modernity, they have come to acquire similar bodily feelings and sensitivities (51). Here it is suggested that the conception of "Asia" should not be derived from some essential Asianness nor from the sharing of a common Other (the West). Most crucially, Lee's music tells people in Japan that if Asian popular music makes Japanese feel that they are Asian, it is because it reminds them of the shared modern experience of ever-cross-fertilizing dynamics in Asia, where Japan does not occupy the position of a transcending center but merely that of a player—one among many—contributing to the production of a new syncretic culture.

Dick Lee and East Asian capitalist cross-fertilization

The drawback of the Japanese appreciation of Dick Lee, however, has become manifest in his transient popularity and, more significantly, in the subsequent, twisted development of Lee's advocacy of cultural hybridization by Japanese media industries. What is significant but missing in Ueda's argument is a critical consideration of how the Japanese appreciation of Lee's music could work collusively with Japan's project of reconfiguring its leading position in a China-centered dynamic space of cultural cross-fertilization in Asia, which I discussed in chapter 3. If "Lee's music is symptomatic, but not directly reflective, of the ongoing reformations of politico-cultural issues in Singapore" (Wee 1996, 503), I would suggest that its greater popularity in Japan than in other Asian countries is symptomatic of the resurgence of Japan's desire to generate a pan-Asian cultural fusion.

After interrogating his impure Asian identity in *The Mad Chinaman* (1989) and *Asia Major* (1990), Lee tried to explore his persona as a modern "banana Asian" in his next album, *Orientalism* (1991). He had come to realize that his trademark style—the subtle and playful interweaving of traditional Asian music with Western pop—could be pursued equally well by Westerners. As Lee commented: "I know that if I re-make well-known Asian old songs in Western contemporary popular music style, the album will be well received by critics and sell. But I do not want to be a spurious 'Asian' artist. I think we should honestly acknowledge that our music style is after all deeply Westernized, that we are no longer as much 'Asian' as we believe. This does not mean that all we can do is copy the West but we should start creating a new Asianness based upon a recognition of the state of affairs" (Ajia pawā 1992, 12).

When Lee produced *Orientalism,* he was thus convinced that Asian popular music should reflect the "cultural impurity" of Asians in a positive way. However, the album was not as popular in Japan as his two previous works. It even disappointed Japanese audiences.[9] As Ueda notes, in *Orientalism* the affirmation of a "banana" identity results in a more sophisticated Westernized music devoid of the juxtaposition of the modern and exotic. Alongside the decline in the popularity of world music in Japan, the discursive value of Lee diminished soon after his music lost its strong "Asian," exotic flavor (Ueda 1994, 48–49; Ajia pawā 1992). Such "Westernized" music is too familiar to Japanese audiences to be portrayed as a spectacular antithesis to Japanese hybridism.

More significantly, the release of *Orientalism* coincided with an increasing interest on the part of Japanese business in the expanding markets of Asia, especially East Asia, where the production of popular music had rapidly developed in the early 1990s under Western and (to a lesser extent) Japanese influence.[10] This coincidence suggests two things about the Dick Lee phenomenon in Japan: First, it drew the attention of the Japanese music industry to the value of combining traditional Asian music and Western pop in a sophisticated way; second, it alerted the industry to the potential of marketing and producing pan-Asian popular music icons with the Japanese initiative (Ongaku sangyō wa Ajia mejā o mezasu 1992, 12). The title of Lee's album *Asia Major* was thus manipulated to connote the pan-Asian market strategy of the Japanese music industry (Ongaku sangyō wa Ajia mejā o mezasu 1992). Ironically, then, at the same time that Lee's music was subverting a Japan-centric conception of pan-Asian cultural fusion, it was encouraging the Japanese music industry to expand into other Asian (notably Chinese) markets by becoming an organizer of cultural hybridization. Dick Lee's dynamic pan-Asianism basically triggered Japan's orchestration of the transnationalization of Asian popular music.

This posture taken by the Japanese music industry casts a shadow over the media representation of Asian popular music. Here, the desire for the creation of a pan-Asian cultural sphere still haunts the Japanese imagination strongly. Stimulated by the Dick Lee boom in Japan, one cultural critic, Kawakami Hideo (1990; 1995), enthusiastically expected that, just as Paris had become the center of world music in the mid-1980s, so would Tokyo become the center of Asian popular music in the 1990s. In 1993 two popular magazines, *Across* and *Spa!*, each ran feature articles on transnational Asian entertainment (Toransu Eijian entāteinmento 1993; Ekkyō suru Ajia geinō 1993). Both articles focused on the interest of young Japanese in Asian popular culture. *Across*'s article related that Asian countries were no longer just places suggestive of mystery and tradition for young Japanese; indeed, young Asians who had been deeply exposed to Western culture had now begun creating new local cultures. Nevertheless, both articles noted the central role being played by the Japanese media industries in the region's cultural ebb and flow.

The legacy of the "Asia is one" ideology is also evident in Japanese media representations of Asian pop music in the 1990s. During this period, Japan conceived of itself as the consumer showcase of hybrid Asian music. Although recent Japanese writing on Asian popular culture has been sensitive to the issue of diversity, it is surprising to see how often Asian countries continue to be lumped together in a single musical category, with the word "*Ajia*" (Asia) featuring in the title—a category from which Japan is omitted (the aforementioned magazine *Poppu Eijia* is no exception). Take, for instance, *AsiaNbeat*, a TV series about Asian pop music that was broadcast between 1993 and 1995. Although its Japanese presenter would shout "Asia is one," the program actually regularly lumped together East and Southeast Asian pop music but exclude music from Japan. In this sense, then, "Asia is one" really means that Asia is one only in and for Japan (Ichikawa 1994, 171). Likewise, NHK broadcast a TV special, *Asia Live Dream* (26 December 1996) which also covered many parts of Asia from a Japan-centric perspective. It featured more than twenty pop singers from ten Asian countries. In one segment, several Asian singers sang the program's theme song together with *Doraemon*, a character from a popular Japanese animation. All of this suggests that "Asia" is re-imagined as a cultural space in which Japan is located in the implicit center, playing the part of the conductor of Asian pop musical cross-fertilization.

In the mid-1990s, as I will discuss later, in accordance with the increase in Japanese music industries' interest in East Asian/Chinese pop music markets, Japanese media attention also shifted to the latter regions from Southeast Asia (Shiraishi 1996). Lee himself quickly adjusted to the changing currents,[11] seemingly always conscious of what the Japanese media industries expected of him. On another TV program that dealt with the Asian popular music scene, *21seiki no Bîtoruzu wa Ajia kara* (The Beatles of the twenty-first century will emerge from Asia) (NHK Educational, 8 March 1997), the main topic was no longer Lee's music but emerging Chinese rock musicians, some of whom well-known Japanese music critics and scholars expected to produce globally acclaimed popular music. That music would reflect social contradictions caused by rapid capitalist development in the region by appropriating Western musical styles (see Hashizume 1994). Dick Lee was once again cast in the program as an Asian musician who embodied the transcendence of the East–West binarism. Lee this time renewed his raison d'etre by introducing a new acronym, "WEAST" (a merging of "West" and "East"), to express the importance of overcoming the old binarism. The intricacy of the Japanese appropriation and appreciation of Dick Lee appears to have culminated with his appointment to the vice-presidency of Sony Music's Asian division in July 1998. Although he quit that job in 2000, Lee officially had worked for a Japanese-owned global conglomerate promoting the cultural hybridization of East and West (Kyōmi shinshin Dikku ga Sonī Ajia no fukushachō ni 1998).

Back to the developmental axis

As the pendulum has again swung from a spectacular modernity embodied by Dick Lee (and some other Southeast Asian pop music) to a more "proximate" (more receptive to Japanese influence) modernity mainly featured in East Asian pop music, there has also been a change in the lexicon deployed to articulate Japan's relation with Asia. Familiar difference has come to be explained mostly in terms of capitalist developmental temporality. Even relatively critical Japanese commentators are not immune to this discursive turn. While warning against the view that "Asia is following the way Japan passed ten years ago," their interpretative frame of reference in dealing with cultural difference in Asia nevertheless tends to pull back from a synchronic spatial axis to a diachronic evolutionist temporality.

A case in point is the reportage of urban Asia, *Ajia wa Machi ni Kike* (Go to the city and understand Asia) (1994), written by Ichikawa Takashi. In the book, Ichikawa uses popular music to reflect on Japan's position in and relationship with Asia, particularly the Chinese cultural regions. While acknowledging Japan's influence by citing the many Japanese songs that have been covered by other Asian musicians, Ichikawa argues that other East Asian countries are rapidly developing their own music styles by earnestly indigenizing foreign (American and Japanese) influences (see also Marume 1994; Chikai kuni kara ippai kita geinōjin 1994). According to Ichikawa, Japan and those Asian countries differ less in terms of the act of indigenization itself than in terms of the latter's advantage in the developmental process. Unlike the modernization of Japan, which was accomplished step by step, the modernization of other East Asian countries can be described as a form of "leap" development, in that they have acquired economic and technological innovations without proceeding methodically. Ichikawa (1994, 144–55) considers popular music development in light of this theory. Japan developed its own musical styles through a long process of indigenizing American pop; the corollary of this was the abundance in other Asian countries of Japanese "cover" songs. Ichikawa considers Asian copies of Japanese songs to be an example of leap development, in that Asian countries now effortlessly appropriate the fruit of Japan's long indigenization of Western pop.

Arguably, this leap development has brought about the condensed coexistence of many temporalities as well as of many cultures in one space, much more intensely than Japan ever experienced. This point is made by a philosopher, Washida Kiyokazu with his observation of the synchronous juxtaposition of many temporalities in Shanghai: "All the temporalities I have experienced are hotchpotched like a soup or lie on top of one another like a kaleidoscope. The disappearance of all the temporal differences leads to an overwhelming sense of synchronicity. . . . It is as if fifty years of our [Japanese] postwar experiences are all arranged in every corner of the city. I can also feel the multiple temporal layers in Japanese cities, but I've never known such a city where many temporalities are compressed in one space as in Shanghai" (1996, 41–42). This argument can be read as a Japanese attempt to displace the Japanese sense of superiority in terms of developmental temporality. The juxtaposition of multiple temporalities testifies to a different mode of constituting non-Western modernity operating in other Asian cities. The idea of a gradual progress does not capture what is going on in other Asian cities, according to Washida, where the development is being achieved from hop to jump, omitting the "skip" stage in China (1996, 43).

This discourse is reminiscent of a familiar argument concerning the situation of non-Western postmodernity. Unlike the postmodernity of the West, non-Western postmodernity cannot be conceived as the subsequent stage of modernity rather, as Buell remarks, it "thrives on incomplete modernization, the result of modernization from the top down. Peripheral sites thus produce cultural situations in which distinct time frames (artificially) constructed by colonialism and Orientalism, and powerfully separated by developmentalism's evolutionary narrative, circulate together" (1994, 335). Buell is apt to see the demise of a grand evolutionary narrative in a peripheral postmodernity which articulates "the clash of differently encoded temporalities," as well as the juxtaposition of many cultures (335–37). However, this kind of view tends to underestimate the deeply uneven nature of global capitalist modernity. The "always already postmodern" situation of the non-Western periphery should not be celebrated uncritically, as it has been brought about and is still deeply affected by the legacies of colonialism and unequal power relations.

Likewise, there is something very problematic in the Japanese views on Asian (post)modernity expressed above. They rarely suggest an awareness that slums and hawkers' stalls might be as much a constitutive part of globalized modernity as high-rise buildings and sophisticated hybridizations of popular music. If recognized at all, the existence of such an unambiguous asymmetry tends to be belittled as a transient stage in capitalist development, which sooner or later will be supplanted by the achievement of material affluence, as happened in Japan (see Washida 1996, 41). The Japanese view thus entrenches the sense of linear progressive development while at the same time rejecting it. The notion of a linear, step-by-step development might be displaced, but the direction of development does not change at all.

Since the allure of the disjunctive juxtaposition of many temporalities in a single place derives from the chimera of a somewhat earlier stage of spectacular economic development in other parts of Asia, it is not surprising that Japanese commentators, in articulating the common but different experience of Asian modernity through Asian pop and urban space, tend to assume a retrospective tone. Ichikawa (1994, 176–77), for example, associates a nation's capacity to absorb foreign cultures with a specific developmental stage of high economic growth—a stage which Japan has passed and which other Asian countries are now approaching and/or experiencing. It is often said that while Japan eagerly absorbed Western cultural influences in the 1970s, it stopped doing so in the 1980s, with the result that its popular culture became centripetal and was confined to the national market (e.g., Kawasaki 1993; Mizukoshi and Baeg 1993). Likewise, Ichikawa (1994, 176–77) asserts that Japan's receptiveness to foreign cultural influences peaked in the 1960s and 1970s, when it was experiencing high economic growth. The prevalence of Japanese cover songs in Hong Kong, he suggests, reveals not the inferiority of its music industry, but its great capacity for cultural absorption—a capacity which Japan once had—and hence demonstrates the stagnant situation of Japanese cultural formation. The discordant temporalities to be found in East Asian pop music or in modernizing Asian cities such as Shanghai prompt the Japanese commentators to reflect on their own vivacious path to economic development.

While Ichikawa's (1994) purpose is not to emphasize the temporal lag between Japan and Asia, we will see that such retrospective tropes have been easily exploited in the Japanese media in a more haughty manner in the representation of Asian societies and rising Asian pop idols in the mid-1990s. The self-critical discourse on Asian popular music, forged among a relatively small community of music critics and (world music) audiences was gradually absorbed by the dominant media discourse; this discourse is distinctive in its disavowal of the claim that Japan and Asia inhabit the same temporal location. Before discussing the Japanese promotion and consumption of East Asian (Hong Kong) popular music and idols, we need to analyze this media discourse, which has been characterized by nostalgia for the vigorous economic development and industrialization of Japan's past.

Capitalist nostalgia for "Asia"

Nostalgia, once regarded as a symptom of extreme homesickness, has become a key term to describe the modern and postmodern cultural conditions (e.g., Davis 1979; Stewart 1993; Frow 1991).[12] Fredric Jameson (1983) argues that nostalgia, together with pastiche, is a central feature of late capitalist image production. Nostalgia is no longer what it was under modernism—the empiricist representation of a historical past; in the postmodern age, it has become the appropriation of "the 'past' through stylistic connotation, conveying 'pastness' by the glossy qualities of the image"

(Jameson 1983, 19). Mass advertising thus often represents "imagined nostalgia" by which people are driven to yearn for a mediated world they have never lost (Appadurai 1996, 77). At the same time, the acceleration of the transnational circulation of images and signs, of contact with other cultures and the expansion of tourist industries have facilitated "the global institutionalization of the nostalgic attitude" (Robertston 1990, 53).[13] The (imagined) past images appropriated are now derived from other cultures and places too. Here evoked is "borrowed nostalgia," in which people's memories are constituted by their experiences of consuming mass-mediated cultural forms from elsewhere. As Buell (1994, 342) points out, "We not only manufacture our present cultures in closer relationship with each other than before, but also more and more overtly commingle the inventions of our memories and pasts."

The politics of the transnational evocation of nostalgia is highlighted when it is employed to confirm a frozen temporal lag between two cultures, when "our" past and memory are found in "their" present. As Turner (1994, 116) argues, the Americans' discovery of their lost frontier in the Australian outback, as represented in the film *Crocodile Dundee*, displays "how effortlessly Australian difference might be appropriated to American ends." This shows a moment when the recognition of cultural difference is immediately transfigured into the comfortable affirmation of unequal relations between superior–inferior and advanced–backward (see Said 1978; Todorov 1984).

Such Orientalist tropes of nostalgia have played a significant part in Japanese representations of an idealized "backward" Asia, in which the Japanese can find their lost purity, energy, and dreams. Dorinne Kondo (1997) has identified two types of Japanese (masculine) nostalgia vis-à-vis Asia in her analysis of magazine articles published in 1990. The first is a nostalgia for a pre-urbanized unspoiled nature in Bali. Bali is represented as a site which can be consumed by an affluent Japanese tourist for "spiritual renewal." Kondo also finds in the representation of the premodern innocence of Thailand what Rosaldo calls "imperialist nostalgia," which describes a Western hypocritical sense of yearning for what uncivilized non-Western societies are losing on the path to Western-led modernization. It is "a particular kind of nostalgia, often found under imperialism, where people mourn the passing of what they themselves have transformed" (Rosaldo 1989, 108). Rosaldo is especially concerned with how an apparently innocent yearning can hide the collusiveness of such a nostalgia with the exercise of cultural and economic domination. The dominant (the West) mourns what the dominated (the non-West) is losing, while knowing that such a loss is inevitable if they are to become civilized and modern like "us." Similarly, the Japanese nostalgic representation of "Asia" can be called imperialist—or more precisely, capitalist—as Japan was not only an imperial power in the past but also plays a major role in the contemporary global spread of capitalism, one which has violently transformed and exploited many parts of the developing Asian countries. In this regard, it should be remembered that Japan's postwar policy has been marked by the forgetfulness of its imperial past, as well as by its active economic advancement into Southeast Asian regions.

Japanese capitalist nostalgia does not just mourn what is destined to be lost in Asia. More emphatically, what is grieved, through the predicted destiny of premodern Asia, is actually what Japan itself has lost or is about to lose. As Kondo argues regarding the Japanese representation of an apparently innocent Thai waitress: "Exposure to Japanization, Westernization, urbanization, and other worldly forces will despoil this Thai flower's shy purity and turn her into a tough, threatening hussy. . . . By mourning the fate of Thailand through his [Japanese journalist] projection of the waitress's fate, the journalist also mourns what he clearly perceives to be the ravages of modernization and the loss of identity undergone in Japan" (1997, 88). Such a capitalist nostalgia, as well as the yearning for unspoiled nature, is firmly based upon Japan's economically dominant position vis-à-vis other Asians. Moreover such a privileged position assures Japan that the loss is revivable, as Kondo observes, that "through consumption, Japanese can (re)experience their lost innocence without jeopardizing the comforts of advanced capitalism that ensured its originary loss. Japan's neocolonial economic dominance assures access to spiritual renewal" (94). In the nostalgic representation of premodern "innocence," Japan is not engaging in a dialogue with "Asia" but consuming it for the transient pleasures of recuperation and refreshment.

The magazine articles Kondo analyses were published in 1990. That year was the apex of the Japanese bubble economy which let many Japanese sense Japan's hegemonic position in the world. Their economic power enabled Japanese to somehow pleasurably indulge themselves in nostalgia for a premodern innocence that Japan had lost. By the mid-1990s, however, this nostalgia had become more related to the deterioration of the Japanese economy and society. It arose in the context of a prolonged economic recession and a series of gloomy social incidents, such as an increasing number of brutal murders by teenagers and the nerve gas attacks in the Tokyo railway system by the Aum Supreme sect. Nostalgia for Asia was no longer just a matter of pleasurable yearning for what Japan had lost; instead, it was now an attempt to regain the energy and vitality Japan had lost by identifying itself with the promising land of "Asia."

In the mid-1990s, Bali was surpassed as a site for spiritual renewal by more mystical, destitute, and chaotic sites in Asia such as Varanasi (India) and Katmandu. Another dominant trend in Asia-related publications in the mid-1990s was the popularity of books depicting backpackers' experiences in Asia. The origin of this genre can be found in Sawaki Kōtarō's trilogy of books entitled *Shinya Tokkyū* (Midnight express) (1986a; 1986b; 1992). Sawaki's backpacker travel from Hong Kong to India, Nepal, and finally London was closely followed in the mid-1990s. TV—Asahi produced a documentary-drama based on the book in 1997, and photojournalist Kobayashi Kisei also followed Sawaki's route in his phenomenally popular travel book *Asian Japanese* (1995), which quickly sold more than fifty thousand copies (Wakamono wa hōrō o mezasu 1996, 35). This photo-travelogue depicts young Japanese wandering through Asia, people Kobayashi calls "Asian Japanese." After resigning from his job as a photographer for a sports newspaper, Kobayashi went to Asia because he was sick of the media-saturated daily life in Japan and he wanted to transform himself. In Asia, he came across many Japanese who, like himself, were searching for their "real" selves through an encounter with life in all its rawness and brutality. While Kobayashi and his followers commented that they indulged in a form of transient escapism from Japanese society (e.g., M. Saitō 1997; Sonoda 1997), he maintains that escape is a powerful riposte to the deficiencies of Japanese society. One supporter of Kobayashi also defended herself, saying that, far from constituting an escape, her journey through Asia proved to be highly enlightening, since life in the dirty alleys of Asia taught her how to lead a simpler and more humane life. She likened Asia to a set of parents who had instructed her in the art of living (Wakamono wa hōrō o mezasu 1996, 35).[14]

This motivation for travel to "premodern" Asia is not new but has been the common reason why some Japanese people have traveled in Asia at least since the 1970s (Nomura 1996). There is surely a positive aspect to this escapism, because it is at least an attempt to take a critical distance from Japan's highly consumerist capitalist modernity. Yet, the problem is that Asian Japanese's ephemeral escape to Asia does not escape an Orientalist gaze on Asia, which is still apt to govern any Japanese encounter with Asia.

Unlike the Western consumption of the non-Western, "primitive" Other (Torgovnick 1990), the articulation of Asia as Japan's chimera is not dissociated from a perceived racial/cultural commonality. Kobayashi writes: "I can feel anywhere in Asia to be an extension of Japan. It is something like Japan pulling strings with me. But in Europe or America, I cannot feel as such. Strings are totally cut from Japan" (1995, 4–5). However, this sense of connection strangely coexists with the rejection of historical coevalness. Kobayashi continues, "A trip to an advanced Western country makes me feel something familiar to Japan. There is every modern commodity such as television, telephone and the recent pop culture in the West, all of which I already know as information. But when I am in Asia, I realize that there is nothing familiar which I can understand" (5). Kobayashi finds something strange but somehow familiar both in Asia and Europe, but in very different ways. Japan does not share its past with the West, but both are living in the same affluent but boring, media-saturated (post)modern age. Asia, in contrast, signifies some primordial commonality with Japan, but both are not living in the same time.[15] Behind the comfortable distance Asian Japanese feel toward Asia, there lies a sense of frozen time-lag between Asia and Japan. Asia is never conceived as an equal interlocutor but only a magic landscape where the Japanese unfulfilled search for a "true" self is pursued. For "Asian Japanese" travelers, Asia is a space "out there" to which they can flee whenever they feel suffocated in Japan.

Nostalgia for modernizing energy

While the site for transient spiritual renewal has gradually shifted from tourist resorts to backpackers' penance, there was another significant change regarding the object of Japan's nostalgia in the mid-1990s. Social and economic crisis and the prevailing pessimistic atmosphere about the future caused people in Japan to turn their attention to the ascendancy of other Asian nations who were enjoying remarkable economic growth. It is not simply Japan's economic development in the past but society's loss of energy in the present and the hope for the future that Japan nostalgically projects onto modernizing Asia. As was represented in a weekly magazine, "When we [Japanese] walked around Hong Kong and Bangkok, we were really overwhelmed by the energy people were releasing. It was the same kind of raw vigor that Japan once had at the time of high economic growth" (Ryokō, shoku dake de naku 1993, 19). While Asia is not conceived as "premodern" here, what Japan endeavors to see is apparently not neighbors inhabiting the same temporality. Rather, it still displays "the kind of sympathy that identifies with the Other and yet denies him 'coevalness,'" which is constitutive of "the Orientalizing of the Other" (Dirlik 1991, 406). Good old Japan is to be found in the landscape of ever-developing Asia. Japan's Asia is marked out by a diminishing but immutable temporal and economic lag.

Kobayashi's capitalist nostalgia for Asia displayed a similar twist when he turned his attention to local Asians in *Asia Road* (1997). When listening to a nineteen-year-old Vietnamese female's dream of visiting Japan someday, Kobayashi (1997, 172) had a strong yearning for her to utter frankly a dream of the future. He envies her for having a vision of a better future, a belief that tomorrow will be better than today and a hope that Hanoi will be as developed as Tokyo in ten years. Such modernizing vigor in Vietnam became the theme of a Japanese popular TV drama, *Doku,* which was broadcast in prime time between October and December 1996 and attracted a wide audience.[16] It dealt with the relationship between a Japanese female language teacher and Doku, her Vietnamese male student in Japan. Modernizing Vietnam, represented by Doku, is assigned the role of savior to hopeless, overmodernized Japan, as the following catchphrase appearing in the publicity for the program shows: "Asian dreams will come true: She teaches Japanese, he teaches hopes and dreams." During shooting in Vietnam, the Japanese actor playing the protagonist[17] and a producer were reputedly overwhelmed by the energy of the Vietnamese, young and old, who were willing to discuss their dreams (*Doku!* 1997, 77).

In the first episode's opening scene, the Japanese heroine who visits Vietnam to see her friend is impressed but overpowered by the liveliness of the Vietnamese, so much so that she is unable to cross a busy street safely without the help of her soon-to-be Vietnamese student Doku. Asked why she suddenly came to Vietnam, she tells the friend that while looking at herself in the mirror in Tokyo, she had realized how her face was expressionless and dull. She confesses that she is now seriously considering the meaning of her life and wonders out loud if she is going to live this dull life permanently. Her friend replies, pointing at the Vietnamese people around them: "People in Vietnam are somehow marvelous. Energetic, forward-looking, never looking back. They'd never give way to the hardship. Their company makes me feel I can become like them. . . . (looking at a Vietnam girl innocently smiling to her) What a wonderful smile, isn't it? I wish I could keep smiling like that for good" (from the first episode of *Doku*, 17 October 1996). As the heroine admits, Vietnamese people's vivacity stands in sharp contrast to the monotonousness of her life in Japan. The vitality of the Vietnamese is at once Japan's vanishing present and her desired future. Because they are still not quite modern, Vietnamese are energetic and can afford to dream of a bright future—hence expected to afford unilaterally the Japanese people spiritual nourishment without complication.

The same nostalgia has been deployed in TV commercial films for the oolong tea drink Suntory, which since 1991 have featured depictions of a peaceful, pastoral life in not-quite-modern China. The 1997 version, however, depicted the fresh, unspoiled image of Chinese female flight attendants. Through scenes of putting on their makeup and preparing for the flight, of their job inexperience during the flight, and of their wandering through the rapidly changing landscape of Shanghai, the several versions of this commercial all depicted the lively faces of two newly recruited Chinese flight attendants who believe in a good future and whose eyes are shining with hope. The commercial symbolically features the theme song of an animation series, *Astro Boy,* that was popular in Japan in the 1960s. Though translated into Chinese, the lyric, "Flying to stars far beyond the sky" is familiar to many Japanese. A modernizing but simpler life in China is represented with a Japanese nostalgia for hope for a brighter future, as Japan once had, and perhaps with a self-projected, remorseful wish that the mistakes Japan has made will not be repeated.

In a well-received film, *Swallowtail Butterfly* (1996), the trope of nostalgia is utilized in relation to Asian immigrants to Japan. This is a fictional tale about Chinese immigrants who are lured to Japan by the prospect of securing a future and who settle in the lawless suburb of a megacity in Japan, Yen Town. The main motif appears to be the power and the energy of the migrants, who participate in every kind of shady business to acquire yen. The film represents multicultural situations within Japan. Chinese, Japanese, English, and a fictional migrant language fly back and forth. "Yen" symbolizes the uneven and destructive forces of globalized capitalism, which intensify the widening gap between the haves and the have-nots, the violence among migrants, Japanese discrimination against them, and their own sense of despair.

In spite of representing multicultural chaos in Japan, however, strikingly absent in the film is any "real" encounter between the Japanese and Asians.[18] The film's director is not interested in engaging with the otherness of Asian migrants; instead, he aims to represent what Japanese have lost through imagined Others. As the director, Iwai Shunji, stated, "I often felt that Tokyo has become something like a hospital which offers the resident every sort of service. We can somehow live our lives without demonstrating our inherent instinct for self-defense and surprise. I feel such a situation so suffocating and irritating that I really want to break through it. I simply have a sense of yearning for the power and energy of migrants coming to Japan who abandon their home country or work in a foreign city for their families. I want to produce a story about them" (Swallowtail Butterfly 1996, 44). *Swallowtail Butterfly* starts and finishes with a superimposed title in a sepia scene overlooking Tokyo: "Once upon a time, when the Japanese yen was the strongest force in the world. . . . " This makes us realize that what Yen really symbolizes in the film is less Japanese violence to Asian Others. The film is actually a story about "us," as Iwai's remark suggests; Yen Town is a kind of amusement park where one can transiently pass a stimulating period of time. Yen Town is where imagined Others live energetic lives full of dreams as well as frustration, but it exists only for Japanese audiences who can no longer live out such a dream.

In the film, as for other media representations mentioned above, nostalgia is projected toward the (imagined) past when Japan was still "Asia," when Japan still displayed "Asian" vigor. However, what is suppressed here is the fact that such vigor itself was the source and manifestation of Japanese imperial and economic domination and exploitation over other Asian regions after the War. Furthermore, Japan's perceived loss of social vigor conceals the reality that Japan's asymmetrical and exploitative relation with other Asian countries has not yet ended. Thus, the Japanese media representation of Asian nostalgia does not simply fail to recognize 'Asia' as an equal interlocutor, it also suppresses the history of subjugation of other Asian countries that has been constitutive of Japanese modernity. The futuristic story is marked by a strong sense of imperialist/capitalist nostalgia, in which Japan's cultural Others are reduced in an ahistorical manner to consumable signs for Japan's lost dreamland.

To recapitulate my discussion so far, I have identified two modes of Japanese discourse and representation of Asia and Asian popular culture. One is an attempt of critics and intellectuals to engage with Asian cultural hybridization on equal terms and to recognize a different mode of Asian modernity, which in turn offers self-critical insights into Japanese modernity and the dominant conception of a Japan/Asia binary. Such an attempt, however, is jeopardized by the tenacious recurrence of misrepresentations of Asia as always "behind." As discussed in chapter 4, the cultural resonance that Taiwanese audiences find in Japanese TV dramas is based upon a sense of coevalness and the articulation of cultural/racial proximity, the interplay of which is brought about by the disappearance of the economic gap, the diffusion of globalized consumer culture, and the information time lag between their country and Japan. Japanese representation of Asian popular music and culture display a rather different time-space configuration. The ever-increasing intraregional cultural flows within Asia and the narrowing economic gap between Japan and some Asian countries have activated a nostalgic longing for modernized/modernizing Asia.

On turning our attention to the consumption of Hong Kong popular culture in Japan, however, we realize that the picture is more intricate than it at first seems. The Japanese fans' reception of Hong Kong popular culture shows that the above two views cannot be clearly separated from each other but are commingled in a complex and contradictory way. It is how this time-space nexus is articulated in the Japanese audience reception of Hong Kong popular culture that I examine next.

Promotion and consumption of modern Hong Kong

Since the early 1990s, as Japanese media industries have extended its activities to other (mainly East) Asian markets, the lively East Asian music scene has captured wide media attention, especially in Japanese men's magazines, which have introduced a number of Asian female idols. Apparently, nostalgic tropes have also dominated the representation of the proliferation of East Asian pop idols in Japanese popular magazines in the mid-1990s, in which the rise of idols is again clearly associated with the rise of other Asian countries and the relative decline of Japan in terms of economic power in the early 1990s. One of the most common words for depicting Asian female pop singers in Japanese media texts is *genki* (Asia is vigorous): "Idols emerge where the society has vigor. The sharp contrast between Japan and Asia in terms of idol markets elucidates a decline in the vigor of Japanese economy and society. Like the economy, Asian idols are threatening the predominance of Japanese idol markets" (Daiyosoku Ajian aidoru 1995).[19]

Even if the flourishing of female pop idols is positively interpreted as a sign of the vitality of their societies, the feminized Asian vigor is represented only to reassure Japan's temporal distance from "Asia." The focus on Asian female idols had much to do with the Japanese music scene in the 1990s. As mentioned in chapter 3, the Japanese idol system culminated in the mid-1980s, but it has been replaced by dance music and band music in the 1990s (Inamasu 1993; Nishino 1996). The void of Japanese idols disposed Japanese media to interpret the rise of idols in other Asian countries in terms of a retrospective sense of déjà vu. Another prevalent trope of Japanese media representation of Asian female pop idols is *hajimetenanoni natsukashii* (something new in a "retro" kind of way).[20] One music critic, Uchimoto Jun'ichi (1995, 120), writes that one of the main reasons why Japanese are attracted to Asian female singers is that these singers evoke a Japanese sense of longing for vanished Japanese popular songs, which he believes still appeal to Japanese emotions. An article on Asian pop music in the popular monthly magazine *Bart* stated that Japanese popular music had become too West-inflicted to retain an Asian flavor, and referred to an "Asian melancholy": "Asian female idols sing the sort of 'Asian' popular songs that Japan has forgotten" (Chikai kuni kara ippai kita geinōjin 1994, 11). Obviously, many writers found a past image of Japanese popular music in the Asian pop music scene of the 1990s. As Uchimoto noted, "the vanished Japanese popular music is to be inherited" by Asian female idols, as if Asia's present is Japan's past (1995, 120). The past image of Japanese popular music is easily found in the Asian pop music scene without the cultural specificity of the latter being appreciated.

Along with the nostalgic representation of "Asian" pop idols, another conspicuous trend of Japan's popular Asianism in the mid-1990s was the heavy promotion of Hong Kong popular culture by the Japanese media (see Tadashii Ajia no hamarikata 1997). This testifies to the fact that the renown of Asian popular culture in Japan is, like the spread of Japanese popular culture in East Asia, in part the result of the promotional strategies of local industries. The Japanese market has joined the intraregional coalition in promoting contemporary popular culture in Asia. The prevalent sales message for Hong Kong popular culture in the Japanese market was, however, significantly different from the nostalgic representation I discussed above. Convinced that the appeal of Hong Kong culture is not fully captured by nostalgic tropes, due to its economic strength and advanced cultural production, the Japanese media adopted the promotional strategy of disseminating "modern" and "fashionable" images of Hong Kong to a public more used to viewing the city as backward and dowdy. Purénon H, a small film distribution company, is one example of a firm that pursued this tactic. To

Japanese pamphlet for the film *Chungking Express* (1984),
whose Japanese title is *Koisuru Wakusei* (1994).

improve the image of Hong Kong films, Purénon H organizes a Hong Kong
film fan club, Honkon Yamucha Kurabu, and established a Hong Kong film
shop, Cine City Hong Kong, in a trendy spot in Tokyo where many young
people enjoy window-shopping in an elegantly decorated space. Purénon H
was the distributor for Wong Kar-wai's film *Chungking Express* in Japan,
which became a phenomenal hit in 1995. The film was admired because it
was the first Asian movie that refrained from playing upon Hong Kong's
alleged exoticism and, instead, made the city look like any other major
European city (say, Paris) (Edagawa 1997, 135–36). The quality of the film
notwithstanding, in its publicity Purénon H worked hard to overcome the
dominant image for Hong Kong films as being full of kung fu or (vulgar)

slapstick. From more than two thousand possibilities, the company chose as the Japanese title, *Koisuru Wakusei* (A loving planet), which was totally unrelated to the original title, *Chungking Express.* It hoped in this way to make the film sound modern and accessible to a wider audience (Tadashii Ajia no hamarikata 1997, 53).

The success of Wong Kar-wai's stylish collage films, as well as the upsurge of Japanese media industry promotion in the lead-up to the return of Hong Kong to China in July 1997, further fanned the flames of the interest in the popular culture of a "modern" Hong Kong in Japan. Japan's biggest cosmetic company, Shiseido, hired two Hong Kong female actors, Michelle Lee and Kelly Chen, to appear in their commercials. Lee had acted in the popular films *Fallen Angels* and *Chinese Ghost Story,* while Chen was a rising star. Thus, two Hong Kong women were depicted as modern Asian beauties, not quite identical yet not totally different from Japanese women (Ima sekai ga Ajian byūtī ni chūmoku 1997). In 1997 Kelly Chen was also chosen as the cover model for a new monthly magazine, *Ginza,* which was to be targeted to trendy women in their twenties.

The rise of Japanese interest in modern Hong Kong culture was not confined to a masculine gaze; on the contrary, women play a leading part in it.[21] Especially keenly promoted by Japanese media industries are Hong Kong male stars such as Jacky Cheung, Andy Lau, Leslie Cheung, and Kaneshiro Takeshi (Jin Cheng Wu in Chinese pronunciation[22]), all of whom have performed in Wong Kar-wai's films. Since December 1995, Hong Kong's "four heavenly gods" have performed in concert in Japan and increased their appearances in the Japanese media.[23] Amuse, a Japanese production company, has contracted several Hong Kong stars for media appearances in Japan (Ajia aidoru ninki no butaiura 1997). In 1995 two Asian pop music magazines, *Pop Asia* and *Asi-pop,* were launched in Japan. Both mostly feature pop idols/stars from Hong Kong and Taiwan. Both magazines rapidly expanded sales—by 1998, 20,000 copies of *Asi-pop* and 40,000 of *Pop Asia* were being sold for each issue (Genki na Ajia ongaku zasshi 1998, 52). Although their names suggest that the magazines deal with Asian pop in a comprehensive manner, in fact they focus mostly on Hong Kong and Taiwanese male singers. With *Pop Asia,* this was not always the case. Initially, it covered a broader range of Asian pop music. However, its editor told me that in order to increase its female audience, which represents more than 85 percent of its readership, the magazine had to place more emphasis on

Cover of *Pop Asia*, a Japanese music magazine,
with Leslie Cheung (no. 13, 1997).

Hong Kong and Taiwanese male pop stars (see also Genki na Ajia ongaku zasshi 1998, 52).

Correspondingly, women's magazines since the mid-1990s have often featured articles on "trendy" Hong Kong male stars.[24] *Elle Japon,* for example, had two feature articles about Asian male stars in 1997. One appeared in June, just before the return of Hong Kong to China. The other, published in November, was titled "Sexy Asian guys." Although also dealing with stars from Indonesia, Thailand, and the Philippines, the article focused on Hong Kong film stars: "Gallant, sexy and with a sensitivity so delicate as to appeal to the maternal instinct . . . Asian stars have all these factors of a seductive guy. They attract attention not only in Asia but also all over the world, because they attain an overwhelming aura of stardom and vigor. . . . Japanese women, who are quite sensitive to new trends, are now sensing male sexiness in Asian guys. Their sexiness is something that Japanese guys do not have. Asian guys are becoming more and more stunning and beautiful with the economic development in the region" (Ajia no sekushī na otokotachi, 89, 95).

These representations in *Elle Japon* show an apparent shift in Japanese attention from "premodern" to "modern" and "cosmopolitan," from Southeast Asia to East Asia. A feature article on Asia in a 1994 issue of another women's magazine, *Crea,* for example, carried a pictorial of attractive young men in Bali and Phuket. These young men were associated with the natural beauty of Bali and Phuket with phrases such as "eyes with purity and tenderness," "calmly conversing with nature," and "their pure heart undisturbed by urban city noise."[25] Likewise, *Elle Japon* also depicted Asian charm as "simple and supple, power articulated in chaos" in its feature article on Asian culture in 1994 (Ima Ajia ni atsui manazashi! 1994). However, such capitalist nostalgia disappears in *Elle Japon* articles from 1997; in that year, the magazine clearly stresses that "modern Asian (Hong Kong) guys" mark a new trend.

Japanese fandom of Hong Kong pop stars

In the course of my research in Japan, I discovered that the Japanese promotion of Hong Kong popular culture has left its twisted mark on the way in which that culture is consumed by Japanese fans.[26] The emerging depictions of Hong Kong as "modern," "trendy," and "cosmopolitan" have endowed it in the eyes of many with great novelty value. Several fans overtly or covertly informed me that their interest in Hong Kong films and stars was motivated in part by a desire to prove their modish and sophisticated tastes. In this regard, it is worth noting that while Wong Kar-wai's movies attract a relatively wide audience, the avid consumption of Hong Kong popular culture is still confined to a small community of aficionados. In Japan, the media recently began covering Hong Kong stars, but access to Hong Kong films and information about their actors is still not readily available. Hence, joining fan clubs and frequently visiting a small number of shops which deal with Hong Kong pop culture is an essential means of obtaining such access, and, equally importantly, of publicly acknowledging that one is a devotee of Hong Kong and Taiwanese movies and stars.[27]

I have observed that Japanese fans are keen to talk to each other about the films and stars and they harbor a passion for them. Like the fan culture depicted by Henry Jenkins (1992), the social communication among fans plays an important role in the Japanese fan community of Hong Kong stars. As Jenkins argues, identification as "members of a group of other fans who shared common interests and confronted common problems" gives them the "pleasure in discovering that they are not 'alone'" (1992, 23). Most fans I interviewed mentioned that their friends and colleagues tend to regard their fondness for Hong Kong pop stars as somewhat odd. Constituting a community of taste is an important part of Japanese fandom, since Hong Kong popular culture is still excluded from the mainstream in Japan and fans experience some difficulty in sharing their interest in Hong Kong stars with their friends, according to my interviews.

However, this does not mean that Japanese fans think they are marginalized, or "labeled a subordinate position within the cultural hierarchy," as suggested in Jenkins's (1992, 23) account of the solidarity and creativity of fan communities in the United States. Apparently, Japanese fans tend to pride themselves on the appreciation of a not-quite mainstream Hong Kong and Asian popular culture. As Fiske (1992, 33) argues: "Fandom offers ways of filling cultural lack and provides the social prestige and self-esteem that go with cultural capital." The consumption of not-yet-mainstream popular culture confers social and cultural distinction on them (Bourdieu 1984). For some fans, Hong Kong popular culture is a resource from which they can obtain cultural capital. Furthermore, the development of media technologies, the internet in particular, and the proliferation of media products has expanded the various kinds of segmented consumer niche markets. Thompson's (1995, 222) argument regarding these developments of media consumption, that "being a fan is an altogether ordinary routine aspect of everyday life," seems too sweeping a generalization, but it cannot be denied that various fans commonly try to play up the idiosyncrasy of their tastes so as to differentiate themselves from the mainstream.

This point is made clearer when we realize that Japanese fans tend to have an ambivalent feeling about the popularization of Hong Kong stars. On the one hand, they want other Japanese to know how attractive Hong Kong stars are. They want to show off their good taste to the mainstream. On the other, they also wish the object of their fascination to remain the best kept secret in Japan and fear that their "real" attraction will be deformed and frivolously consumed as their idols are commercially promoted by Japanese media industries. A female fan in her late twenties of Taiwanese star Kaneshiro Takeshi expressed to me her a sense of disappointment over a collection of his photographs published in 1997: "Kaneshiro in this book looks stylish, but that's all. I like him because he looks at once dazed and sturdy, but these characteristics are totally lost in those pictures. I think Japanese publishing companies made Kaneshiro a cheap commodity without understanding his real unaffected but cosmopolitan charm."[28]

The interviewee's anxiety is that Kaneshiro may become another garish, throwaway commodity, shared by vulgar teenagers. She told me that she was upset that *Olive*, a popular teenage magazine, had run a feature story on him, and that another teenage magazine had elected him as the fourth most popular male idol amongst its readers (Kaneshiro Takeshi, anata shika mienai! 1997). Betraying a sense of elitism, she remarked: "Kaneshiro should not have been covered in *Olive*. Its readers are mostly high school students. They are too young to appreciate his real charm. They wrongly regard Kaneshiro among other Japanese idols." My interviewee's conceit was based on the relative scarcity of exposure which Hong Kong and Taiwanese stars and films receive and on the small number of fans who follow them. A common comment made by my interviewees was that they were proud to have known of a particular performer before he became famous. A woman in her early twenties who enjoys Asian pop music expressed this point succinctly: "My interest in Hong Kong and Asian pop music in general has not much to do with sympathy. I think I am more motivated by a desire to create my own world, which is different from something given by the mass media. I tend to feel that I am losing my own individuality in standardized Japanese society. So I need to be absorbed in something minor, I mean, something others are not following, so that I can maintain my own individuality." It is thus a sense of one's precious uniqueness, a knowledge of one's individuality, that justifies all the effort involved in being a serious fan of Asian popular culture. Indeed, the arduousness of a fan's calling—the information that must be collected, the fan clubs that must be established and maintained, the media texts that must be sought after outside the mainstream Japanese media—only enhances the pleasure of these self-styled sophisticates who wish to differentiate themselves from the cultural "dupes" of the mass media.

The truth is, however, that these fans are closer to those "dupes" than they care to admit. As noted earlier, it was in part the return of Hong Kong to China on 1 July 1997 that motivated some people to take an interest in its popular culture. This is obvious from the fact that most fans first began following Hong Kong films and stars around 1995, after the intensive promotion of these products in the media (Adachi 1998, 16–22). This media coverage has bolstered the confidence of fans in their taste and judgment, as it gives them the sense that they are at the vanguard of the latest trend. As a woman in her late twenties told me, "I felt I am going ahead of others by appreciating the unknown Hong Kong stars as Hong Kong is now attracting much media attention." For all their attempts, then, to distance themselves from the "mindless" consumerism of the mainstream media, the interests of such fans have themselves been shaped to an extent by that media.

Reflexive nostalgia for a different Asian modernity

The Japanese media industry's promotional strategy stressing the stunning contemporaneity of Hong Kong popular culture apparently generates interest among people hunting for novelty. However, the Japanese fascination with Hong Kong popular culture is more than the familiar story of a freak subculture attempting to carve out a distinctive place for itself in a media-saturated society. As I will show below, it is also engendered by a positive appreciation of Hong Kong's social and cultural formations, which sharply contrast with Japanese counterparts. This contrastive idealization of Hong Kong is reminiscent of Karen Kelsky's (1996, 1999) argument of how "internationalist" Japanese women's sexualized desire for Western men is closely related to their strong sense of frustration with the male-dominated structure of Japanese society and workplaces. Although Japanese fans of Hong Kong popular culture were not much expressive of this kind of feminist agenda in my interviews with them, the strong sense of dissatisfaction with present-day Japan (which is unambiguously male-dominated) seemed to evoke their sexualized longing for Hong Kong and to motivate the extra-investment of money and effort required to be fans. Yet, while the West is conceived as a "progressive" Other in contrast to "backward" and "feudalistic" Japan by Kelsky's "internationalist women," the appreciation of Hong Kong is intertwined with the perception of the overlap between Hong Kong's present and Japan's past, hence evoking what Japan used to be. Here, in spite of the gendered inversion of the Japanese consumption of Asian popular culture, we can see that the female following of Hong Kong male stars still shares a nostalgic orientation toward them.

This posture is hinted at in the aforementioned representation of Hong Kong male stars in *Elle Japon*. In the article, the emphasis is seemingly placed not on temporal distance but on modern contemporaneousness. Nevertheless, the "modern-ness" of Hong Kong is still marked by a sense of "not-quite." As described in the article, "Japanese women are sick of Japanese men, who have become too effeminate to attain strong masculinity" (Ajia no sekushī na otokotachi 1997, 95). Together with the emphasis on economic development as the main cause for the emergence of sexy Asian guys, this suggests Japan's loss: What Japanese masculinity has given up in the course of Japan's high economic development is projected onto modern yet still behind-the-times Hong Kong male stars and media texts.

Such a contradictory nostalgic longing for "modern" Hong Kong stars represented in popular media texts is discerned in my interviews with Japanese female fans. Hong Kong stars satisfy fans' appetite for recuperating the lost stardom of Japanese performers. The most common response to a question about the attraction of Hong Kong stars during my interviews was their charismatic aura of stardom. According to their fans, Hong Kong stars are professional in a complete sense, as they are well trained to sing and act, always wear the mask of stardom, and are extremely skillful at entertaining the audience. Their sincere and friendly attitude toward fans is also interpreted as an aspect of true stardom, as it shows their willingness to value fans. These two aspects, the aura of stars and their friendliness, are regarded as two sides of the same coin. In contrast, Japanese idols look too casual to be identified as stars and they are not at all friendly, as Japanese agents are very fussy about protecting their commodities from direct contact with anonymous fans. These criticisms are thus, again, directed to the way the Japanese media industries manufactures idols and entertainment.

This aura of stardom is, according to Japanese female fans of Hong Kong stars, what Japanese idols used to attain, at least until the mid-1980s. Most fans I observed in Japan were in their late twenties and thirties, and some were even in their fifties (see also Hara 1996; Adachi 1998). The relatively high average age might be due mainly to the fact that Hong Kong stars are in their thirties, while the target audience of the Japanese idol system are predominantly in their teens and early twenties. Yet mature-aged Japanese women often explain the attraction of Hong Kong idols by referring to the good old days of the Japanese entertainment world which they themselves enjoyed in their teens or early twenties. A female fan in her mid-thirties told me that she became fascinated with Hong Kong male stars around 1990. This was a time when her generation, who were then in their late twenties, no longer found Japanese popular music and idols appealing. She was then excited to find in Hong Kong a world of pop music idols that, in her experience, was similar to the one that had existed in Japan in the 1980s. As the organizer of the Japanese fan club for Leon Lai explained to me in an interview, "Hong Kong stars remind us of a half-forgotten longing for heroes of our generation." Hanaoka (1997, 63), in her essay in a popular weekly magazine, describes the image of Japan's lost idols as follows: "Not very radical music style as now; the existence of idols who unashamedly maintained their own narcissistic world; and who never betrayed the idealized image fans had of them, looking intimate at the same time." The adolescent memory of a glittering Japanese entertainment world is apparently evoked by Hong Kong stars today (see also Hara 1996; Murata 1996).

More importantly, the nostalgic yearning for Hong Kong popular culture is also being fueled by a deep sense of disillusionment and discontent with Japanese society as well as the entertainment business. The attraction of the aforementioned films and performers, again, tends to be linked to the loss of energy and power of Japanese society in general, as two women, one in their late twenties and the other in her late thirties each explained:

> Japanese TV dramas do not have dreams or passions. I sometimes enjoy watching them, but still feel [compared with Hong Kong actors] Japanese young actors lack a basic power and hunger for life.

> Wong Kar-wai's films always tell me how human beings are wonderful creatures and how love and affection for others are important for us to live. All of those are, I think, what Japan has lost and forgotten.

Through the consumption of Hong Kong popular culture, Japanese fans feel they have regained the vigor and hope lost in their daily lives, as two interviewees in their mid-twenties and late thirties remarked:

> I think people in Hong Kong really have a positive attitude to life. My image is that even if they know they are dying soon, they would not be pessimistic. This is in sharp contrast to present-day Japan. I can become vigorous when watching Hong Kong films and pop stars on video. Hong Kong and its films are the source of my vitality.

> Leslie Cheung makes me realize my virtue, something I forgot and gave up. I can get energy and courage to do what I could do in my twenties through Leslie.

These associations of present-day Hong Kong with Japan's loss, it can be argued, still testify to Japan's refusal to consider other Asian nations as dwelling in the same temporality. However, as I listened carefully to these fans, I came to think that the sense of longing for vanished popular cultural styles and social vigor does not exclusively attest to the perception of a time lag. It also displays the Japanese fans' appreciation for the difference between Japanese and Hong Kong cultural modernity. Here, we can see an ambivalence in Japan's nostalgia for a different Asian modernity: The conflation of a nostalgic longing for "what Japan has lost" and a longing for "what Japanese modernity has never achieved." What matters is Japan's lack as well as Japan's loss.

Almost all the interviewees told me that they, like Taiwanese audiences of Japanese TV dramas, can more easily relate to Hong Kong stars and films than to Western ones due to perceived cultural and physical similarities. Western popular culture looks too remote from their everyday lives. However, unlike Taiwanese audiences of Japanese TV dramas, the sense of cultural and racial proximity tends to strengthen the Japanese fans' perception of socio-cultural difference between Japan and Hong Kong. What is crucial here is that such perception is facilitated by recognition of the disappearance of temporal distance between Japan and Hong Kong. As a female in her late twenties told me: "I think that Hong Kong films are powerful and energetic. Hong Kong is apparently similar to Japan in terms of physical appearances, but I realized that its society and culture are actually completely different from us. [This is clearly shown by the fact that] Hong Kong has also achieved a high economic development, but still retains the vitality that Japan has lost." It is not assumed that Hong Kong is also losing something important, becoming more like "us," precisely because Hong Kong has already attained the same degree of modernization and material affluence as "ours."

Thus, what sets Hong Kong apart is neither solely attributed to some primordial cultural difference nor to some developmental difference. Rather, it is suggested that the difference between Hong Kong and Japan has become evident in the course of modernization, especially in the way in which Western cultural influence is negotiated. A commercial film producer, Higuchi Takafumi (1997), has argued that recent interest in Hong Kong and its popular culture reflects the increasing numbers of young people who sense a resonance between Japan and Hong Kong in terms of "the aesthetics of cultural borrowing." However, what Japanese fans positively find in Hong Kong popular culture is, I would suggest, rather, a different mode of Asian modernity, which antithetically demonstrates that something went wrong with the process of Japan's modernization. And this is closely related to the wholesale way in which Japan has absorbed Western culture. As a women in her late twenties observed: "I think Japan is looking to the West too much. Many people in Japan look down on Asia, but this does not match the reality. Japan has been too influenced by the West to retain its own way, but Hong Kong still has its own style and system. In this sense, Hong Kong is even culturally superior."

Like Dick Lee's music, Hong Kong's modernity has resisted the erasure of its "Asian odor," while Japan has neither retained its own odor nor become truly "Western." Japan has simply kept up its modern appearance, according to an early thirties informant: "In Hong Kong and perhaps in Taiwan as well, things traditional and modern subtly coexist even after they achieved high economic growth. Japan has thrown away the good old things so much so that everything looks merely quasi-Western."

In relation to this, the appeal of Hong Kong stars and popular culture was also expressed in terms of its "cosmopolitan" feature. It is suggested that the Japanese mode of cultural absorption of Western culture have promoted the insularity of its society and culture. Hong Kong, in contrast, is very cosmopolitan, and the market for Hong Kong stars is really pan-Asian. A woman in her late twenties remarked: "I do not think Japan is superior to Hong Kong. On the contrary, in Hong Kong, East and West coexist without melding with each other. Japan, in contrast, has absorbed and indigenized Western cultures at its convenience (attempting to supress traces of the original to make them exclusively "Japanese"). As a result, Japanese culture has become closed and lost a meeting point with other cultures. I am very wary of this. It seems that Japan has come to a kind of dead-end situation and has no further possibility." Like the criticism uttered by Japanese cultural producers and academics, Japan's cultural modernity is considered by Japanese fans of Hong Kong popular culture not to match that of Hong Kong's, because Japan has been reluctant to link itself to the outside world. In contrast, Hong Kong seems to the Japanese woman to have always been in touch with the outside world, while the fact that this "openness" was an involuntary one, as Hong Kong itself was as a former British colony —is not well acknowledged.

It is thus the perceived crisis in Japanese national identity that underlies Japanese fans' determination to transcend the narrow-minded life of a self-contained society and to become more cosmopolitan and connected to the larger world by consuming Hong Kong pop culture. Thus, an introspective apprehension of Japan's relations with other Asian nations is not just expressed by Japanese critics. "Ordinary" consumers of Hong Kong popular culture also experience it. "Hong Kong" presents Japanese female fans with an opportunity to realize that the idea of Japan being superior to Hong Kong is not just politically incorrect but also emotionally and culturally untrue.

Here, I suggest that like the Taiwanese audiences of Japanese TV dramas, a sense of coevalness perceived by Japanese fans toward Hong Kong finds its expression in the critical reflection on Japanese cultural modernity but even more urgently accompanied efforts of self-transformation. A working woman in her early thirties expressed how she had been transformed by Hong Kong popular culture:

> Of course, I cannot one hundred percent devote myself to Hong Kong. I simply observe myself consuming Hong Kong stars and films. I know I am looking for something I cannot get in my boring company life [through fictional, dreamlike worlds of Hong Kong stars and films]. But, by so doing, I have become more positive than before. I am now more interested in knowing about the language, the history of Japanese invasion, and Japanese prejudice against Hong Kong. My view of Japan has also changed a lot. I realize how we, Japanese, are shortsighted and that our affluence has been achieved at the expense of so many important things of life.

Japanese fans, unlike Japanese women who have "real" contacts with Asian men and immigrate to other Asian nations via international marriage (Yamashita 1996; Nomura 1996), might neither wish to transform their lives by leaving Japan or encountering cultural Others in real situations. Nevertheless, their exposure to Hong Kong popular culture has encouraged at least some of these women to become more critically aware of Japan's modern experiences and imperialist history. An accompanied self-reflexive praxis thus marks out their appreciation of the different cultural modernity of Hong Kong.

Capitalist coevalness in East Asia

The Japanese representation and consumption of "Asia" in the 1990s shows that many Japanese are attempting to recuperate something they think their country allegedly either is losing or has lost. Whether Japan ever had the social vigor projected on Asian popular culture is highly debatable—and ultimately irrelevant. As many have pointed out, the object of nostalgia is not necessarily some "real" past—the things that used to be (see Davis 1979; Stewart 1993).[29] The important point here is that nostalgia arises out of a sense of insecurity and anguish in the present.

In the face of rapid modernization and globalization, nostalgia has played a significant role in the imagining of Japan's cultural authenticity and identity. These processes have intensified the country's cultural encounters with the West, and these, in turn, have generated a nostalgic desire in Japan, "a longing for a pre-modernity, a time before the West, before the catastrophic imprint of Westernization" (Ivy 1995, 241).[30] A similar longing for the purity and authenticity of primordial life underpins Japanese media representations of, and backpacking trips to, "premodern" Asia. However, in the Japanese reception of Hong Kong popular culture, nostalgia is projected onto a more recent past, not before but after the West, or, more precisely, a past that is conjoined with the West's presence. This nostalgia for a modern Asia is not fed by a nationalistic impulse to rid Japan of Western influence or to recuperate an "authentic" Japan. Rather, the issue is how to live with Western-induced capitalist modernity, how to make life in actual, modern Japan more promising and humane.

A mounting sense of urgency explains, if only partly, why the object of nostalgia is directed to Asia's present. Japan's newly imagined "Asia" serves as a contraposition to its own society—one which is commonly regarded as suffocating, closed, and rigidly structured, as well as worn down by a pessimism about the future instilled by a prolonged economic recession. Here, "Asia" is not simply idealized as the way things were in Japan. Some people in Japan also appreciate it, for the purpose of self-reformation, as representing an alternate, more uplifting cultural modernity.

I have tried to show the ambivalence of Japanese consumption of "Asia" by identifying just such a reflexive mode of nostalgia. Nevertheless, I conclude this chapter by suggesting that personal feelings and anguish do not commonly overlap with the critical consciousness of the Japanese national history as an imperial power in Japan's appreciation of Hong Kong modernity. It is, as we have seen in Japanese media representations, more often than not at the risk of the effortless reproduction of tamed cultural Others. Murai's (1990) observation concerning the "Asia boom" in late 1980s Japan still holds true here; a Japanese consumerist gaze on Asia is enticed by Asian exoticism and is not concerned with the asymmetrical relations between Japan and other Asian countries. Kelsky (1996, 187) argues, concerning Japanese women who seek out foreign (American) male lovers, that their border-transgressing penchant might have demolished the reigning stereotype of the submissive Japanese woman; nevertheless, at the same time, it reinscribes a clearly drawn boundary between the Japanese and the Other, for such women "transform the foreigner into a signifier whose primary purpose is to further their domestic agendas." This point is illustrated by Japanese female fans' mediated consumption of Hong Kong stars. Even if the nostalgic gaze on Hong Kong might be replaced by the realization that "they" are just as modern as "we" are, but in a different way, it cannot be denied that these fans reduce Hong Kong to a convenient and desirable Asian Other. In her book *On Longing*, Susan Stewart argues that the collection of souvenirs generates a sense of temporal (antique) and spatial (exotic) longing for authenticity. Similarly, "Hong Kong" is easily rendered Other, an Other which is, like the souvenir, located spatially and temporally "within an intimate distance," so that Japanese can "appropriate, consume, and thereby 'tame'" it for the narcissistic search for self (Stewart 1993, 146–47).

The admiration for Hong Kong in terms of its subtle juxtaposition of East and West, like views about Chinese leap development discussed earlier, has much in common with Western stereotypical images of the chaotic vulgarity of East Asian (mainly Japanese) cities which have, since the 1980s, been represented in Hollywood futuristic films such as *Blade Runner* and *Black Rain*. These Western films represented the chaotic coexistence of West and East, high-tech landscapes and premodern, traditional and vulgar lives, in an Orientalist fashion (Yoshimoto 1989). Likewise, the animation director, Oshii Mamoru, in producing a futuristic animation, *The Ghost in the Shell,* changed the animation's location from Tokyo in the original comic version to Hong Kong in order to depict a futuristic cyber-city where the traditional and the high-modern disjunctively coexist (Oshii, Itō, and Ueno 1996). A computer game, *Kowloon's Gate,* also represented Hong Kong as a modern but chaotic space where rationality and irrationality are fused together, as the distinctions between good and bad, reality and fantasy, are blurred (Tsunagime Honkon 1997). According to the game's creator (Pia info-pack 1997), Hong Kong is a model for modern Japan that is neither Asia nor the West while at the same time embodying both. Japanese modernity has been so keen to keep the social order that it has institutionalized and tamed the chaotic coexistence of the rational and the irrational, but Hong Kong has the possibility of producing something totally new out of such chaos. It is untenable to ignore the existence of an Orientalist imagination behind such an idealized image of Hong Kong.

Furthermore, while showing the possibility of transcending Japan's denial of coevalness with Hong Kong, the Japanese appreciation of Hong Kong cultural modernity at the same time reproduces a "backward" Asia. Being critical of the Japanese mode of negotiation with the West nonetheless affirms Western-dominated capitalist modernity. As Morris-Suzuki (1998a, 20) argues, the new Asianism in Japan "no longer implies rejection of material wealth and economic success, but rather represents a yearning for a wealth and success which will be somehow *different*" (emphasis in original). The fans' armchair engagement with "Hong Kong" modernity depends crucially on its imagined capitalist "sophistication," as opposed to the lack thereof in "Asia." Many Japanese fans of Hong Kong popular culture emphasize the difference between "Hong Kong" and "Asia." This, on the one hand, looks a promising corrective to the construction of an abstract, totalizing conception of "Asia." These Japanese fans reject the dominant media's tendency to use the term "Asia" to refer to Hong Kong male stars.[31] However, in such a conception, other Asian nations are still reduced to entities that are undifferentiatedly represented by urban middle-class strata, the main players in consumerism. Moreover, the demarcation between Hong Kong and Asia is imperative for many fans, as the latter is predominantly associated with the image of backwardness.[32] I have often heard interviewees remark that premodern China would corrupt Hong Kong's charm:

> I am afraid that Hong Kong might be more Sinicized after the return to China. Hong Kong is losing a liberal atmosphere of 'anything goes' by political self-restriction and is influenced by more traditional mainland Chinese culture which is definitely old-fashioned.

> The British presence has made Hong Kong sophisticated and something special. But I think Hong Kong is becoming dirtier and losing its vigor after its return to China.

China is threatening to destroy the cosmopolitan attraction of Hong Kong not only because of its rigid communist policy, as pointed out by Japanese commentators (e.g., Edagawa 1997), but because of its "premodern" Chineseness. The imagining of a modern, intimate Asian fellow is still based upon the reconstruction of an oriental Orientalism. As observed in the depiction of Asian male stars in *Elle Japon*, "Asian guys are becoming more and more stunning and beautiful with economic development in the region." A certain degree of economic development is thus a minimum condition for other Asian cultures to enter "our" realm of modernity. "Pre-modern" Asia never occupies a coeval space with capitalist Asia but represents a place and a time that some Japanese fans of Hong Kong popular culture have no desire to identify with. It is not temporally proximate enough to evoke a nostalgic longing for a (different) Asian modernity.

6

Japan's Asian dreamworld

In this book, I have explored the various aspects of transnational popular cultural flows—intellectual discourses, marketing strategies, and audience consumption—through which Japan's conception of being "in but above" or "similar but superior" to Asia is asserted, displaced, and rearticulated. Regarding Japan's cultural return to Asia in the 1990s, one cannot help but be struck by its multifaceted and contradictory dimensions. However, these dimensions have been obscured by a historically constructed taxonomy of binary oppositioning between "Asia" and "Japan"—with "the West" as a powerful third Other—which still strongly curbs the Japanese transnational imagination. Various discursive tropes—both positive and negative, self-congratulatory and self-critical, unequivocal and ambivalent—have been employed by Japanese observers in asserting Japan's transnational cultural significance and in expressing Japan's (asymmetrical) relationships with other Asian nations. Nevertheless, they all ultimately tend to be contained by an all-absorbing idea of "Asia," which only provides further momentum for framing the discussion in binary terms.

It is all too tempting to dismiss Japan's totalizing conception of Asia with the theoretical assertion that "Asia" is merely a discursive construct, devoid of any substance or coherence, and that therefore there is no Asia. Yet to do so is beside the point, for the issue is not the appropriateness of the term *Asia*. If we recognize the impossibility of talking about Asia in a generalized manner in the first place, then what we should focus on is the question of why Japan's psychic investment in imagining "Asia" has been rearticulated in the last decade of the twentieth century.

The reason might be readily sought in the resurgence in the 1990s of the idea of a supra-national cultural/civilizational regional bloc. Admittedly, the newly articulated Japanese interest in Asia has much to do with per-ceived cultural and racial commonalities, age-old historical connections, and geographical proximity. Nevertheless, commercialized transnational cultural flows now also play a significant role in the demarcation of the cultural boundaries—although porous and transient—of Japan's Asia. While conservative theorists are busy essentializing civilizational blocs as the largest cultural entities in the world (e.g., Huntington 1993), such concentration on the sense of cultural immediacy and proximity that is inherent in the formation of supra-national regional popular culture markets has created an incongruity between what is the actual, concrete geographical reach of Japan's Asia and the region defined by traditional cultural/civilizational commonalities.

There is a clear tendency, discussed in this book, to say that as the traditional high cultures of Asia have been replaced by a capitalist consumer culture (Ching 2000), Japan's reach in Asia, in terms of transcultural resonance and imagination, has also gradually shrunk and intensified. In the pan-Asianist idea of Okakura Tenshin, Asia was defined by its non-Westernness, included Arab chivalry, Persian poetry, and Indian philosophy, but by the early 1990s the idea of a pan-Asian entity encompassed only Southeast and East Asia. Furthermore, by the late 1990s, this idea tended to embrace mostly East Asia. This grouping of East Asian nations or cities easily provokes assertions of primordial cultural commonality (for example, a shared Chinese cultural legacy). However, the relatively minor role China currently plays in the intensified East Asian popular cultural flow—though China's weight has been articulated in terms of its huge market size—highlights the significance of the penetration of West-dominated global capitalist culture in the spatial demarcation and formation of transnational regional modernity in the 1990s. In light of that culture's pervasiveness, it has become untenable to continue regarding the West as the object of Othering against which a totalizing idea of Asia can be advocated. In the 1990s the deep inscription of globalized capitalist modernity has played a significant role in framing the exploration of the meaning of being Asian. In this regard, it is important to note that Asian interconnections being forged by the flows of popular culture are not national ones. They are predominantly between urban spaces, between global cites—Tokyo, Seoul, Hong Kong, Taipei, Shanghai, and so on.

In this emerging Asian capitalist sphere, Japan's exploitative articulation of Asian cultural commonality has been reframed to accommodate itself to the entangled transnational flows of capital, cultural products, and imagination (Appadurai 1996). In the 1990s a singular cultural geography called Asia, with its rich diversity and contradictions, has emerged for Japan as a "dreamworld" in which Japanese can imagine things in the way they want them to be. It was Walter Benjamin who coined the term *dreamworld* in the 1930s to describe the emergent sites of that era, such as department stores and arcades, which stirred capitalist consumer desire. As Featherstone (1991, 23) remarks, "The vast phantasmagoria of commodities on display, constantly renewed as part of the capitalist and modernist drive for novelty, was the source of dream images which summoned up associations and half-forgotten illusions." Likewise, in the 1990s, "Asia" has served to fuel Japan's imagination of a phantasmagoric capitalist dreamworld, one which transcends (if only temporally) the contradictions and limitations of containing intensified transnational flows within a nationalist framework.

Spectacular capitalist development and the ever-changing urban landscapes in Asia have exhilarated the Japanese capitalist desire for Asia in multiple ways. For conservative thinkers, capitalist modernizing Asia is a site where Japan's long-standing nationalist project for extending its cultural reach to a pan-Asian sphere has been reactivated. In this case, Japanese capitalist consumer culture has not simply offered a sense of nationalistic pride, it has also played a diplomatic role in healing the wounds inflicted on Asia by Japan's imperialist history. For Japanese cultural industries, Asia has offered a business opportunity for the trying out of the transnational reach of Japanese popular cultural production methods. It has stimulated an unfulfilled fantasy of Japanese media industries that one day a trans-Asian—and possibly global—pop star will emerge from the region through Japanese initiative. Finally, Japanese audiences have been attracted to various sorts of Asian popular culture, which inspire nostalgia for the glory days of Japanese capitalist development. As the exploitative transnational dynamic of cultural and capital flows has moved from the Japanese archipelago to other parts of Asia, Asia has come to remind some people in Japan of a half-forgotten social vigor and hope. All of this indicates that Japan's Asian dreamworld is a product of globalizing forces, which have made it no longer tenable for Japan to contain its cultural orientation and agenda within clearly demarcated national boundaries. In this sense, Japan's "return to Asia" project demonstrates that transnational popular cultural flows at once displace and redemarcate national/cultural boundaries.

However, it is important to note that the resurfacing of Japan's nationalistic project to extend its cultural horizon to East and Southeast Asia is not simply discursive or ideological. It is structurally backed by a general increase in Japan's transnational cultural presence and influence under the forces of cultural globalization. Tomlinson (1997) enumerates three reasons why we should reframe the issues posed by the "cultural imperialism" thesis with a perspective of cultural globalization. They are (1) the question of the impact and the ubiquity of Western cultural products in the world; (2) the dialectical nexus between global and local in terms of ongoing cultural hybridization; and (3) the decentering process of Western cultural hegemony. The ascent of Japanese media industries in the process of media globalization seems to be a testimony to all three. The increasing flow of Japanese TV programs into other Asian markets refutes the unambiguous power of Western cultural products in the world; the localization strategies of Japanese cultural industries are grounded upon the exploitation of global–local dynamics; the global circulation of Japanese animations and the involvement of Japanese corporations in global media conglomerates shows the diffusion of cultural power. The activities of Japanese media industries at three levels—global, regional, local—suggest that the decentered process of cultural globalization has given added weight to their transnational activities. Here, we should remember that while the main corporate actors of cultural globalization disregard the rigid boundaries of nation-states, their national origins are limited to a small number of powerful nations including Japan, and that transnational corporations still operate most of their transnational business from their home country, hence their profits are enjoyed largely within national boundaries (Hirst and Thompson 1997). The framework of the nation-state, both as a spatially controlled entity and as a discursively articulated geography, does not lose its prominence in the analysis of uneven global cultural flows (Sreberny-Mohammadi 1991; Ang and Stratton 1996).

I hope I have also been able to show that the allure of Asian capitalist phantasmagoria cannot be entirely contained by the national imaginary and hence it embodies a potential for mustering up a progressive transnational imagination. Japan's dreamworld Asia offers the site of concrete—both actual and mediated—encounters with the ever-changing landscapes of other Asian modernities, in which people in Japan are driven to realize that Japan and other Asian nations have been deeply inscribed by each other and that their relations are becoming more and more immediate and complexly interlocked in the multilayered web of "transnational connections" (Hannerz 1996). While we know theoretically that Asia is culturally diverse and that Japanese relations with Asian nations are marked by variations, the Japanese engagement in dreamworld Asia has illustrated how diversity works concretely in the way in which transnational encounters and imaginations generate the (partial) demise of the Japanese nationalist project.

The empirical analysis of the expansion of Japanese media industries into Asian markets shows the impossibility of dealing with Asia as a singular entity. Through their actual encounter with producers and audiences of Asian cultural markets, Japanese media industry representatives and critics have come to realize that the idea of Japan orchestrating the construction of a pan-Asian cultural sphere is illusionary, and that the actual conditions on the ground in Asia do not equate with Japan's perception of its cultural influence in the region. Through its inroads into Asian markets, the Japanese media industries have been forced to recognize that Japan's cultural reach in each Asian nation varies according to such factors as its historical legacy and the particular political, economic, and cultural conditions in that nation. The industries now more readily acknowledge the active agency of other Asian nations, as those nations negotiate with transnational flows in ways different from Japan's own past experiences.

It is in the encounter with a concretized Asia (e.g., in the appreciation of Wong Kar-wai, Dick Lee, or Leslie Cheung and not of "Asian" film or music in general) that we can detect self-reflexive voices and the realization that Japanese must meet other Asians on equal terms. Japanese (mostly female) audiences of Asian popular culture overtly or covertly reject the singular notion of Asia, which occupies the dominant discourse in Japan, to appreciate the cultural specificity of particular Asian cultural productions and the different modes of Asian cultural modernity articulated in them. The capitalist Asian dreamworld feeds on Japan's transnational regional imagination through popular cultural consumption, which goes beyond the mere reconfirmation of what has already been known about Asia and Japan. Here, the idea of Japanese cultural superiority to other Asian nations is displaced, facilitating a more dialogic engagement with other Asian cultural modernities; dialogic in the sense that it involves self-transformation and a redefinition of one's own culture through a developed consciousness of a shared temporality with different Asian modernities.

Appadurai (1996) argues that the acceleration of transnational cultural flows, through the development of communication technologies as well as the escalation of the trans-border movement of people, has dramatically transformed the role of social imagination in the texture of people's everyday life (see also García Canclini 1995). As "more persons throughout the world see their lives through the prism of the possible lives offered by mass media in all their forms" (Appadurai 1996, 53–54), the consumption of transnationally mediated fantasy and imagination has become deeply inscribed in social practice and identity construction.

While Appadurai (1996, 55) argues that "the link between the imagination and social life . . . is increasingly a global and deterritorialized one," I have tried to show in this book that such a transnational imagination still needs to be articulated within a specific cultural geography. The reception of Japanese TV dramas in Taiwan and Japanese popular Asianism highlight the imperative of developing a new conceptual toolkit for the analysis of intraregional dynamics among Asian peoples and nations, other than those which have been concerned with the ubiquity of Western media and popular culture in the formation of non-Western modernities. Non-Western countries have tended to look to the West when gauging their nearness to or distance from modernity. The non-West's encounter with the West has always been based upon the expectation of difference and time lag. However, some "modern" East Asian nations are now bypassing the West and finding a resonance in other Asian modernities while simultaneously recognizing their differences. What is occurring does not have much to do with an exclusive and essentialist Asian values discourse. The emerging resonance has become conspicuous with the discovery of neighbors sharing similar experiences of indigenizing Western capitalist modernity. The transnationalization of commodified popular culture has generated an intra-Asian search for a common frame of reference for cultural emulation and social praxis. Transnational media consumption articulates "a new social and communicative space" in which people can positively and reflexively rethink their own cultures and those of others (Gillespie 1995, 206). It helps transform people's views of "their" as well as "our" modern experiences and reconceive the cultural boundaries, "not to divide, to exclude, but to interface and construct" transnational alliances (Buell 1994, 341).

Having said all this, it remains a highly contested issue whether or to what extent transcultural encounters through popular cultural flows really lead to constructive dialogues between Japan and other Asian nations. By examining cultural flows in both directions—from Japan to Taiwan and from Hong Kong to Japan—I have argued that the transnational imagination is unevenly and unequally experienced via media consumption. While the intraregional cultural flows and consumption among East Asian nations such as Taiwan, Japan, and Hong Kong make young people in the region realize some familiar difference in other Asian cultural modernities, the capitalist exploitation of cultural resonance in Asian regions has produced a new asymmetry, one which works in favor of Japan. The mediated encounter with other Asians will continue to feed new modes of transnational imagination among people in Japan and other Asian nations. Yet, as transnational media and cultural flows are always already deeply inscribed in uneven and unequal power relations, nothing guarantees any promising future that the synchronously mediated consumption of information and images of other Asian nations under the structural forces of globalization will construct a more egalitarian and transnational connection.[1]

Benjamin once tried to discern in the capitalist dreamworld " 'dialectical images' with the power to cause a political 'awakening' " (Buck-Morss 1983, 215). Likewise, there is no need to entirely abandon in advance the radical—and unforeseeable—possibility unleashed by the proliferation of transnational imagination through media popular culture. Precisely in order to foster such a potential, however, the recognition of and critical engagement with the inequality of transnational interconnections and interpenetrations is more imperative than before.

In many ways, the 1990s has been the decade of Asia. The decade opened with the spectacular economic development of the region which has made Asian nations more assertive against Western powers. The Asian economic miracle was followed by a dramatic downfall due to the recent financial and economic crisis in the region, which occurred in the year of the historical event of Hong Kong's return to China. And the millennium came and went with no optimistic sign of economic recovery in most Asian countries. While the crisis has highlighted the persistence of Western (particularly American) economic and financial power, it has not stopped Japan's engagement with Asia as well as the intra-Asian cultural flows and interconnections.

A prolonged recession and financial crisis in Japan and many parts of Asia has apparently put a damper on self-congratulatory discourses of Asianism. The Japanese craze for the capitalist Asian dreamworld is no exception. The Asian boom in Japan seems to have culminated around 1997, when Hong Kong was returned to China and the economic crisis hit many Asian countries. However, the economic crisis in Asia, far from discouraging Japan from engaging with the region, has activated nationalistic discourses and facilitated intra-Asian popular cultural connections in new ways. In the intellectual field, discussion of Japan's leading role in Asia is still capturing attention. Right-wing ex-politician, Ishihara Shintaro, who was elected governor of Tokyo in 1999, has published another book in "The-Japan-That-Can-Say-No!" series, entitled *Sensen Fukoku: "No" to ieru Nihon keizai* (A proclamation of war: The Japanese economy that can say no!: For the liberation from American financial slavery) (Ishihara and Hitotsubashi Sōgō Kenkūjo 1998). This time the demonized enemy is the American financial system. Ishihara argues that Japan should fight against the system for the sake of Asian recovery. Hence, once again, Japan is depicted as the champion of the Asian cause. A strong emphasis on Asian solidarity is again accompanied by the assumed leadership of Japan. Similarly, another eloquent Asianist, Kazuo Ogura (1999), has restated his position by calling for Japan to take a leading role in the "creation of new Asia"; collective action, rather than the mere discursive articulation of "Asia," is needed, he claims, to check American global domination and make shared Asian political and economic interests more explicit in the international community.[2]

The new century has begun in a retrospective atmosphere, even with strong pessimism for the future, in Japan. The economic recession no longer seems temporary and the breakdown of other social institutions such as education and family have also become obvious. Yet, the Japanese government has repeatedly shown its inability to take the initiative to effectively restructure the impoverished systems, so much so that there is a prevalent feeling of living in a stifling straitjacket among the populace—living in a materially affluent country that nevertheless lacks hope.[3] In this gloomy situation, connecting to outer worlds, particularly to "Asia," comes to have a renewed significance for Japan to find its way out of the current wretched condition. In the feature article emblazoned across the front page of the *Asahi Shinbun* for 1 January 2001, the necessity and significance of "fusioning with Asia" was again stressed, so that Japan can cope with a new century of globalism and thus can create a bright future. Here again, the optimistic picture that the dissolution of clearly demarcated national boundaries between Japan and other Asian nations facilitated by transnational flows will lead to the solution of various problems within Japanese society is all too easily depicted. However, the article also shows that Japan's desire for connecting (with) Asia has come to be driven by necessity and is becoming more desperately future-oriented than before.

In accordance with this dire need, cross-cultural fertilization between Japan and East Asian nations in popular cultural production has been strengthened since the late 1990s. More Japanese pop music artists now regularly tour Hong Kong and Taiwan. A "hybrid" male pop group, Y2K (made up of two Japanese and one South Korean), became top idols in South Korea in 1999. One of the most popular Japanese drama series in 1998 featured Taiwanese-Japanese actor, Kaneshiro Takeshi; this TV drama series was broadcast almost simultaneously every week in Japan and Taiwan (Nihon no dorama eiga higashi Ajia e 1998). Beijing-born pop singer Faye Wong sings the theme music of the Japanese computer game, *Final Fantasy VIII*; the song reached the Top 10 in Japan (Hitto daijesuto 1999). In summer 2001, Faye Wong played a heroine in a Japanese TV drama for the first time. Coproduction among East Asian film industries has become more frequent (The birth of Asiawood 2001). In 1998, the second biggest advertising agency in Japan, Hakuhōdō, organized a feature film's coproduction with seven Asian countries. It starred a Hong Kong actor, Leslie Cheung, and a Japanese actress, Tokiwa Takako. Wong Kar-wai's forthcoming film *2046* in turn features today's most popular Japanese actor, Kimura Takuya.

Generated by the South Korean government's decision to partly relax its regulation policies on the import of Japanese popular culture in late 1998, and its cohosting of World Cup Soccer in 2002 with Japan, cultural exchange between Japan and South Korea has been increasing. In 2000, the Korean film *Shiri* had more than one million viewers in Japan; correspondingly, in the same year the Japanese film *Love Letter* attracted an audience of more than one million in Korea. Japan and South Korea also coproduced and nearly concurrently broadcast the TV drama *Friends*, a love story between a Korean man and a Japanese woman in their early twenties, drawing a large audience from both countries.

The cross-fertilization of popular cultural does not readily lead to the creation of an egalitarian relationship among Asian nations, however. The uneven expansion of Japanese popular culture in East Asian markets has even been increasing. It is true that the economic crisis has to some extent inhibited the spread of Japanese popular culture in Southeast Asian countries such as Thailand, Indonesia, and Malaysia. It has deterred local TV stations from buying Japanese and other foreign TV programs, whose prices soared due to the drastic fall of the local currencies.[4] In contrast, the crisis has not curbed the spread of Japanese popular culture to East Asia, which has continued to gather momentum in this century (e.g. Pop passions 2001). In Hong Kong, we have seen a Japan-boom escalating since 1998. Young people wear T-shirts with (meaningless) Japanese characters on them, and Japanese TV dramas have captured a wider spectrum of young audiences than ever before (Nihon būmu no urajijō 1998; "Nichishiki" ninki Honkon de kanetsu 1998). In Taiwan, Japanese TV dramas are still attracting broad strata of young people, and TV commercials featuring Japanese culture and language are in vogue (NHK *News 11* 23 April 1999). In 1999 sales of CDs— both single and album—for rising Japanese pop star Utada Hikaru—had been at the top for seven consecutive weeks (IFPI Taiwan hit chart, 16–22 August 1999). In tourism, the economic downturn has brought Japan's geographical as well as cultural proximity into relief and has led to an increase in the numbers of tourists traveling from Hong Kong and Taiwan to experience "trendy" dramas in Japan since 1998 (Yasui Nippon e Honkon no wakamono sattō 1998). A similar trend has been observed in Singapore. According to a survey conducted by the *Strait Times* in Singapore, more than 8 percent of young Chinese-Singaporean respondents agreed that they would have preferred to be Japanese (No kidding! S'pore youth are into J-pop 1999).

The increasing export of Japanese popular culture has continued to stimulate excessive expectations in Japan of an expanded role for the country in cultural diplomacy, particularly with two former colonies of Japan. In both cases, Japanese popular culture in East Asia is again politicized opportunistically in the way in which the complexity of transnational popular cultural flows is never seriously attended. Since 1999, there has been massive Japanese media coverage about the influx of Japanese popular culture into South Korea and the overall tone of the argument is unambiguously welcoming (e.g., Fukamaraka kōryū 2000; Souru ga hamaru Tokyo fasshon 2000). This tendency was highlighted in August 2000, when the Japanese duo Chage & Aska, who have been self-conscious of their mission as cultural diplomats in Asian regions, finally performed in concert in Seoul. The event was highly celebrated as signifying the beginning of the new era of reconciliation between neighbors (Atarashii mirai kizuko 2000). It is effortlessly assumed that popular culture can perform the belated historical reconciliation between Japan and South Korea, terminating the long-standing Korean antagonism and agony caused by Japanese colonialism.

The mission assigned to Japanese popular culture in Taiwan takes a different postcolonial trajectory. Japanese media coverage of the Taiwanese craze for Japanese popular culture has also been increasing, but, in contrast to the case of South Korea, the excessively passionate consumption of Japanese popular culture by Taiwanese youth works only to intensify Japanese nostalgic desire for legitimizing Japanese supremacy as colonial master. As

Japan lost socio-economic vigor and confidence, the 1990s also saw the rise of reactionary nationalism in Japan (Yoda 2001). Most notably was the movement to revise primary- and secondary-school history textbooks, whose self-critical view of the history of Japanese imperial and colonial violence in Asian regions is condemned as "self-torturing" and derogatory to Japanese national pride by the group called *Atarashii Rekisikyōkasho o Tsukuru Kai* (Association for making a new history textbook), Taiwan has gradually attracted wider attention as it is regarded as the nation that cherishes and fosters the Japanese colonial legacy. In a notorious cartoon on Taiwan by a core member of the movement, it is jingoistically argued that Japan has lost Taiwan's unreciprocated love due to the intervention of "evil China," which signifies both the KMT and the Chinese Communist Party, but that, even so, the good old Japanese spirit and Japanese values are still alive in Taiwan in even more sophisticated ways (Kobayashi 2000). In this outrageously self-justifying view of Japanese colonial rule in Taiwan, the current passionate reception of Japanese popular culture in Taiwan is viewed ambivalently. While the phenomenon is narcissistically observed, the recent craze for Japanese popular culture among Taiwan youth is also regarded as too trivial to match Taiwan's historically constituted "affectionate" relationship with Japan—though Kobayashi strangely ignores the fact that his cartoon is also part of such trivial cultural forms. Yet, "superficial" consumption of Japanese popular culture in Taiwan is less denounced than taken advantage of in reinforcing his point that young people in Taiwan as well as in Japan should learn the deep history underlying the Taiwanese crush on Japan (Kobayashi 2000; see also Hsieh 2000).

Thus, since the recent economic crisis and upon entering the new century, the main features of the intraregional cultural flow in East Asia that this book has examined have been illuminated in a number of new guises: the lingering American cultural and economic supremacy in the world; the significant Japanese cultural presence in Asia; the capitalization of regional cultural resonance and proximity, and the intensification of cross-fertilization among affluent East Asian cities, whose cultural connections are increasingly separate from other segments of Asia; and the growing Japanese nationalist desire to connect (with) "Asia" and the reactionary use of Japanese popular culture for this purpose.

Needless to say, we should not expect that popular cultural phenomena will remain the same or will have a long-lasting significance, as the trend of popular culture is only temporary. While Japanese popular culture is still well-received in East Asian markets, the rise of Korean popular culture such as TV dramas, pop music, and films, has become even more conspicuous in the early twenty-first century. It also remains to be seen whether the perimeters of Asia will shrink further or expand again, and whether China will fully join the capitalist club in the years to come. In any case, it seems untenable to expect revolutionary modes of Asian resistance against the global proliferation of capitalist popular culture. Globalization processes flows will continue to relentlessly capitalize on intra-Asian cultural resonance, at the same time reproducing unequal cultural power relations in multiple and multilayered ways. This book just begins to grapple with the fascinating but underexplored study of cultural globalization in the context of intra-Asian interactions. No clear-cut, armchair speculation—be it optimistic or pessimistic—would be able to fully capture these contradictory and unforeseeable processes. We need to continue to attend to what is going on in the real world to critically examine the way in which cultural (a)symmetry and dialogue are articulated through transnational cultural flows between Asian nations; and above all, to the way in which the phantasmagoria of dreamworld Asia holds an allure for the Japanese transnational imagination.

Notes

1 *Doraemon* is one of the most popular animation series in many Asian countries, but it has never become popular in Western countries.
2 European countries have also denounced American cultural influence.
   However, their critique is different from the Asian reaction in that it is
   based upon a strong conviction of Europe's cultural superiority to America
   and its centrality in the world, rather than upon a sense of the threat posed
   by the culturally dominant center (see Ang 1998).
3 STAR TV was the first satellite network to have a significant impact on
   Japanese policies of transnational broadcasting. When STAR TV broadcasts
   first reached Japan in 1992, the Japanese government banned the commercial distribution of intercepted transnational broadcasts within Japanese
   territories, although it did not prohibit private viewing for people with
   their own satellite dishes. The STAR TV incident prompted the Japanese
   government and Japanese media industries to face the age of global communications seriously. Further impact on Japan by transnational satellite TV
   came from global player Rupert Murdoch. In June 1996 Murdoch announced his plan to launch JSkyB, stating that Japan was the last unexca-
   vated gold mine in the world of satellite broadcasting. Just ten days later, his
   company, News Corp.—together with a Japanese computer software company, Softbank—bought some 20 percent of the shares in TV Asahi, one of
   the five key commercial TV stations in Japan. The threat posed by Murdoch
   was not that of transnational broadcasting, as with STAR TV, but rather the
   possibility that control of the Japanese media industry could be assumed by
   foreign capital. It soon became clear, when Murdoch suddenly decided in
   March 1997 to sell the shares of TV Asahi to its parent company, Asahi
   Shinbun, that Murdoch's intention was not to control a free-to-air TV
   station in Japan. Murdoch had concluded that the acquisition of shares in a
   particular Japanese TV station would deter other stations from cooperating
   with JSkyB and thus would do more harm than good in securing good
   Japanese programs. Two months after Murdoch sold his TV Asahi shares in
   1997, Fuji TV, which is a more popular TV station, and Sony, which

owns Columbia, decided to join JSkyB (which is currently named Sky-Perfect TV).

4   While media globalization on the one hand promotes the influx of foreign media products and industries into the Japanese market, it does not seem to be posing a real threat to Japanese national identity. Japan has kept its doors open to foreign cultural goods such as TV programs, films, and popular music since World War II. It imports many films, particularly from the United States. In the last ten years, foreign films have generated 60 to 70 percent of total box office sales (Kakeo 2001). As for the TV market, Japan is one of the few countries that has no quota on importing programs. Nevertheless, the Japanese TV market shifted from a high dependence on American programs in the 1960s to a high level of self-sufficiency in the 1970s (Kawatake and Hara 1994). The relative absence of a defensive discussion about the protection of national culture in Japan, in contrast even with many other developed countries (e.g., France and Australia), is a testimony to the confidence of the Japanese government as well as media industries that the influx of foreign programs does not have a great impact on audience preference for domestic programs (see Ajia eisei ga sofuto ryūtsū o kaeru 1993).

5   Murai, Kido, and Koshida (1988) found in their survey of Japanese high school students that almost 60 percent of the respondents said that Japan is not a part of Asia.

6   The most famous statement on the matter has been Okakura Tenshin's "Asia is one" (Okakura 1904; see also Ching 1998). I will discuss Okakura's assertion in greater detail in chapter 5.

7   This was an ideology forged by Japanese academics in the 1930s and formalized in 1940. It attempted to conceive a coherent Asian space in order to counter Western imperial power. However, the unambiguous assumption of Japanese superiority in the sphere inevitably resulted in justifying Japanese imperialism in the region under the name of the solidarity and self-sufficiency of Asia and liberation from Western imperial power.

8   Kawamura Minato (1993, 133), writing about Japanese prewar literature which depicted other Asian people in an Orientalist manner, argues that Japanese authors mistook Japanese military and economic superiority for cultural and racial superiority. Japanese Orientalism was, according to him, based upon a groundless conviction of cultural superiority to other Asians. It is argued that Western Orientalism cannot be dissociated from its unambiguous military and economic hegemony, and that culture played a significant constitutive role in the Western imperial expansion and colonization of Others. As Thomas (1994, 2) argues: "Colonialism has always, equally importantly and deeply, been a cultural process. . . . Colonial cultures are not simply ideologies that mask, mystify or rationalize forms of oppression

that are external to them; they are also expressive and constitutive of colonial relationships in themselves." Japanese colonial power is instead interpreted as conceited and self-satisfied. Japanese dehumanizing discourse on Asian Others is not seen to be productive as an instrument of colonial domination. Kawamura seems to suggest that because Japanese cultural power is always secondary and borrowed from the West, Japanese Asian colonies could not be regarded as less civilized than Japan itself, especially in light of a long-standing Chinese influence across the region, including Japan (see also Komagome 1996).

9   Needless to say, this process is not unique to Japan. We can find dual meanings in "Americanization," too. As Ewen and Ewen (1982) argue, Americanization was originally about the assimilation of immigrants into the American melting pot through the spread of consumer culture. This mode has expanded internationally since the 1920s. The spread of American-style consumerism and American media products became the most familiar usage of "Americanization." The meaning of any "nationalization" includes internal assimilation and external domination, both of which are necessary to the construction of imperial nationhood.

10 This is not to affirm the effectiveness of Japanese assimilation policy. See Komagome's (1996) excellent analysis of the contradictory and ambivalent nature of Japanese assimilation policies and its implementation.

11 This is an ideal pattern of economic development in Asia, as argued by the Japanese economist Akamatsu Kaname (1959). As flying geese form a group headed by a leading goose, this pattern refers to Japan's role as guiding other Asian countries so that they can form an economic group based upon a cooperative relation.

12 They are Western, Confucian, Japanese, Islamic, Hindu, Slavic-Orthodox, Latin American, and possibly African civilizations.

13 In this respect, Asian values discourses are surprisingly similar to the debate on the uniqueness of Japanese culture, in which Confucian values or consensus-oriented groupism are attributed as the secret of the Japanese economic "miracle" in the 1970s and early 1980s. It seems that no lesson has been learned from the debate.

14 In the 1990s the rise of civilization discourse in Japan coincided with the relative decline of Nihonjinron literature, which emphasized Japan's unique cultural traits in essentializing ways. Nihonjinron was powerful and popular during the 1970s and 1980s. It explained the secret of the Japanese economic miracle and defended Japan's point of view in its trade disagreements with the United States (Iwabuchi 1994). In the late 1980s, when the trade friction between Japan and the United States became a serious issue, however, so-called revisionists came to the center stage of American foreign policy (e.g., Fallows 1989, Wolferen 1989). They insisted that Japan

was indeed different in terms of its inhumane and undemocratic social systems and institutions, and they accused Japan of utilizing cultural difference to justify an unfair trade game (Miyoshi 1991). Japan's supposed cultural uniqueness had changed from an object of admiration to one of criticism. Under these circumstances, as I will discuss in chapter 2, it is not a coincidence that the discourse on Japanese national identity departed from the discourse on particularistic culture and became more concerned with Japan's overseas cultural influence in the 1990s (see Kawakatsu 1991, 244–47).

15 The original Japanese version was published in 1994.

16 Several Japanese journals have published special issues on the "clash of civilizations" debate. For example, the title of a 1994 issue of *Hikaku Bunmei* is "Towards the Coexistence of Civilizations: Beyond the Clash of Civilizations." In this issue, Yuasa (1994) convincingly criticizes Huntington for his totalizing view of cultures and civilizations and his essentialist assumption of a West–East dichotomy. However, Yuasa then argues that the shortcomings of Huntington's thesis have much to do with the underestimation of the role of Japanese civilization in world history. Huntington, according to Yuasa, cannot offer a productive vision for the future because he does not take seriously Japan's successful experience of fusing Western and non-Western civilizations. Yuasa emphasizes that Japan's unique cultural capacity of absorbing multiple cultural values should be reevaluated in terms of the reconciliation of cultural and civilizational differences.

17 A scholar of international relations, Iokibe Makoto (1994) also refers to Japan's experience of indigenizing foreign civilizations, refuting Huntington's binary opposition between the West and the non-West. In Iokibe's view, the lesson learned from Japan's experience of antagonistic confrontation with Western culture or civilization in the prewar era might confer on Japan the role of accommodating the antagonistic schism between the West and the non-West. Iokibe finds in APEC the best opportunity for Japan to play such a role in reconciling the relationship between "Asia" and "the West" (see also Takenaka 1995; Funabashi 1995). To be fair, the imagining of Japan's mission as a mediating leader is not necessarily motivated by reactive or chauvinistic sentiment. Iokibe (1994) makes the good point that the prevalence of Western values and institutions in the modern world is not just the victory of Western civilization but also the victory of the non-West for its successful indigenization of Western civilizations. He tries to reject a zero-sum view of the encounter of different civilizations and cultures, basing his argument on the recognition that the world is always-already inter-contaminated. Nevertheless, these discourses on Japan's role in reconciling world disorder are reminiscent of the ideological collusion of

two seemingly competing Asianist discourses in prewar Japan. Koschmann (1997) distinguishes two kinds of Asianism in prewar Japan: "exoteric" and "esoteric." "Exoteric" Asianism stressed a harmonious, natural, organic, quasi-family Asian entity that is based upon cultural and racial commonalities. "Esoteric" Asianism instead emphasized the constructive process of an inclusive Asian community which is based less upon natural ties than upon the creation of new culture. A leading proponent of the "esoteric" view, Miki Kiyoshi, referred to the Japanese cultural capacity of assimilating foreign cultures as a significant spirit for the creation of an inclusive Asian community appreciative of cultural particularities: "Indeed, the depth and breadth of the Japanese mind are aptly revealed in this practical unification of objectively incompatible entities" (quoted in Koschmann 1997, 92). Over the course of Japan's imperialism, however, as Koschmann points out, the esoteric view was utilized to justify Japan's invasion of Asia by representing Japan not as an imperial exploiter but as a mediating leader. The impetus for complicity between an esoteric view and Japanese imperialism at the time requires a comprehensive historical research on contemporary political, economic, and social elements. However, remembering Japan's rejection of an exclusivist Asianism and its proposal for an inclusive globalism, the advocate of Japan's role as an editor, translator, or mediator in creating a new civilizational space in the 1990s has much in common with the prewar version of esoteric Asianism, hence involving the similar danger. Both assert Japan's unique leading role in Asia, both possess the motivation to counter a Eurocentric view and structure, and both articulate "certain world-historical pretensions, according to which Japan is destined [in the twenty-first century] to transcend the modern era and move to the forefront of not only Asia but the world" (Koschmann 1997, 106).

18 As a prominent scholar of Japanese Asian studies, Tsurumi Yoshiyuki once clearly stated, Asia must be conceived as a poor victim in order for Japanese to engage the issue of Japan's imperial history and lingering economic exploitation (Kadota 1998).

1 Taking "Japanization" seriously: Cultural globalization reconsidered

1 The term *mukokuseki* was first used in the early 1960s by a Japanese newspaper film critic to describe a new film genre (Koi 1989, 290). Parodying Hollywood Western films such as *Shane*, the Japanese film production house Nikkatsu produced a series of action films which featured a (Japanese) guitar-toting, wandering gunman.

2 As Classen, Howes, and Synnott (1994) show, while "odor," or "smell," seems to be a natural phenomenon, the perceived attraction of any particular odor is, in fact, closely associated with the historical and so-

cial construction of various kinds of hierarchies such as class, ethnicity, and gender.

3   In the book, such a shift in Japanese cultural exports toward software is addressed, symbolically, by the designer of the Walkman, Kuroki Yasuo. While Kuroki (1995) stresses the necessity for Japanese manufacturers to change their corporate culture in order to develop the creativity of Japanese designers, he also laments Japan's inability to produce the software that people consume with the Walkman. Yet, he sees hope, in the success of animation and computer games, that Japan is shifting from being a hardware superpower to a software superpower (Kuroki 1995, 14).

4   Japanese animation and comics have been more popular in Asia than in the West, but their popularity in Asia has not been enough to affirm the emerging hegemony of Japanese animation or comics (see, for example, *Nihonjin wa yunīku ka* 1990). In this sense, it can be argued that Japan's nationalistic view of the global spread of animation is still deeply dependent on and collusive with Western Orientalism. Japanese hyper-real culture, in which comics, animation, and computer games feature, has simply replaced Western Orientalist icons such as the geisha or the samurai in the complicit exoticization of Japan (Ueno 1996a; Mōri 1996).

5   With respect to the Japanese romantic comedy animation, *Kimagure Orenjirōdo,* in which the hero and heroine never confess their love for each other and their relationship is full of misunderstanding to the end, Okada observed that American fans wish to experience this Japanese way of love (Eikoku ga mitometa Nihonbunka 1996, 30–31). An American researcher similarly observed about American fans' fascination with the Japanese mode of romance represented in *Kimagure Orenjirōdo* that it was "a form of heterosexual masculinity which is not rooted in sexual prowess, but romantic feelings" (Newitz 1995: 6). Nevertheless, Newitz's analysis shows that this ardent American consumption is articulated in the form of a nostalgia for "gender roles Americans associate with the 1950s and 60s." (13). It can be argued that this nostalgic longing displays an Americans' refusal to acknowledge that they inhabit the same temporality as Japan (see Fabian 1983). Here, as in the Japanese consumption of Asian popular culture which I will discuss in chapter 5, it might be the case that Japan is marked by temporal lag and consumed in terms of a sense of loss; hence the articulation of America's dominant position.

6   See Mitsui and Hosokawa (1998) for this line of discussion concerning the global diffusion of karaoke.

7   Clearly, animation and computer game characters play a significant role in the packaged multimedia business. The comic book characters are intertextual and can be used in a variety of media such as computer games, movies, TV series, CD-ROMS, and toys. Kinder (1991) describes the multi-

ple possibilities of transmedia intertextuality as representing a "supersystem of entertainment" which has come to be a dominant force in the global entertainment business (see especially ch. 4). The worldwide success of Pokémon clearly testifies to the efficacy of such a supersystem. The popularity of Pokémon depends on the multimedia strategy, in which the game, comics, animation, and playing cards interlink with each other.

8　Its Japanese box office revenue exceeded 10 billion yen, surpassing the until-then record amount earned by *E. T.* This record was easily broken by *Titanic* in June 1998, but Myazaki's latest film, *Sen to Chihiro no Kamikakushi* (2001) established a new record. Actually Miyazaki's relationship with Disney has never been peaceful. His stories tend to be long and complicated, defying a simplified distinction between good and evil, as is commonly seen in Hollywood films. He refused Disney's request to shorten the three-hour long *Mononokehime*, and its box-office results in the U.S. market were not successful. However, as evinced by the fact that *Sen to Chihiro no Kamikakushi* won the Best Film prize at the 2002 Berlin Film Festival, the international appreciation of Miyazaki's animated films has been enhanced (Jiburi no mahō 2002).

9　In this regard, Japanese animation is often compared by the Japanese media to Ukiyoe—premodern Japanese color prints depicting ordinary people's everyday lives. Their beauty and value were appreciated as Japanesque by the West, and they had a significant impact on Western artists. It is often suggested that animation faces the same dilemma as Ukiyoe, many of which were taken out of Japan and exhibited in Western art galleries from the mid–nineteenth century onward. The West (America) may again deprive Japan of animation if Japan fails to recognize its (commercial) value (e.g., Hariwuddo ni nerawareru sofuto taikoku Nippon 1994; Nihon anime no sekai seiha 1996; Nihonhatsu no otaku bunka ga sekken 1996). Precisely because they have come to be universally consumed, they are destined to be copied, studied, and indigenized outside Japan. Thus, Hollywood is trying to develop a new global genre by making use of Japanese animation. American film producers and directors are recruiting Japanese animators to develop American animation and computer graphics (Nihon anime ni sekai ga netsushisen 1996; 2020nen kara no keishō 1997). American production companies, with the help of Japanese animators, have begun producing Japanimation in the United States (Ōhata 1996; Nihonhatsu no otaku bunka ga sekken 1996). Also, the South Korean government has begun to support the promotion of the local animation industry for the sake of the future development of the national economy. A Korean conglomerate has entered the animation business by investing in domestic as well as Japanese animation industries (Nihon anime ni tōshi 1996; Nihon anime ni sekai ga netsushisen 1996). In the face of the increasing number of competitors, the

Japanese government has been criticized for its failure to promote Japan's most lucrative cultural software industry (*Kaigai bunka ikusei seisaku* 1997). Responding to such criticism, the Agency for Cultural Affairs belatedly decided to support multimedia software content in 1997 and began a media arts festival in Tokyo in February 1998. Its purpose was to encourage the domestic production of animation, comics, computer graphics, and computer game software. However, there is strong doubt among the industries as to the scale and efficacy of such governmental support to enhance the international competitiveness of Japanese animation.

10 Taiwan removed its ban on broadcasting Japanese-language TV programs and music in late 1993, and in 1998 South Korea also began a step-by-step process that will eventually abolish all restrictions on importing Japanese cultural products.

2 Trans/nationalism: The discourse on Japan in the global cultural flow

1 One criticism of the concept of hybridity lies in its excessive popularity, which risks turning the theoretical tool into what Morelli calls "a fashionable theoretical passport" (quoted in Trinh 1996, 9). Detractors (e.g., Parry 1994; Thomas 1994; Young 1994) are critical of the indiscriminate and celebratory overuse of the concept of hybridity. They find problematic the concept's implicit assumption of two (or more) pure "origins" to be mixed, as well as its negation of agency, neglect of materiality in favor of textual performance, racial and biologist connotations, and failure to discuss the specific applicability of the concept in different and unique contexts. There is also a tendency to employ and examine the concept of hybridity or hybridization only in certain contexts and geographies. For example, hybridity is discussed mostly in terms of non-Western cultural mixing under Western influences. The whole subject of hybridity as it relates to cultural exchange and cross-fertilization among different areas of the non-West remains to be explored.

2 Hybridization and hybridity remain the most common terms, despite criticisms against them. It is argued that "creolization" too closely suggests Caribbean and Latin American experiences of cultural mixing. "Indigenization," or the appropriation of the foreign into one's own culture, is intimately interrelated with "hybridization" or "creolization." In this book, I am not much concerned with the subtle theoretical differences between these concepts and will use them interchangeably. For conceptual arguments, see, for example, Ashcroft et al. 1998; Hannerz 1996; Lull 1995; Appadurai 1996; Young 1994; and Friedman 1994.

3 See also Dower (1986) for an excellent analysis of Japan's representation of its racial purity during the Pacific war.

4 Shohat and Stam (1994, 33) argue that hybridity is "cooptable," referring to Latin American nations, which often subtly smooth over the existence of racial hierarchies, officially priding themselves on their racial hybridity as a source of national identity.

5 For example, in seeking the secret of the Japanese capacity for cultural absorption in Japanese religious syncretism, Robertson (1992, 94) hints at the difference between hybridity and hybridism by pointing out that Japanese religious syncretism is "indeed an 'ism,' in the sense that it is a kind of 'ideology.'" Nevertheless, he argues that the traditional Shinto rituals, Japan's indigenous religion, of purification helped minimize contamination from foreign ideas. As Robertson sees it, Japanese boundary-making between the self and the Other when importing the foreign is never an innocent cultural practice but a highly nationalistic discursive strategy to "purify" foreignness. It is quite another thing to say, however, that this strategy has been successful enough to minimize Japan's contamination. Robertson seems to subsume any actual "contamination" or influence in the discursive construction of Japaneseness as the skillful domestication of foreign influence.

6 Similarly, exploring cultural hybridity and syncretism in the non-West, Pico Iyer writes that whereas other Asian nations appropriate and indigenize the West in creative and enjoyable ways, "Japan had taken in the West only, so it seemed, to take it over" (1988, 410). Iyer points to the example of baseball, which was imported from the United States and sufficiently domesticated in Japan for an American ex-baseball player to say, "They've out-Americanized America," based on Japan's victory over the United States at the Los Angeles Olympics (405). By claiming its superiority over the West, so the theory goes, Japan has violated the postmodern mode of enjoyable spectacle of non-Western cultural hybridization.

7 Naoki Sakai's critique of David Pollack's (1986) book, *The Fracture of Meaning,* is a useful reminder here. Sakai severely criticizes Pollack's essentialist equation of "the three unities of Japanese language, Japanese culture and the Japanese nation" (1989, 481). He rejects the implicit assertion that "Japan has been from the outset a 'natural' community, [that] has never constituted itself as a 'modern' nation" (484). It seems a similar sort of essentialism at work in Featherstone's discussion. In highlighting the relativity of the Eurocentric modern worldview with the ascent of non-Western power, Featherstone (1995) actually refers to Sakai's article, in which the difference between monistic and world history is argued; history is "not only temporal and chronological but spatial and relational" (Sakai 1989, 488). Featherstone quotes Sakai to emphasize that Eurocentric monistic history cannot appropriately deal with a world in which difference and heterogeneity are irreducible.

However, the wider context in which Sakai discusses world history is missing from Featherstone's account. It was in the 1930s that Japanese intellectuals argued strongly for the demise of monistic history and the emergence of world history. However, world history was a conceptual tool for Japanese intellectuals, enabling them to imagine Japan's position in the center of the world, a position which was denied by Eurocentric monistic history. Sakai criticizes Kōyama Iwao, a young Japanese philosopher of the 1930s, whose view of world history, due to his essentialist conception of heterogeneity and Otherness, easily became another version of monistic history that justified Japanese imperial power. Sakai (1989, 489) argues that "this notion of otherness and heterogeneity was always defined in terms of differences among or between nations, cultures, and histories as if there had been no differences and heterogeneity within one nation, culture, and history." Thus, Sakai's main argument is less about the conceptual shift from monistic (modern) to world, pluralistic (postmodern) history than about the difficulty of transcending the former and the danger of the latter being subsumed in the former by equating the subject of world history with the nation. As will be discussed subsequently, such a danger becomes an urgent issue when Japanese hybridism extends its reach to external geopolitical relations, as was the case in the 1930s.

8 For a good overview and critique of Japanese discussion of "civilization," see Morris-Suzuki 1993, 1995, 1998b.

9 Likewise, a sociologist, Kōtō (1998) argues that the universal transportability of Western modernity is the basis of non-Western modernity. He depicts the latter as "hybrid modern," which is created by indigenizing the former. Kōtō stresses the difference between "hybrid modern" and "postmodern" in terms of the transformation of modernity: while in the former, modernity is transfigured by spatial movement from Western origin to other cultures, the latter is a product of the passage of time and historical change in the West. The examination of Japanese hybrid modernity, Kōtō (1998, 396) argues, is significant in deconstructing the "modern" from an Asian perspective, as it would lead to a better understanding of the rise of East Asian economic power and its modern constitution.

10 The Japanese public is often informed that Japan is not trusted and liked by other Asians, particularly Chinese and Koreans who experienced violent Japanese imperial invasion (e.g., Nikkanchūbei 4 kakoku yoron chōsa 2000, 2001; Nicchū kyūdō yoron chōsa 1997; "Ajia to no kyōsei" 1997; "Ajia to no kyōsei" 1996; Sengo 50 nen Ajia 7 toshi yoron chōsa 1995; Nihon girai Kankoku de 69 percent 1995). A featured article of popular biweekly magazine *Views* (A report from 12 Japanized Asian countries 1993) which dealt with the spread of Japanese department stores, fashion

magazines, food, TV programs, animation, and karaoke in Asia; it was subtitled, "They hate Japan but want to copy us."

11 People in South Korea have the strongest resistance to the spread of Japanese popular culture in Asia. According to a survey conducted by *Asahi Shinbun* (Nihon girai Kankoku de 69 percent 1995), almost half of the respondents objected to the abolition of the restriction on importing Japanese popular culture; more than half of the respondents had a strong aversion to watching Japanese films, and two-thirds felt this way about singing Japanese popular songs. These trends were still observed in a similar survey conducted in 2000 (Ajia no mirai 2000).

12 In 1988 the Takeshita government for the first time established a discussion panel on international cultural exchange with the aim to examine the possibility of exporting TV programs to Asian countries. In 1991 the Ministry of Foreign Affairs and the Ministry of Post and Telecommunications jointly established JAMCO (Japan Media Communication Center) to subsidize the import of Japanese TV programs to developing countries.

13 A prominent cartoonist in Japan, Satonaka Machiko, similarly argues that Japan should be proud of its cartoons and animations, because they are "the first Japanese cultural products spontaneously received by those [Asian] countries without Japan's cultural, militaristic, and economic impositions" (quoted in Kuwahara 1997, 44).

14 In this sense, while Honda does not clearly state it, apparently *Oshin* is not included in this kind of mukokuseki popular culture.

15 Honda's argument is supported by the then–dramatic rise in market share of Japanese comics in Hong Kong, from 20 percent in 1992 to about 60 percent in 1995. According to a *Reuter's* report (13 September 1995), Japanese comics keep up with the changes of lifestyle in Hong Kong and attract new middle-class and more educated readers who have not read them before.

16 The film was described as a "quite likely" story in the Japanese media (Eiga Sotsugyō Ryokō 1993, 26).

17 This is the same kind of discursive strategy that has been often deployed in Japanese self-Orientalism vis-à-vis the West, in which there is an intriguing interplay between "the non-Japanese seen through Japanese eyes" and "Japan seen through westerners" (Ivy 1995, 50; see also Iwabuchi 1994). John Caughie, in an analysis of American media domination of the world, defines the process of the subordinated's double identification with see-er and seen as "playing at being American." The subordinated empowers himself/herself by objectifying the center and rendering it as its own other; these are "the permitted games of subordination" (1990, 44). In the game of television viewing, the subordinated adopts a tactical "'ironic knowing-

ness" that "may escape the obedience of interpellation or cultural colonialism and may offer a way of thinking subjectivity free of subjection" (54). In Japanese self-Orientalism, however, what occurs is less "playing at being American" than "playing at being (America's) 'Japan,'" as the game is played through the objectification of the Western colonizing gaze. In this objectification, "Japan" as the object of Western cultural domination is suspended by setting up the subject position of "Japan" outside the ground of domination. It is not a double identification with subject and object but a substitution of the unstable doubleness articulated in the relationship between games and tactics by a pleasurable game overlooked by otherwise subordinated Japanese spectators. By suspending Japan's position as the object of domination, "Japan" is kept out of reach of the colonizer; the game attempts to claim that there is no "Japan" that can be the dominated object of the Western Orientalizing gaze.

18 Such a line of reasoning is clearly found in two books, Inoue (1996) and Shirahata (1996), both of which were published by researchers of the International Research Center for Japanese Culture, which was established in 1986 by then Prime Minister Nakasone Yasuhiro for research on Japan's unique, traditional culture. Both were displays of an appreciation of and indulgence in the spread of Japanese cultural products through the inversion of the subject and the object in the global cultural consumption and localization process. Inoue's *Grotesque Japan* is mostly interested in an exploration of the "grotesquely" distorted international consumption of Japanese culture that could undo the expectation contained by the West-dominated Orientalist cultural hierarchy. Inoue (1996) attempts to reconsider the essence of Japanese culture through the exploration of distorted international consumption of Japanese culture. Inoue claims that he is no longer surprised at the spread of made-in-Japan commodities in the world, nor interested in the Western Orientalist image of Japanese exoticism. Rather, he is fascinated to find things of Japanese "origin" grotesquely localized and indigenized in different parts of the world—for example, the transformation of the rules and rituals of Jūdō and the decontextualized use of "zen" for the name of department stores (215–18). Inoue distinguishes himself from hard-liner nationalists who become angry at seeing Japan misunderstood or distorted in the world and insist on the importance of exporting a correct image of Japan. His intention in writing the essays is not to deplore, but to enjoy, the ridiculously distorted image of Japan and the foreign (mainly Western) misappropriation of a Japanese exotic image. Inoue's fascination with a distorted "Japan" is a kind of nationalist strategy that claims Japanese transnational cultural power, a power which simultaneously allows for the preservation of a "pure Japan" in a hermetically sealed space (217–18). Inoue wrote that some commodities, such as tatami

mats or tanuki dolls (folk-culture figures of well-endowed badgers which are said to bring fortune and wealth), might embody essential "Japaneseness," precisely because of the fact that they are not exportable (23–29, 54–60).

Shirahata (1996), like Honda, stresses the culturally odorless, or mukokuseki, nature of Japanese cultural products that are globally well received. Shirahata (1996, 240) argues that unlike traditional Japanese high culture, the internationally consumed Japanese cultural products are not self-assertive about their "authentic Japaneseness." Rather, they leave their use-value to consumer tastes and cultural traditions outside Japan. The universal appeal of Japanese cultural products, in this instance, is demonstrated by their openness for local appropriation in other parts of the world. The discourse of hybridism confers a global cultural power status on Japan in terms of its own capacity for cultural hybridization and indigenization by denying the occurrence of other modes of cross-fertilization elsewhere. Likewise, the narcissistic discourse on Japanese cultural export, as exemplified by Shirahata (1996), endeavors to elevate the mukokuseki, that is, the non-self-assertive, nature of Japanese cultural products to Japan's distinctive, universally appreciated cultural traits by discounting the disjunctiveness of global cultural flows. Shirahata (1996, 1–3; 242–43) compares Japanese cultural export to *kaitenzushi* (fast-food sushi rotating on a conveyer belt), where customers choose anything at their will: "All those Westerners who seek sashimi and tofu for health reasons, Asian children who passionately read *Doraemon* comic books, and boys and girls around the world who watch Japanese animation with a gleam of interest remind me of my own childhood. At that time, kaitenzushi plates were full of American culture. . . . Japan, which was a poor but ardent customer of American culture, has become a shop owner and a powerful purveyor of culture into the world." With the kaitenzushi metaphor, Shirahata does not simply stress the capacity of Japanese culture and cultural products to be appropriated in each locale. The global consumption of Japanese mukokuseki culture reminds Shirahata (1996, 242–43) of his own past, when Japan eagerly pursued American cultures and commodities—hence, he suggests that Japan's global power status today is analogous to its American counterpart in the past.

3 Localizing "Japan" in the booming Asian markets

1 The film industry, for example, has begun to seriously explore the export potential of Japanese audiovisual software. In 1992, an annual Tokyo film market was set up to promote the sale of Japanese programs, though this was replaced by MIP–Asia (which is the Asian version of an annual international TV program trade fair in France), held for the first time in De-

cember 1994 in Hong Kong. Sony Music Entertainment also started a TV program, *Big Gig Japan* on STAR TV's Channel [V] in 1994, and a radio program, *Postcard from Tokyo,* which promoted Japanese pop music in Asia and was broadcast in Hong Kong, Taiwan, Singapore, and Thailand in 1995.

2 For example, the business earnings of Nippon Television Network for the 1997 fiscal year were 283 billion yen. However, according to my interview with the station, international sales earnings were less than 1 billion yen.

3 It is interesting to note that McDonald's derived its firm conviction in the effectiveness of the multilocal strategy from its local-owner operation in Japan (Watson 1997, 13).

4 The recent prominent example is the global spread of the aforementioned British quiz show, *Who Wants to Be a Millionaire?*

5 The commercial TV network TBS has also been active in the format business; it has sold several variety shows and quiz shows to Europe, Asia, and the United States.

6 In 1997, NTV, a popular commercial TV station in Japan, also coproduced a program to promote the syndication business in Asian markets. The program was called *Chō Ajiaryū* (Super Asians), and it was produced in association with Hong Kong (TVB), Taiwan (CTV), South Korea (SBS), Thailand (ITV), and Singapore (TCS−8). Each week's program content consisted of a main topic, such as fashion, idols, or karaoke, and each station covered the topic on the local cultural scene. What is interesting, however, is that each of the TV stations used the footage differently. Only CTV broadcast the same program as NTV, with subtitles. SBS, ITV and TCS−8 incorporated some film coverage in local information programs so as to make the program look like it was locally produced.

7 Taiwan joined the program in 1994 after the Taiwanese government abolished its ban on broadcasting Japanese-language programs at the end of 1993. South Korea joined the program in 1997, but could not broadcast it in South Korea due to government policies regulating the broadcasting of the Japanese language on TV. The program finally ended in late 2000.

8 Another commercial film shows a Sony karaoke machine that features Maribeth's song, "Born to Sing." In the film Maribeth is scouted by a Sony Music manager when she sings for a nightclub bar. The Sony manager is not Japanese but Caucasian (seemingly American). This also articulates the propensity of Japanese media industries to suppress the visible presence of Japanese in the products.

9 The producer of *Asia Bagus!* told me in an interview that they often urge the contestants to choose one of the latest hit songs or a song from a trendy genre such as rap or dance music.

10 The most dramatic examples are that TVRI quit the program in 1995 be-

cause the Indonesian government did not like to broadcast Mandarin, and that Taiwan left the program in 1997 due to its strong Southeast Asian flavor, which did not appeal to Taiwanese audiences.

11 It should be noted that Fuji TV could not make a profit by producing the program, as *Asia Bagus!* was not produced for the Japanese market. On the contrary, Fuji TV was responsible for covering most of the production costs. The main reason for co-production was to establish a corporate tie with other Asian industries and make a trial run of searching for pan-Asian pop singers (Kanemitsu 1993).

12 This is not exclusive to media industries. The same problem and contradictions in the strategy of global localization is often observed among manufacturing companies such as Sony (e.g., Emnott 1992, ch.7; du Gay et al. 1997, 80).

13 Even Japanese consumer and household electrical appliances are increasingly overwhelmed by domestically produced products from China (Mo 1999).

14 The program was broadcast in China in 1995 and 1996 and scored high ratings (Nicchū Gassaku dorama 1996).

15 The director and the protagonist of *Shanghai People in Tokyo* are both Chinese, but Amuse provided the entire production budget of four hundred million yen (Amyūzu Chūgoku to 1996). Amuse sold commercial time for various sponsors, including South Korean and Chinese companies, but allegedly could not cover the production costs. According to my interview with the director of Amuse, the main purpose was to establish a relationship with the Chinese TV industry, to learn the Chinese production system, and to gain the know-how of selling programs and advertising time in China.

16 In the early 1990s the Japanese music industry attempted to promote unknown Japanese artists in East Asian markets by showing their professional acts intensively in the local market. The artists tried to become local idols by singing songs in Mandarin and frequently appearing on local media programs and commercials (Ajia aidoru ninki no butaiura 1997). As a Taiwanese producer commented to a Japanese newspaper, this represented a Taiwanization of Japanese culture. Unlike the Japanization of Taiwan through colonial rule, Japan engaged with Taiwan by adopting the local culture and language (Chikayotte kita Nihon bunka 1995). According to my interview with Japanese and Taiwanese music producers in Taiwan, the success of the Taiwanization strategy, however, did not last long because the idols did not have fame in Japan.

17 The huge success of Japanese popular music in Taiwan pushed Avex Inc. to establish Avex Taiwan in 1998. Avex Inc. further established Avex Holdings Ltd. in Hong Kong in May 2001 in order to integrate the management of Avex Asia Limited (established in 1996) and Avex Taiwan.

18 Komuro Tetsuya also tried to launch several Chinese, Hong Kong, and Taiwanese pop singers in the American market. This movement from regional (Asia) to global (the West) was forged by his joint venture with News Corp., TK NEWS, and Komuro established a new record label, rojam com, within Sony Music Entertainment, for the American market (Hitto no mukōgawa 1998).

19 Shiraishi (1997) coins the term "image alliance" in the cooperative promotion of Japanese animations in Indonesia.

4 Becoming culturally proximate: Japanese TV dramas in Taiwan

1 For a detailed analysis of the film, see Liao (1997) and Marukawa (2000).

2 See Hu (forthcoming) and Davis and Yeh (forthcoming) for detailed analysis of VCDs. In September 1998 the Japanese TV industry and the Hong Kong Customs and Excise Department finally carried out a raid on the shops of Sino Center, which sold pirate videos and VCDs of Japanese TV dramas and animation (Japan TV team joins customs in piracy fight 1998; Mass swoop nets 200,000 pirated VCDs 1998).

3 It should be noted that this strategy was deployed by STAR TV as early as 1992, well before Murdoch's takeover of STAR TV and the beginning of his localizing strategy.

4 Po-shin Channel ended its operation in 2000 due to financial difficulty.

5 In 1998 the number of cable channels was 96 and there were 103 licensed cable system operators in Taiwan (The Republic of China Yearbook 1999).

6 The collection of letters and columns was published in book form in 1997.

7 I thank Su Herng for giving me a copy of this research paper.

8 McKinley (1997, 92) finds that young American audiences sense that *Beverly Hills, 90210* is a story about themselves, even though they clearly recognize the gap between the extravagant lifestyle represented in the drama series and their own. McKinley (1997, 92) suggests that what prevents American audiences from emotionally identifying with *Beverly Hills, 90210* is not the unrealistic materialistic affluence presented but the lack of realism in the representation of characters and the symbolic meaning associated with general life experiences.

9 For similar observations for Thailand, see Yoshioka 1992, 1993; for Indonesia, Kurasawa 1998.

5 Popular Asianism in Japan: Nostalgia for (different) Asian modernity

1 Around 1980 two influential travelogues that dealt with everyday life in Asia were published: Yamaguchi Fuminori's *Hong Kong Tabi no Zatsugaku Nōto* (Jumbled notes on a trip to Hong Kong) (1979) and Sekikawa Nat-

suo's *Souru no Renshū Mondai* (Doing exercises in Seoul) (1984). Both featured personal reportage on their experiences with the peoples and cultures of the region. The popularity of Asia as a tourist destination for younger Japanese has grown, with more than 60 percent of overseas travelers now choosing individual trips (Ajia no tabi wa yonde jibunryū 1996). This trend has led to the increasing prevalence of travelogues. Now there are several series of personal travel guides, such as *Asia Rakuen Manyuaru* (Manual for Asian paradise), *Asia Karuchā Gaido* (Asian cultural guide), and *Wonderland Traveler.* The original series was *Chikyū no Arukikata* (How to wander around the world), the first issue of which was published in 1981. This series quickly became the bible of Japanese backpackers in the 1980s.

2 The regional divide between East and Southeast Asia can be seen in terms of the popularity of Japanese songs. For example, there were two phenomenally popular Japanese songs in the late 1980s, but one was popular in East Asia and the other in Southeast Asia (Shinozaki 1990a; Morieda 1988).

3 Given that many authors (Shinozaki 1990b; Kubota 1990; Saitō 1990b; Kawakami 1990) refer to him, the publication of *Poppu Eijia* was itself apparently caused by Lee's popularity in Japan.

4 These amount to about 100,000 copies, according to representatives of Japanese recording companies. While these numbers are impressive for an Asian musician, they are trivial compared to those of popular Japanese musicians, who sometimes enjoy sales of more than three million in the local market.

5 A similar comment on the difference between takokuseki and mukokuseki was made concerning Japanese animation production by a prominent Japanese animator, Oshii Mamoru (Oshii, Itō, and Ueno 1996).

6 A notable exception is Shinozaki (1990a), who places Dick Lee's music in the political and sociocultural context of Singapore.

7 Okakura, it should be noted, wrote mostly in English and thus was writing for a predominantly Western audience. In his writings in Japanese, he stressed a difference that existed between Japan and China (see Ching 1998; Kinoshita 1973).

8 Okakura was specifically concerned with the arts, but his saying, "Asia is one," became infamous when it was appropriated by the ideologues of Japanese imperialism in Asia in the 1930s. Hosokawa (1998) demonstrates that they used Okakura's ideas in their attempts to forge an Asian unity through traditional music. For instance, an ethnomusicologist of that time depicted Japanese music as the repository of all Asian music, since it "contained all the significant characteristics found in Asian music traditions [*sic*]" (Hosokawa 1998, 16). Music was thus the medium par excellence in which the truth of the adage "Asia is one" was manifest.

9 Dick Lee's Singaporean producer admitted that he consciously attempted

to sell a new cross-fertilized sound for the most important market, Japan, but could not really catch up with the changing tastes of Japanese audiences (Kawakami 1995, 103).

10 In Hong Kong, for example, the maturity of the music industry in this period was marked by the emergence of local pop stars such as the Four Heavenly Kings (Jacky Cheung, Leon Lai, Andy Lau, and Aaron Kwok), who dominated the Chinese music markets in Hong Kong, Taiwan, and Singapore.

11 Although he apparently does not care for Canto-pop musical forms and does not speak Cantonese fluently, Lee released a Canto-pop album (Wee 1996).

12 For an account of how nostalgia has framed sociological discussions of modernity, see Turner (1994).

13 For the exploitation of nostalgia on tourism, see MacCannell (1976), Urry (1990), Frow (1991), and Graburn (1995).

14 Ironically, Kobayashi's romanticization of traveling Asian Japanese was exposed by a TV program's commodification of backpackers' travel. In 1996, an unknown comic duo, Saruganseki, began tracing the same path by hitchhiking. They had just 100,000 yen at the beginning of their trip and had to find casual jobs and endure fasting and frequently sleeping in the open. Their trip was documented in detail and broadcast on a variety TV show every week. The audience at first just ridiculed wretched conditions that the duo suffered through, but as they saw Saruganseki experience "real" life through their heartwarming communication with local people, crying over the physical threats and emotional fears they faced and being almost starved to death during the trip, Saruganseki became an object of applause and envy. The young audiences were jealous of Saruganseki in that the duo experienced something substantial in life which could not be experienced in Japan (Wakamono wa hōrō o mezasu 1996, 34–35).

15 Kobayashi's sense of a commonality with Asia is more apparent in his subsequently published *Asian Japanese 2* (1996). Kobayashi this time went from Asia to Paris, the place Kobayashi felt would be most different from Asia. He repeatedly juxtaposed Paris and Asia in a binary opposition: Paris is the place where he uses sophisticated and established cultural and artistic knowledge, values, and materials to think things through, whereas Asia is where modern wisdom is superseded by bodily sensations—all he can do there is feel, watch, and hear something fundamental to life in a chaotic, nasty alley (Kobayashi 1996, 365–68); Paris is the place from which Asian Japanese can no longer escape, whereas Asian Japanese are allowed to indulge in the search for their real self in the affection and depth of Asia (Kobayashi 1996, 74); Paris is the place where Kobayashi stands apart, whereas he can comfortably "dissolve into Asia" (Morris-Suzuki 1998a) due to its physical and cultural proximity and the disappearance of a sense

of inferiority. In the final instance, however, Paris and Asia converge to Kobayashi's narcissistic search for self, as he is convinced that Asian Japanese, no matter which foreign countries they are in, are traveling away from a homeland called "Japan" (Kobayashi 1996, 373).

16 The ratings were between 15 and 20 percent, which are well above the average rating for Japanese TV dramas.

17 All the main characters, including the Vietnamese hero, were played by Japanese actors.

18 Like *Doku,* most main characters were also played by popular Japanese actors.

19 For the use of the term *genki* in the media representation of Asian pop music, see also Ajian poppusu o kike 1994; Marume 1994; Nippon seifuku bijo zukan 1995; Kitanaka 1995).

20 This phrase is also used for other commodities which exploit the image of "Asia," such as the Japanese alcohol labeled "Asian."

21 Young women also seem to take the lead in the consumption of Japanese TV dramas in East Asia, but Japanese consumption of Hong Kong films and pop stars appears clearly more gendered. While it is beyond the scope of this book, the gendered transnational desire apparent in the intra–East Asian cultural flows is a significant issue for further investigation.

22 Kaneshiro is Taiwanese-Japanese, mainly brought up in Taipei, but he has actively appeared in Hong Kong films and other media productions.

23 Following the successful concerts in Japan of Jacky Cheung in 1995 and Andy Lau in 1996, Leslie Cheung and Aaron Kwok also held their first concerts in 1997.

24 For example, *Elle Japon* (Ima Honkon ga shigekiteki June 1997; Ajia no sekusī na otokotachi 1997; Chainīzu binan danyū ni meromero!! 1997; Sakimonogai! 1996; and Tadashii Ajia no hamarikata 1997. Japanese newspapers also cover the popularity of Hong Kong male stars (e.g., Kajinteki Meisei 21 October 1995; "Honkon meisei" 19 April 1997; CM, zasshi de hikatteru anohito wa Honkon geinōjin 1997).

25 In the early 1990s, the fascination of Japanese women for "pure" beach boys in Southeast Asia attracted media attention. They are often described in a derogatory way as the women's equivalent of Japanese "sex tourism." However, it was not just a "pick-up-a-man" phenomenon. Some women actually migrated to Bali through marriage (see Yamashita 1996; Ajia karuchā ryūnyū no 30 nen 1994; Hanayome wa kamigami no shima o mezasu 1994; Bari no gensō ni hamaru Nihonjin 1996).

26 I use the term *fan,* as I will show, not just because interviewees made extra efforts to consume Hong Kong popular culture, but also because they were quite self-conscious of the fact that their tastes were not (yet) shared by the majority of people in Japan.

27 There are many fan clubs for Hong Kong and Taiwan stars and for Hong Kong film and music lovers. The largest one by far is a fan club for Hong Kong films, Honkon Yamucha Kurabu, which has more than 12,000 members (Adachi 1998, 5). Other large fan clubs are those for Leslie Cheung (about 900 members), Leon Lei's Leon Family (about 800 members), Jacky Cheung (about 500 members), and Aaron Kwok (about 480 members) (see Poppu na Ajia no fan kurabu in Japan 1998, 72–74).

28 Given that Kaneshiro's father is Japanese (Okinawan), it can be argued that his appeal is also related to the fact that he has "Japanese blood." Kaneshiro, who is Taiwanese-Japanese, speaks five languages (Japanese, English, Taiwanese, Mandarin, Cantonese) and takes an active role in Hong Kong films, in a sense represents a favorable "cosmopolitan" attribute that cannot be attained by Japanese.

29 Stewart (1993, 26) argues: "Nostalgia, like any form of narrative, is always ideological: the past it seeks has never existed except as narrative, and hence, always absent, that past continually threatens to reproduce itself as a felt lack." That the director of *Swallowtail Butterfly* is conscious of this is evident from his comments about certain scenes he saw in Shanghai, where people were cooking outdoors while chatting with their neighbors: "I am not sure if I really experienced the same thing as a child, but I somehow felt nostalgic for the scene. . . . [Cooking outside] has little to do with vitality, but the scene might be associated with my faint memory of a vulgar and energetic Japan on the path of high economic growth" (Iwai 1997, 6).

30 Such a nostalgic search for an "authentic" Japan has been relentlessly provoked by domestic tourism (e.g., Robertson 1998a; Ivy 1995; Creighton 1997; Graburn 1983).

31 For example, *Nikkei Entertainment* featured an article on how to become addicted to Asia (Tadashii Ajia no hamarikata 1997). The article predominantly dealt with Hong Kong and Taiwanese popular culture and idols, but the magazine used the term *Asia* rather than *Hong Kong* or *Chinese*. The same was true for an the article in *Elle Japon* (Ajia no sekushī na otokotachi 1997).

32 Adachi (1998) also found the same tendency.

6 Japan's Asian dreamworld

1 This point became acute at the beginning of the twenty-first century, especially since 11 September 2001, as we were compelled to recognize through the sudden, massive media attention to the hitherto forgotten Asian country, Afghanistan, how the disparity between the haves and have-nots has been widened and how the disparity itself has been left out of global issues. The development of communication technologies and the

intensification of media and cultural flows simultaneously interconnecting many parts of the world have also brought forward global indifference toward many deprived peoples and regions. Facing such a grave situation, a view that negatively equates globalization with Americanization has accordingly regained momentum. It is true that a series of events since 11 September 2001 has highlighted anew U.S. economic and military supremacy. However, I would suggest that such a view is misleading and irresponsible, as it conceals the fact that the unevenness in transnational connections has been intensified not solely by U.S. dominance but also by the various kinds of collusive alliances among the developed countries under the patronage of the dominant U.S. military power. It cannot be overemphasized that the decentering process of globalization has not dissolved global power structures: Globalization has been subtly diffused and even solidified, producing asymmetry and indifference on a global scale. See Hardt and Negri (2000) for a sweeping theorization of new form of global goverance that is not founded on the sovereignity or the hegemonic power of a single nation.

2　It should be noted that Ishihara's anti–American Asianism coexists with xenophobia against Asian residents in Japan whom Ishihara demonizes as internal threats to a Japanese national community. This posture was made clear by racist remarks he publicly made at the event of the Ground Self-Defense Force in April 2000. Ishihara stated that illegal Asian migrants and foreigners were responsible for the recent increase in vicious crimes and potential rioters and looters at the time of disaster, and used a word, *sangokujin*, which discriminatorily referred to Chinese, Koreans, and Taiwanese in the postwar period under the U.S. occupation.

3　This is a main motif of a popular novel by Murakami Ryū, *Kibou no kuni no eguzodasu* (Exodus to the country full of hope) (2000).

4　From my November 1998 conversation with Kurasawa Aiko, who was conducting research on Japanese popular culture in Indonesia.

References

2020nen kara no keishō: Nihon ga kieru 4. 1997. *Nihon Keizai Shinbun,* 5 January.

Adachi Miki. 1998. Honkon no kigō shōhi: Gendai nihon no "Ajia" shōhi no ichi kōsatsu. Undergraduate graduation thesis, Department of Sociology, University of Tokyo.

Aidoru sangyō nimo kūdōka no nami? 1994. *Mainichi Shinbun,* 9 November, evening edition.

Ajia aidoru ninki no butaiura. 1997. *Nikkei Trendy,* June, 97–104.

Ajia de kageki ni shōhi sareru Nippon bunka. *Spa!* 1 September, 39–49.

Ajia eisei ga sofuto ryūtsū o kaeru. 1993. *Nikkei Entertainment,* 28 April/5 May, 4–11.

Ajia ga miteiru Nihon no terebi. 1995. *Kōkoku,* May/June, 3–24.

Ajia karuchā ryūnyū no 30 nen. 1994. *Across,* November, 12–21.

Ajia mo watashi no ikiru michi! 1997. *Bart,* 10 March, 28–35.

Ajia no sekushī na otokotachi. 1997. *Elle Japon,* November, 88–99.

Ajia no tabi wa yonde jibunryū. 1996. *Nihon Keizai Shinbun,* 29 January, evening edition.

Ajia pawā: sofuto wa kō kawaru. 1992. *Nikkei Entertainment,* 5 February, 4–15.

Ajia poppusu gutto mijikani. 1996. *Nihon Keizai Shinbun,* 30 July, evening edition.

Ajia to Nihon no zure egaku. 1993. *Asahi Shinbun,* 22 September, evening edition.

"Ajia to no kyōsei" yoron chōsa. 1996. *Asahi Shinbun,* 9 November.

"Ajia to no kyōsei" yoron chōsa. 1997. *Asahi Shinbun,* 9 June.

Ajiabon no shuppan kakkyō. 1994. *Asahi Shinbun,* 17 September, evening edition.

Ajian poppusu o kike. 1994. *Views,* 23 March, 28–37.

Akamatsu Kaname. 1959. Wagakuni sangyō hatten no gankō keitai: Kikai kigu kōgyō ni tsuite. *Hitotsubashi Rongyō* 11: 514–26.

Aksoy, Asu, and Kevin Robins. 1992. Hollywood for the twenty-first century: Global competition for critical mass in image markets. *Cambridge Journal of Economics* 16: 1–22.

Akurosu Henshūshitsu, eds. 1995. *Sekai Shōhin no Tsukurikata: Nihon media ga sekai o seishita hi.* Tokyo: Parco Shuppan.

Amerika nimo otaku ga daihassei. 1996. *Shūkan Bunshun,* 5 September, 190–91.

Amyūzu, Chūgoku to renzoku terebi dorama. 1996. *Nihon Keizai Shinbun,* 12 January.

Amyūzu, Honkon ōte to eiga gappei. 1997. *Nihon Keizai Shinbun,* 11 December.

Anderson, Benedict. 1983. *Imagined communities.* London: Verso.

Ang, Ien. 1985. *Watching Dallas: Soap opera and the melodramatic imagination.* London: Methuen.

———. 1994. In the realm of uncertainty: The global village and capitalist postmodernity. In *Communication theory today,* edited by D. Crowley and D. Mitchell, 192–213. Cambridge: Polity Press.

———. 1996. *Living room wars: Rethinking media audiences for a postmodern world.* London: Routledge.

———. 1998. Eurocentric reluctance: Notes for a cultural studies of "the new Europe." In *Trajectories: Inter-Asian cultural studies,* edited by K.-H. Chen, 87–108. London: Routledge.

Ang, Ien, and Jon Stratton. 1996. Asianizing Australia: Notes toward a critical transnationalism in cultural studies. *Cultural Studies* 10 (1): 16–36.

———. 1997. The Singaporean way of multi-culturalism: Western concepts/Asian cultures. *New Formations* 31: 51–66.

Ansart, Olivier, Cyryl Raphael Veliath, Bruce L. Batten, and Satō Shun'ichi. 1994. Jibun o rikai saseru koto ga fuete na Nihon. *Gaiko Forum* 74 (November): 52–62.

Aoki Tamotsu. 1990. *Nihon bunkaron no hen'yō.* Tokyo: Chūō Kōronsha.

———. 1993. Ajia Jirenma. *Asuteion* 27: 16–43.

Appadurai, Arjun. 1990. Disjuncture and difference in the global cultural economy. *Public Culture* 2 (2): 1–24.

———. 1996. *Modernity at large: Cultural dimensions of globalization.* Minneapolis: University of Minnesota Press.

Asai Masayoshi. 1997. Ajia eisei hōsō shijō ni deokureta Nihon. *Shinbun Kenkyū* 551: 67–70.

Ashcroft, Bill, Gareth Griffiths, and Helen Tiffin. 1998. *Key concepts in postcolonial studies.* London: Routledge.

Asia says Japan is top of the pops, 1996. *Asiaweek,* 5 January, 35–39.

Asia strikes back: Local TV takes on the satellite giants. 1996. *Asiaweek,* 8 November, 38–46.

Atkins, Will. 1995. "Friendly and useful": Rupert Murdoch and the politics of television in Southeast Asia, 1993–1995. *Media International Australia* 77: 54–64.

"Atarashii mirai kizukou" atsui hakushu. 2000. *Asahi Shinbun,* 28 August.

"Bangumi urimasu," Bei shinshutsu nerau minpō. 1993. *Asahi Shinbun,* 10 September, evening edition.

Bari no gensō ni hamaru Nihonjin. 1996. *Aera,* 17 June, 33–47.

Barker, Chris. 1997. *Global television: An introduction.* Oxford: Blackwell Publishers.

Barnet, Richard, and John Cavanagh. 1994. *Global dreams: Imperial corporations and the new world order.* New York: Simon and Schuster.

Barrett, James. 1996. World music, nation, and postcolonialism. *Cultural Studies* 10 (2): 237–47.

Bartu, Friedmann. 1992. *The ugly Japanese: Nippon's economic empire in Asia.* Singapore: Longman.

Baudrillard, Jean. 1981. *For a critique of the political economy of the sign.* St. Louis, Mo.: Telos Press.

———. 1983. *Simulations.* New York: Semiotexte.

———. 1988. *America.* London: Verso.

Befu Harumi. 1987. *Ideorogī to shite no Nihonbunkaron.* Tokyo: Shisō no Kagakusha.

Beilharz, Peter. 1991. Louis Althusser. In *Social theory: A guide to central thinkers,* edited by P. Beilharz, 16–19. Sydney: Allen and Unwin.

Bell, Philip, and Roger Bell. 1995. The "Americanization" of Australia. *Journal of International Communication* 2 (1): 120–33.

Benjamin, Walter. 1973. *Illuminations.* London: Fontana.

Berger, Mark, and Douglas A. Borer. 1997. *The rise of East Asia: Critical visions of the Pacific century.* London: Routledge.

Berland, Jody. 1992. Angels dancing: Cultural technologies and the production of space. In *Cultural Studies,* edited by L. Grossberg et al., 38–55. New York: Routledge.

Berry, Chris. 1994. *A bit on the side: East-West topographies of desire.* Sydney: Empress.

Bhabha, Homi. 1985. Of mimicry and man: The ambivalence of colonial discourse. *Journal Name?* October 28: 125–133.

———. 1990. The third space. In *Identity: Community, Culture, Difference,* edited by J. Rutherford, 207–21. London: Lawrence and Wishart.

———. 1994. *The Location of Culture.* London: Routledge.

The birth of Asiawood. 2001. *Newsweek,* 21 May, 52–56.

Bosche, Marc. 1997. Nihon ni yoru hisokana shokuminchika. Translated by M. Shimazaki. *Sekai,* February, 231–35.

Bourdieu, Pierre. 1984. *Distinction: Social critique of the judgement of taste,* translated by R. Nice. Cambridge, Mass.: Harvard University Press.

Boyd, Douglas A., Joseph D. Straubhaar, and John A. Lent. 1989. *Videocassette recorders in the Third World.* New York: Longman.

Brannen, Mary Yoko. 1992. "Bwana Mickey": Constructing cultural consumption at Tokyo Disneyland. In *Re-made in Japan: Everyday life and consumer taste in a changing society,* edited by J. Tobin, 216–34. New Haven, Conn.: Yale University Press.

Bratton, John. 1992. *Japanization at work: Managerial studies for the 1990s.* London: Macmillan Press.

Buck, Elizabeth B. 1992. Asia and the global film industry. *East-West Film Journal* 6 (2): 116–33.

Buck-Morss, Susan. 1983. Benjamin's *Passanger-werk*: Redeeming mass culture for the revolution. *New German Critique* 29: 211–40.

Buell, Frederick. 1994. *National culture and the new global system.* Baltimore, Md.: John Hopkins University Press.

Cast of thousands. 1994. *Far Eastern Economic Review,* 27 January.

Caughie, John. 1990. Playing at being American: Games and tactics. In *Logics of Television,* edited by P. Mellencamp, 44–58. London: British Film Institute.

Chainīzu binan dan'yū ni meromero!! 1997. *Crea,* January, 97–101.

Chakrabarty, Dipesh. 1992. Postcoloniality and the artifice of history: Who speaks for the "Indian" past? *Representation* 37: 1–26.

Chambers, Iain. 1990. A miniature history of the Walkman. *New Formations* 11: 1–4.

———. 1994. *Migrancy, culture, identity.* London: Routledge.

Chan, Joseph Man. 1996. Television in greater China: Structure, exports, and market formation. In *New patterns in global television: Peripheral vision,* edited by J. Sinclair et al., 126–160. New York: Oxford University Press.

Chatterjee, Partha. 1986. *Nationalist thought and the colonial world: A derivative discourse?* London: Zed Books.

Chen Kuan-Hsing. 1996. Not yet the postcolonial era: The super nation-state and transnationalism of cultural studies (Response to Ang and Stratton). *Cultural Studies* 10 (1): 37–70.

Chiiki wo musubu kakehashi. 1994. *Mainichi Shinbun,* 8 December.

Chikai kuni kara ippai kita geinōjin. 1994. *Bart,* 27 June, 8–13.

Chikayotte kita Nihon bunka. 1995. *Asahi Shinbun,* 15 November, evening edition.

Ching, Leo. 1994. Imagining in the empire of the sun: Japanese mass culture in Asia. *boundary 2* 21 (1): 199–219.

———. 1998. Yellow skin, white masks: Race, class, and identification in Japanese colonial discourse. In *Trajectories: Inter-Asia cultural studies,* edited by K.-H. Chen, 65–86. London: Routledge.

———. 2000. Aesthetic and mass culture: Asianism in the age of global capital. *Public Culture* 12 (1): 233–57.

Chō Kyō. 1998. Bunka ga jōhō ni natta toki. *Sekai,* April: 82–107.

Choi Il-nam. 1994. Japan: America of Asia. *Korea Focus* 2 (2): 146–48.

Chow, Rey. 1993. Listening otherwise, music miniaturized: A different type of question about revolution. In *The cultural studies reader,* edited by S. During, 382–99. London: Routledge.

Chua, Beng-Huat. 1998. Globalization: Finding the appropriate words and levels. *Communal / Plural* 6 (1): 117–24.

Chūgoku māketto no neraime wa kono bijinesu da! 1994. *Sandē Mainichi,* 13 November, 144–47.

Chūgoku tairiku de yūbō tarento o hakkutsu seyo. 1993. *Aera,* 14 September, 65.

Classen, Constance, David Howes, and Anthony Synnott. 1994. *Aroma: The cultural history of smell.* London: Routledge.

CM, zasshi de hikatteru anohito wa Honkon geinōjin. 1997. *Asahi Shinbun,* 24 May, evening edition.

Creighton, Millie. 1997. Consuming rural Japan: The marketing of tradition and nostalgia in the Japanese travel industry. *Ethnology* 36 (3): 239–54.

Cute power! 1999. *Newsweek Asia,* 8 November.

Daitōa atsuzoko kyōeiken. 2001. *Nikkei Business,* 15 January.

Daiyosoku Ajian aidoru uresuji katarogu. 1995. *Dime,* 5 October, 21.

Dale, Peter. 1986. *The myth of Japanese uniqueness.* London: Croom Helm.

Davis, Darrell, and Yeh Yueh-yu. Forthcoming. Flexible accumulation, flexible consumption: VCD and class consciousness in Asia-Pacific. In *Feeling "Asian" modernities: Transnational consumption of Japanese TV dramas,* edited by K. Iwabuchi. Hong Kong: Hong Kong University Press.

Davis, Fred. 1979. *Yearning for yesterday: A sociology of nostalgia.* New York: The Free Press.

Dentsū, and Dentsū Sōken. 1994. Eizō Sofuto Yushutsu Shinkō Kenyiukai Hōkokusho. Report submitted to the Japanese Ministry of International Trade and Industry.

Dirlik, Arif. 1991. Culturalism as a sign of the modern. In *The nature and context of minority discourse,* edited by A. R. Jan-Mohamed and D. Lloyd, 394–431. New York: Oxford University Press.

——. 1994. *After the Revolution: Waking to global capitalism.* Middletown, N.H.: Wesleyan University Press.

The divas of pop. 1996. *Time Asia,* 4 October.

Dohse, Knuth, Ulrich Jurgens, and Thomas Malsch. 1985. From "Fordism" to "Toyotism"? The social organization of the labor process in the Japanese automobile industry. *Politics and Society* 14 (2): 115–46.

Doku! by Katori Shingo in Vietnam. 1997. *Uno!,* January, 69–78.

Dore, Ronald P. 1973. *British factory—Japanese factory: The origins of diversity in industrial relations.* Berkeley: University of California Press.

Dower, John W. 1986. *War without mercy: Race and power in the Pacific War.* New York: Panthenon Books.

du Gay, Paul, et al. 1997. *Doing cultural studies: The story of the Sony Walkman.* London: Sage.

Duus, Peter. 1995. *The abacus and the sword: The Japanese penetration of Korea, 1895–1910.* Berkeley: University of California Press.

Dyer, Richard. 1992. *Only entertainment.* London: Routledge.

Edagawa Kōichi. 1997. Honkon bunka wa Tokyo no atama o tobikoeta. *Ushio,* August 1997, 132–39.

Eiga *Sotsugyō Ryokō: Nihon kara kimashita.* 1993. *Shūkan Posuto,* 30 July, 23.

Eikoku ga mitometa Nihonbunka wa manga to terebi gēmu. 1996. *Shūkan Yomiuri,* 2 June, 29–31.

Eisei: Kaigai de tamesareru terebi taikoku Nippon no jitsuryoku. 1995. *Nikkei Trendy,* March, 31–42.

Ekkyō suru Ajia geinō. 1993. *Spa!,* 24 February, 36–45.

Elger, Tony, and Chris Smith. 1994. *Global Japanization: The transnational transformation of the labor process.* London: Routledge.

Emnott, Bill. 1992. *Japan's global reach.* London: Random House.

Ewen, Stuart, and Elizabeth Ewen. 1982. *Channels of desire: Mass images and the shaping of American consciousness.* New York: McGraw-Hill.

Export machines: The culture club. 1999. *Time Asia,* 3 May.

Fabian, Johannes. 1983. *Time and the other: How anthropology makes its object.* New York: Columbia University Press.

Fallows, James. 1989. Containing Japan. *The Atlantic Monthly,* May.

Featherstone, Mike. 1991. *Consumer culture and postmodernism.* London: Sage.

———. 1995. *Undoing culture: Globalization, postmodernism, and identity.* London: Sage.

Featherstone, Mike, Scot Lash, and Roland Robertson, eds. 1995. *Global modernities.* London: Sage

Ferguson, Majorine. 1992. The mythology about globalization. *European Journal of Communication* 7: 69–93.

Fiske, John. 1992. The cultural economy of fandom. In *The adoring audience: Fan culture and popular media,* edited by L. A. Lewis, 30–49. London: Routledge.

Forester, Tom. 1993. Consuming electronics: Japan's strategy for control. *Media Information Australia* 67: 4–16.

Friedman, Jonathan. 1994. *Cultural identity and global process.* London: Sage

Frith, Simon. 1982. *Sound effect: Youth: Leisure and the politics of rock 'n' roll.* New York: Panthenon.

Frow, John. 1991. Tourism and the semiotics of nostalgia. *October* 57: 123–51.

Fukamaruka kōryū, ryōkoku ni kitaikan. 2000. *Asahi Shinbun,* 28 June.

Funabashi Yoichi. 1993. The Asianization of Asia. *Foreign Affairs* 72 (5): 75–85.

———. 1995. *Asia Pacific fusion: Japans role in APEC.* Washington, D.C.: Institute of International Economics.

Furansu de kosupure kontesuto nekkyō. 1997. *Asahi Shinbun*, 23 October, evening edition.

Furuki Morie, and Higuchi Masahiro. 1996. Eisei kurofune no shūrai de nemutte irarenakunatta terebikyoku. *Hōsō Bunka*, July, 56–71.

Gaiko Forum. 1994. Bunka Kōryū no atarashii chihei, no. 74 (November).

Ganley, Gladys D., and Oswald H. Ganley. 1987. *Global political fallout: The VCR's first decade*. Cambridge, Mass.: Program on Information Resources Policy, Harvard University, Center for Information Policy Research.

García Canclini, Néstor. 1995. *Hybrid cultures: Strategies for entering and leaving modernity*, translated by C. L. Chiappari and S. L. López. Minneapolis: University of Minnesota Press.

Garnham, Nicholas. 1990. *Capitalism and communication: Global culture and the economics of information*. London: Sage.

Genki na Ajia ongaku zasshi. 1998. *Aera*, 9 March, 52.

Gillespie, Marie. 1995. *Television, ethnicity, and cultural change*. London: Routledge.

Gluck, Carol. 1993. The past in the present. In *Postwar Japan as History*, edited by A. Gordon, 64–95. Berkeley: University of California Press.

———. 1997. The end of the postwar: Japan at the turn of the millennium. *Public Culture* 10 (1): 1–23.

Gomery, Douglas. 1988. Hollywood's hold on the new television technologies. *Screen* 29 (2): 82–88.

Government Information Office, Republic of China. 1999. *The Republic of China Yearbook*. Taipei: Government Information Office.

Graburn, Nelson H. H. 1983. *To pray, pay, and play: The cultural structure of Japanese domestic tourism*. Aix-en-Provence: Centres des Hautes Etudes Touristiques.

———. 1995. Tourism, modernity, and nostalgia. In *The future of anthropology: Its relevance to the contemporary world*, edited by A. S. Ahmed and C. N. Shore, 158–78. London: Athlone.

Grewal, Inderpal, Akhil Gupta, and Aihwa Ong. 1999. Guest editors' introduction, Special issue on Asian transnationalities. *positions* 7 (3): 653–66.

Gupta, Akhil, and James Ferguson. 1992. Beyond "culture": Space, identity, and the politics of difference. *Cultural Anthropology* 7 (1): 6–23.

Hall, Stuart. 1991. The local and the global: Globalization and ethnicity. In *Culture, globalization, and the world-system*, edited by A. King, 19–39. London: Macmillan.

———. 1992. The question of cultural identity. In *Modernity and its futures*, edited by S. Hall et al. London: Polity Press.

———. 1995. New cultures for old. In *A place in the world? Places, cultures, and globalization*, edited by D. Massey and P. Jess, 175–214. Oxford: Oxford University Press:

———. 1996a. On postmodernism and articulation: An interview with Stuart Hall. In *Stuart Hall: Critical dialogue in cultural studies,* edited by D. Morley and K.-H. Chen, 131–50. London: Routledge.

———. 1996b. When was "the post-colonial"? Thinking at the limit. In *The post-colonial question: Common skies, divided horizons,* edited by I. Chambers and L. Curti, 242–60. London: Routledge.

Hall, Robert K., ed. 1949. *Kokutai no Hongi: Cardinal principles of the national entity of Japan.* Cambridge, Mass.: Harvard University Press.

Hamelink, Cees. 1983. *Cultural autonomy in global communications.* New York: Longman.

Hamilton, Annette. 1997. Looking for love in all the wrong places: The production of Thailand in recent Australian cinema. In *Australia and Asia: Cultural transactions,* edited by M. Dever, 143–61. London: Curzon Press.

Hanaoka Takako. 1997. Dokusen! Machi no uwasa. *Shûkan Bunshun* 25 (3 July): 62–63.

Hanayome wa kamigami no shima o mezasu. 1994. *Asahi Shinbun,* 19 August.

Hannerz, Ulf. 1989. Notes on the global ecumene. *Public Culture* 1 (2): 66–75.

———. 1991. Scenarios for peripheral cultures. In *Culture, globalization, and the world-system,* edited by A. King, 107–28. London: Macmillan.

———. 1992. *Cultural complexity.* New York: Columbia University Press.

———. 1996. *Transnational connections: Culture, people, places.* London: Routledge.

Hara Tomoko. 1996. *Honkon chûdoku.* Tokyo: Japan Times.

Hardt, Michael, and Antonio Negri. 2000. *Empire.* Cambridge, Mass.: Harvard University Press.

Hariwuddo ni nerawareru sofuto taikoku Nippon. 1994. *Dime,* 6 October, 21–25.

Harootunian, D. Harry. 1993. America's Japan/Japan's Japan. In *Japan in the world,* edited by M. Miyoshi and H. D. Harootunian, 196–221. Durham, N.C.: Duke University Press.

Harvey, David. 1989. *The condition of postmodernity.* Oxford: Basil Blackwell.

Harvey, Paul A. S. 1995. Interpreting *Oshin:* War, history, and women in modern Japan. In *Women, media, and consumption in Japan,* edited by L. Skov and B. Moeran, 75–110. London: Curzon Press.

Hashizume Daizaburō. 1994. *Cui Jian: Gekidō Chūgoku no sūpā sutā.* Tokyo: Iwanami Shoten.

Hatakeyama Kenji, and Kubo Masaichi. 2000. *Pokemon story.* Tokyo: Nikkei BP.

Hatsunetsu Aija. 1994. TBS *News 23.*

Hattori Hiroshi, and Hara Yumiko. 1997. Tachanneruka no naka no terebi to shichōsha: Taiwan kēburu terebi no baai. *Hōsō Kenkyū to Chōsa,* February, 22–37.

Hawkins, Richard. 1997. Prospects for a global communication infrastructure in the twenty-first century: Institutional restructuring and network development. In *Media in global context: A reader*, edited by A. Sreberny-Mohammadi et al., 177–93. London: Arnold.

Hebdige, Dick. 1988. *Hiding in the light: On images and things*. London: Comedia.

Hein, Laura, and Ellen H. Hammond. 1995. Homing in on Asia: Identity in contemporary Japan. *Bulletin of Concerned Asian Scholars* 27 (3): 3–17.

Hendry, Joy. 1993. *Wrapping culture: Politeness, presentation, and power in Japan and other societies*. Oxford: Clarendon Press.

Herman, Edward, and Robert McChesney. 1998. *The global media: The new missionaries of global capitalism*. London: Cassell.

Higashi Ajia konketsu eiga no tanjō. 1997. *Aera*, 1 December, 53–54.

Higuchi Takafumi. 1997. Nihon no media no naka no Honkon. *Kinema Junpō*, July 1997, 44–46.

Hirano Ken'ichirō. 1994. Bunmei no shōtotsu ka bunka no masatsu ka? Hanchinton ronbun hihan. *Hikaku Bunmei*, October, 21–37.

Hirst, Paul, and Grahame Thompson. 1996. *Globalization in question: The international economy and the possibilities of governance*. Cambridge: Polity Press.

Hitto daijesuto. 1999. *Nikkei Entertainment*, May, 9.

Hitto no mukōgawa 7. 1998. *Asahi Shinbun*, 16 January, evening edition.

Hobsbawm, Eric J., and Terence Ranger, eds. 1983. *The invention of tradition*. Cambridge: Cambridge University Press.

Honda Shirō. 1994a. Higashi Ajia ni hirogaru Nihon no popyurā bunka. *Gaiko Forum*, September, 63–70.

Honda Shirō. 1994b. East Asia's middle class tunes into today's Japan. *Japan Echo* 21 (4): 75–79.

Honkon de chō ninki no Nihonjin aidoru tachi. 1992. *Mainichi Gurafu*, 29 November.

Honkon eiga ga tsumugu bimyō na kokoro. 1997. *Nihon Keizai Shinbun*, 27 September.

"Honkon meisei" kagayaki masu. 1997. *Nihon Keizai Shinbun*, 19 April.

Honkon, Taiwan sutā okkake masu. 1994. *Nihon Keizai Shinbun*, 7 July, evening edition.

Honkon TVB no chōsen. 1994. *Mainichi Shinbun*, 21 April.

Hoskins, Colin, and Rolf Mirus. 1988. Reasons for the U.S. dominance of the international trade in television programs. *Media, Culture, and Society* 10: 499–515.

Hōsō sofuto no Shinkō ni Kansuru Chōsa Kenkyūkai. 1997. Hōsō sofuto no Shinkō ni Kansurue Chōsa Kenkyūkai Hōkokusho. Research report submitted to the Japanese Ministry of Posts and Telecommunications.

Hosokawa Shuhei. 1989. The Walkman effect. In *Popular music 4: Performances and audiences,* edited by R. Middleton and D. Horn. Cambridge: Cambridge University Press.

——. 1998. In search of the sound of Empire: Tanabe Hisao and the foundation of Japanese ethnomusicology. *Japanese Studies* 18 (1): 5–20.

Howes, David. 1996. Introduction: Commodities and cultural borders. In *Cross-cultural consumption: Global markets, local realities,* edited by D. Howes, 1–16. London: Routledge.

Hsieh Yamai. 2000. *Nihon ni koishita Taiwanjin.* Tokyo: Sōgō Hōrei.

Hu Hsing-chi. Forthcoming. Japanese VCDs (Video CDs): Chinese remakings of Japanese audio-visual products. In *Feeling "Asian" modernities: Transnational consumption of Japanese TV dramas,* edited by K. Iwabuchi. Hong Kong: Hong Kong University Press.

Huntington, Samuel P. 1993. The clash of civilizations. *Foreign Affairs* 72 (3): 22–49.

Ichikawa Takashi. 1994. *Ajia wa Machi ni kike!* Tokyo: Tōyō Keizaisha.

——. 1995. In'yu to shiteno Chainīzu poppusu. *Chūgoku bijinesu daikyōsō jidai* (special issue of *Chūō Kōron*), October, 318–34.

Igarashi Akio. 1997. From Americanization to "Japanization" in East Asia? *Journal of Pacific Asia* 4: 3–20.

——, ed. 1998. *Hen'yō suru Ajia to Nihon: Ajia shakai ni shintō suru Nihon no popyurā karuchā.* Tokyo: Seori Shobō.

Igarashi Akio, Saitō Eisuke, Wun'geo Srichai, and Chung Daekyun. 1995. Bōdaresuka suru Ajia no taishū bunka. *Ushio,* October, 238–47.

Ima Ajia ni atsui manazashi! 1994. *Elle Japon,* 5 March, 24–45.

Ima Honkon ga shigekiteki. 1997. *Elle Japon,* June, 40–55.

Ima sekai ga Ajian byūtī ni chūmoku. 1997. *Elle Japon,* August, 60–63.

Imada Takatoshi. 1994. *Konton no chikara.* Tokyo: Kōdansha.

Imamura Yōichi. 1995. Nihon hatsu sofuto no hādoru. *Hōsō Hihyō* 307: 14–17.

Inamasu Tatsuo. 1993. Aidoru kōgaku. Rev. ed. Tokyo: Chikuma Shobō.

Indonesia ban de Oshin rimōku. 1997. *Asahi Shinbun,* 7 July, evening edition.

Inoue Shōichi. 1996. *Gurotesuku Japan.* Tokyo: Yōsensha.

Invasion of the pocket monsters. 1999. *Time,* 22 November, 62–69.

Iokibe Makoto. 1994. Shin sekai muchitsujoron o koete. *Asuteion* 31: 16–33.

Ishida Takeshi. 1995. *Shakaikagaku saikō: Haisen kara hanseiki no dōjidaishi.* Tokyo: Tokyo Daigaku Shuppankai.

Ishihara Shintaro, and Hitotsubashi Sōgō Kenkyūjo. 1998. *Sensen Gukoku "No" to ieru Nihonkeizai.* Tokyo: Kōbunsha.

Ishii Ken'ichi, and Watanabe Satoshi. 1998. Honkon ni okeru Nihon no popyurā bunka to shōhi kōdō. *Burēn,* April: 118–24.

Ishii Ken'ichi, Watanabe Satoshi, and Su Hearng. 1996. Taiwan ni okeru

Nihonbangumi no shichōsha bunseki. Discussion Papers series, no. 701, University of Tsukuba, Tsukuba.

Ivy, Marilyn. 1993. Formations of mass culture. In *Postwar Japan as history,* edited by A. Gordon, 239–58. Berkeley: University of California Press.

———. 1995. *Discourses of the vanishing: Modernity, phantasm, Japan.* Chicago: University of Chicago Press.

Iwabuchi, Koichi. 1994. Complicit exoticism: Japan and its other. *Continuum* 8 (2): 49–82.

———. 2000. Political correctness, postcolonialism, and the self-representation of "Koreanness" in Japan. In *Koreans in Japan: Critical voices from the margin,* edited by S. Ryan, 55–73. London: Routledge.

———, ed. Forthcoming. *Feeling "Asian" Modernities: Transnational consumption of Japanese TV dramas.* Hong Kong: Hong Kong University Press.

Iwai Shunji. 1997. Nihonjin ga ushinatta pawā o kanki suru kakūtoshi "Yen Town." *Shin Chōsa Jōhō* 3: 4–7.

Iyer, Pico. 1988. *Video night in Kathmandu: And other reports from the not-so-far East.* New York: Knopf.

Jameson, Frederic. 1983. *Postmodernism, or, the cultural logic of late capitalism.* Durham, N.C.: Duke University Press.

Japan TV team joins customs in piracy fight. 1998. *South China Morning Post,* 8 September.

Japanese Ministry of Posts and Telecommunications. 1997. Heisei 9 nendoban Tsūshin Hakusho. Tokyo: Japanese Ministry of Posts and Telecommunications.

Jenkins, Henry. 1992. *Textual poachers: Television fans and participatory culture.* London: Routledge.

Jiburi no mahō. 2002. *Newsweek Japan,* 3 April, 52–62.

Kadota Osamu. 1998. Kaisetsu: Tsurumi san e no tegami. In Ajia no Arukikata, by Y. Tsurumi, 271–77. Tokyo: Chikuma Bunko.

Kakeo Yoshio. 2001. Nihon no eiga jijō. *Asuteion,* 104–17.

Kaigai bunka ikusei seisaku. 1997. Dime, 3 June, 105–7.

Kajinteki meisei. 1995. *Nihon Keizai Shinbun,* 21 October.

Kamo Yoshinori. 2000. Pokemon ga yushutsu shita "kūru" na Nihon to Nihonjin. *Asahi Shinbun,* 20 January, evening edition.

Kanemitsu Osamu. 1993. Takokuseki bangumi Asia Bagus! kara mita Ajia terebi jijō. *Aura,* August, 22–29.

Kaneshiro Takeshi, anata shika mienai! Koi no ondo wa 37.2° C. 1997. *Olive,* 3 July, 96–103.

Kang Sang-jung. 1996. *Orientarizumu no Kanata e.* Tokyo: Iwanami Shoten.

Karatani Kōjin. 1994. Bijutsukan to shite no Nihon. Hihyō Kūkan 2 (1): 68–75.

Katō Shūichi. 1979. Katō Shūichi Chosakuū 7, Kindai Nihon no Bunmeishiteki Ichi. Tokyo: Heibonsha.

Kawakami Hideo. 1990. Kyokutō Ajia to Nihon no taishū ongaku kōryū. *Poppu Eijia, WAVE* 7: 113–20.

——. 1995. *Gekidō suru Ajia ongaku shijō.* Tokyo: Shinema Hausu.

Kawakatsu Heita. 1991. *Nihon Bunmei to Kindai Seiyō.* Tokyo: NHK Shuppan.

——. 1995. *Fukoku Utokuron.* Tokyo: Kinokuniya Shoten.

——, ed. 1994. *Atarashii Ajia no dorama.* Tokyo: Chikuma Shobō.

Kawamura Minato. 1993. Taishū orientarizumu to Ajia ninshiki. In *Kindai Nihon to Shokuminchi,* vol. 7, edited by S. Ōe, et al, 107–36. Tokyo: Iwanami Shoten.

Kawamura Nozomu. 1982. *Nihon bunkaron no shūhen.* Tokyo: Ningen no Kagakusha.

Kawasaki Ken'ichi. 1993. Nihon no hasshin suru popyurā bunka towa. *Sekai,* December, 202–9.

Kawatake Kazuo. 1994. Nihon o chūshin to suru terebi jōhō furō no genjō to mondaiten. *Jōhō Tsūshin Gakkaishi* 12 (1): 54–63.

——. 1995. Ajia kyōtsū no terebi bunka kōchiku ni mukete. *Kōkoku,* May–June, 20–24.

Kawatake Kazuo, and Hara Yumiko. 1994. Nihon o chūshin to suru terebi bangumi no ryūtsū jijyō. *Hōsō Kenkyū to Chōsa,* November, 2–17.

Kelly, William W. 1993. Finding a place in metropolitan Japan: Ideologies, institutions, and everyday life. In *Postwar Japan as history,* edited by A. Gordon, 189–216. Berkeley: University of California Press.

Kelsky, Karen. 1996. Flirting with the foreign: Interracial sex in Japan's "international" age. In *Global/local: Cultural production and the transnational imaginary,* edited by R. Wilson and W. Dissanayake, 173–92. Durham, N.C.: Duke University Press.

——. 1999. Gender, modernity, and eroticized internationalism in Japan. *Cultural Anthropology* 14(2): 229–55.

Kinder, Marsha. 1991. *Playing with power in movies, television, and video games.* Berkeley: University of California Press.

Kinoshita Nagahiro. 1973. *Okakura Tenshin.* Tokyo: Kinokuniya Shoten.

Kitanaka Masakazu. 1994. Kosei ga bakuhatsu suru Ajian poppusu. *Elle Japon,* March, 34–35.

——. 1995. Hitomukashimae no mūdo kayō mitai!? Ieie, Chainīzu poppu wa tottemo genki nan desu. *Hanako,* 13 April, 102.

Kobayashi Akiyoshi. 1994. Terebi bangumi no kokusai idō. *Kokusai Kōryū* 64: 33–38.

Kobayashi Kisei. 1995. *Asian Japanese.* Tokyo: Jōhō Sentā Shuppankyoku.

——. 1996. *Asian Japanese 2.* Tokyo: Jōhō Sentā Shuppankyoku.

——. 1997 *Asia Road.* Tokyo: Kōdansha.

Kobayashi Yoshinori. 2000. *Taiwanron.* Tokyo: Shōgakkan.

Kogawa Tetsuo. 1984. Beyond electronic individualism. *Canadian Journal of Political and Social Theory* 8 (3): 15–19.

———. 1988. New trends in Japanese popular culture. In *Modernization and beyond: The Japanese trajectory,* edited by G. McCormack and Y. Sugimoto, 54–66. Cambridge: Cambridge University Press.

Koi Eisei. 1989. *Den Nihon eiga no ōgonjidai.* Tokyo: Bungei Shunjū.

Kōkami Shōji, and Chikushi Tetsuya. 1992. Ajia to dō tsukiauka. In *Sazan Uindo: Ajia eiga no atsui kaze,* edited by Gaifūsha Henshūbu, 1–22. Tokyo: Gaifūsha.

Kokusai hōsō Ajia de hibana. 1994. *Nihon Keizai Shinbun,* 14 July.

Kokusai Kōryū. 1994. Denshi Media to Kokusai Kōryū, vol. 64.

Komagome Takeshi. 1996. *Shokuminchi teikoku nihon no bunka tōgō.* Tokyo: Iwanami Shoten.

Kondo, Dorinne. 1997. *About face: Performing race in fashion and theater.* New York: Routledge.

Kong, Lily. 1996. Popular music in Singapore: Exploring local cultures, global resources, and regional identities. *Environment and Planning D: Society and Space* 14: 273–92.

Korhonen, Pekka. 1994. *Japan and the Pacific free trade area.* London: Routledge.

Koschmann, Victor J. 1997. Asianism's ambivalent legacy. In *Network power: Japan and Asia,* edited by P. J. Katzenstein and T. Shiraishi, 83–110. Ithaca, N.Y.: Cornell University Press.

Kōtō Yusuke. 1998. Posutomodan to haiburiddo modan. *Shakaigaku Hyōron* 48 (4): 391–406.

Kozakai Toshiaki. 1996. *Ibunka juyō no paradokkusu.* Tokyo: Asahi Shinbunsha.

Kubota Makoto. 1990. Chanpurū myūjikku wa sekai o mezasu. *Poppu Eijia, WAVE* 27: 38–47.

Kuisel, Richard. 1993. *Seducing French: The dilemma of Americanization.* Berkeley: University of California Press.

Kumamoto Shin'ichi. 1993a. Sutā wuōzu kara sofuto wuōzu e. *Aura* 100: 10–17.

———. 1993b. Nihon no mediaryoku o dō hirogeruka. *Sekai,* December, 210–18.

Kurasawa Aiko. 1996. "Doraemon" vs. chūkan kaikyū: Indonesia ni okeru Japanimēshon. *Yuriika,* August, 107–11.

———. 1998. Ajia wa wakon o juyō dekiruka. In *Ajiateki kachi to wa nanika,* edited by T. Aoki and K. Saeki, 171–90. Tokyo: TBS Buritanika.

Kuroki Yasuo. 1995. Nihon no monozukuri wa sekai ni eikyō o ataete iruka. In *Sekai shōhin no tsukurikata,* edited by Akurosu Henshūshitsu, 10–17. Tokyo: Parco Shuppan.

Kuwahara, Yasue. 1997. Japanese culture and popular consciousness: Disney's

The Lion King vs. Tezuka's *Jungle Emperor. Journal of Popular Culture* 31 (1): 37–47.

Kyōmi shinshin Dikku ga Sonī Ajia no fukushachō ni. 1998. *Pop Asia*, no. 20 44.

Kyūseichō Ajia nerau ongaku sangyō. 1994. *Asahi Shinbun,* 11 February.

Lardner, James. 1987. *Fast forward: Hollywood, the Japanese, and the onslaught of the VCR.* New York: W. W. Norton.

Lash, Scott, and John Urry. 1994. *Economies of signs and space.* London: Sage.

Lebra, Joyce C., ed. 1975. *Japan's greater East Asian co-prosperity sphere in World War II.* Kuala Lumpur: Oxford University Press.

Lee, Chun-Chuan. 1980. *Media imperialism reconsidered: The homogenizing of television culture.* Beverly Hills, Calif.: Sage.

Lee, Paul S.-N. 1991. The absorption and indigenization of foreign media cultures: A study on a cultural meeting points of East and West: Hong Kong. *Asian Journal of Communication* 1 (2): 52–72.

Lee, Paul S.-N., and Georgette Wang. 1995. Satellite TV in Asia: Forming a new ecology. *Telecommunications Policy* 19 (2): 135–49.

Levi, Antonia. 1996. *Samurai from outer space: Understanding Japanese animation.* Chicago: Open Court.

Levitt, Theodore. 1983. *The marketing imagination.* New York: The Free Press.

Lewis, Glen, et al. 1994. Television globalization in Taiwan and Australia. *Media Asia* 21 (4): 184–89.

Li Zhen-Yiet al. 1995. *Tokyo love story: A study on the reason of the popularity and audience motivations in Taiwan.* Undergraduate research paper, National University of Politics, Taiwan.

Liao, Chaoyang. 1997. Borrowed modernity: History and the subject in *A Borrowed Life. boundary 2* 24 (3): 225–45.

Liao, Ping-hui. 1996. Chinese nationalism or Taiwanese localism? *Culture and Policy* 7 (2): 74–92.

Liebes, Tamar, and Elihu Katz, eds. 1993. *The export of meaning: Cross-cultural readings of "Dallas."* Oxford: Oxford University Press.

Liechty, Mark. 1995. Media, markets, and modernization: Youth identities and the experience of modernity in Kathmandu, Nepal. In *Youth culture: A cross-cultural perspective,* edited by V. Amit-Talai and H. Wulff, 166–201. London: Routledge.

Lii, Ding-Tzann. 1998. A colonized empire: Reflections on the expansion of Hong Kong films in Asian countries. In *Trajectories: Inter-Asian cultural studies,* edited by K.-H. Chen, 122–41. London: Routledge.

Lull, James. 1991. *China turned on: Television, reform, and resistance.* London: Routledge.

———. 1995. *Media, communication, culture: A global approach.* Cambridge: Polity Press.

MacCannell, Dean. 1976. *The tourist: A new theory of the leisure class.* New York: Schocken.

Mādokku to kunde Komuro Tetsuya no daitōa kyōeiken. 1996. *Focus,* 18 December, 8–9.

Maekawa Kenichi, and Ōno Shin'ichi. 1997. Ippansho to shiteno Ajiabon ga detehosii. *Nukunuku* 7: 38–49.

Mahathir, Mohamad, and Ishihara Shintarō. 1994. *"No" to ieru Ajia.* Tokyo: Kōbunsha.

———. 1995. *The voice of Asia.* Tokyo: Kōdansha International.

Manabe Masami. 1997. The wonderful world of *anime. Look Japan* (May): 17.

Manga mo aidoru mo NIEs sei. 1990. *Box,* March, 115–29.

Marukawa Tetsushi. 2000. *Taiwan, posutokoroniaru no shintai.* Tokyo: Seidosha.

Marume Kuraudo. 1994. Ajia no sūpā aidoru 63nin. *DENiM,* April, 92–97.

Maruyama Masao. 1961. *Nihon no shisō.* Tokyo: Iwanami Shoten.

———. 1991. Genkei, kosō, shitsuyōteion. In *Nihonbunka no kakureta kata,* edited by K. Takeda, 91–159. Tokyo: Iwanami Shoten.

Mass swoop nets 200,000 pirated VCDs. 1998. *South China Morning Post,* 11 September.

Massey, Doreen. 1991. A global sense of place. *Marxism Today,* June.

Mattelart, Armand, Xavier Delcourt, and Michelle Mattelart. 1984. *International image markets: In search of an alternative perspective,* translated by D. Buxton. London: Comedia.

Maxwell, Richard. 1997. International communication: The control of difference and the global market. In *International communication and globalization: A critical introduction,* edited by A. Mohammadi, 191–209. London: Sage.

McCormack, Gavan. 1996. *The emptiness of Japanese affluence.* Armonk, N.Y.: M. E. Sharpe.

———. 1998. From number one to number nothing: Japan's fin de siècle blues. *Japanese Studies* 18 (1): 31–44.

McKinley, Graham E. 1997. *Beverly Hills, 90210: Television, gender, and identity.* Philadelphia: University of Pennsylvania Press.

McNeely, Connie, and Yasemin N. Soysal. 1989. International flows of television programming: A revisionist research orientation. *Public Culture* 2 (1): 136–44.

Mediamatic. 1991. Special issue: *Otaku* radical boredom, 5 (4).

Meyrowitz, Joshua. 1985. *No sense of place: The impact of electronic media on social behavior.* Oxford: Oxford University Press.

Miller, Daniel. 1992. The young and restless in Trinidad: A case of the local and global in mass consumption. In *Consuming technologies: Media and information in domestic spaces,* edited by R. Silverstone and E. Hirsch, 163–82. London: Routledge.

———, ed. 1995. *Worlds apart: Modernity through the prism of the local.* London: Routledge

Minami Hiroshi. 1994. *Nihonjinron: Meiji kara kon'nichi made.* Tokyo: Iwanami Shoten.

Mitsui, Toru, and Shuhei Hosokawa, eds. 1998. *Karaoke around the world: Global technology, local singing.* London: Routledge.

Miyoshi, Masao. 1991. *Off center: Power and culture relations between Japan and the United States.* Cambridge, Mass.: Harvard University Press.

Mizukoshi Shin. 1998. Ajia no media, media no Ajia. In *Jōhō shakai no bunka 3: Dezain, tekunorojī, shijō,* edited by A. Shimada, 199–226. Tokyo: Tokyo Daigaku Shuppan.

———. 1999. *Digitaru media shakai.* Tokyo: Iwanami Shoten.

Mizukoshi Shin, and Baeg Seong Soo. 1993. Ajia media bunkaron kakusho: Gyakushōsha sareru Nihon. *Aura* 100: 37–43.

Mo Bang-Fu. 1999. Nihon kadenmēkā shinwa no hōkai. *Chūō Kōron,* April, 154–61.

Mononokehime, datsu Miyazaki anime de 100 okuen. 1998. *Nikkei Entertainment,* January, 42–43.

Mooij, Marieke de. 1998. *Global marketing and advertising: Understanding cultural paradoxes.* London: Sage.

Mōri Yoshitaka. 1996. Japanimēshon to Japanaizēshon. *Yuriika,* August, 150–57.

Morieda Takashi. 1988. *Chūkanzu de mita Ajia.* Tokyo: Tokuma Shoten.

Morita Akio. 1987. *Made in Japan.* Tokyo: Asahi Shinbunsha.

Morita Akio, and Ishihara Shintarō. 1989. *"No" to ieru nihon.* Tokyo: Kōbunsha.

Morley, David. 1980. *The nationwide audience: Structure and decoding.* British Film Institute Television Monograph no. 11. London: British Film Institute.

———. 1992. *Television, audiences, and cultural studies.* London: Routledge.

———. 1996. EurAm, modernity, reason, and alterity: or, Postmodernism, the highest stage of cultural imperialism? In *Stuart Hall: Critical dialogues in cultural studies,* edited by D. Morley and K.-H. Chen, 326–60. London: Routledge.

Morley, David, and Kevin Robins. 1995. *Spaces of identities: Global media, electronic landscapes, and cultural boundaries.* London: Routledge.

Morris-Suzuki, Tessa. 1993. Rewriting history: Civilization theory in contemporary Japan. *positions* 1 (2): 526–49.

———. 1995. The invention and reinvention of "Japanese culture." *The Journal of Asian Studies* 54 (3): 759–80.

———. 1998a. Invisible countries: Japan and the Asian dream. *Asian Studies Review* 22 (1): 5–22.

———. 1998b. *Re-inventing Japan: Time, space, nation.* New York: M. E. Sharpe.

Mouer, Ross, and Yoshio Sugimoto. 1986. *Images of Japanese society: A study in the structure of social reality.* London: Routledge and Kegan Paul.

Murai Yoshinori. 1987. *Ebi to Nihonjin.* Tokyo: Iwanami Shinsho.

———. 1990. Nihon no nakano Ajia, Ajia no nakano Nihon. *Mado,* summer, 87–100.

———. 1993. Oshin, Doraemon wa kakehashi to nareruka. *Views,* 10 March, 26–27.

Murai Yoshinori, Kido Kazuo, and Koshida Takashi. 1988. *Ajia to Watashitachi.* Tokyo: Sanichi Shobō.

Murakami Ryū. 2000. *Kibou no kuni no eguzodasu.* Tokyo: Bungei Shunjū.

Murata Junko. 1996. Ajian aidoru jijō. *Aura* 115: 25–28.

———. 1997. Shin meisei densetsu no. 20. *Gekkan Kadokawa,* August, 298–99.

Mure Yōko. 1994. *Ajia fumufumu ryokō.* Tokyo: Shinchōsha.

Nakazawa Shin'ichi. 1990. Itoshi no maddo chainaman. *Yuriika* 22 (5): 214–18.

Nakazora Mana. 1994. Hōsō bangumi sofuto no kokusai ryūtsū jōkyō. *Jōhō Tsūshin Gakkaishi* 12 (8): 48–53.

Negus, Keith. 1997. The production of culture. In *Production of culture / Cultures of production,* edited by P. du Gay, 67–104. London: Sage.

Newitz, Annalee. 1995. Magical girls and atomic bomb sperm: Japanese animation in America. *Film Quarterly* 49 (1): 2–15.

NHK International, ed. 1991. *Sekai wa Oshin o dō mitaka.* Tokyo: NHK International.

Nicchū gassaku dorama "Tokyo no Shanhaijin." 1996. *Asahi Shinbun,* 24 February, evening edition.

Nicchū kyōdō yoron chōsa. 1997. *Asahi Shinbun,* 22 September.

"Nichishiki" ninki Honkon de kanetsu. 1998. *Asahi Shinbun,* 12 September.

Nihon anime ni sekai ga netsushisen. 1996. *Aera,* 29 July, 6–9.

Nihon anime ni tōshi. 1996. *Nihon Keizai Shinbun,* 3 September.

Nihon anime no sekai seiha. 1996. *Bart,* 22 January, 20–29.

Nihon būmu no urajijō. 1998. *Honkon Posuto,* 18 September.

Nihon burando Chūgoku no shōhisha ni shintō. 1995. *Nihon Keizai Shinbun,* 17 February, evening edition.

Nihon girai Kankoku de 69%. 1995. *Asahi Shinbun,* 29 July.

Nihon hatsu no bangumi Ajia kakeru? 1994. *Nihon Keizai Shinbun,* 26 November, evening edition.

Nihon kizzu karuchd ga sekai o seifuku suru! 1997. *Bart,* 23 June, 34–43.

Nihon no bangumi, Ajia kakuchi de hipparidako. 1994. *Yomiuri Shinbun,* 27 October, evening edition.

Nihon no dorama eiga Higashi Ajia e. 1998. *Aera,* 19 October, 56–57.

Nihon no manga ga sekai o seifuku!? 1996. *Elle Japon* (April): 70–73.

Nihon no terebi dorama Tōnan Ajia de torendī. 1998. *Asahi Shinbun,* 14 April.

Nihon otaku to yobitai hitobito. 1996. *Honkon Tsūshin,* July, 5–19.

Nihonbunka kosupure Amerika yushutsu. 1996. *Shūkan Shinchō,* 24 July, 171–75.

Nihonhatsu no otaku bunka ga sekken: Beikoku saishin anime jijō. 1996. *Nikkei Trendy,* October, 86–91.

Nihonjin wa yunīku ka. Vol. 4, Manga. 1990. *Aera,* 12 June, 29–67.

Nihonka suru Ajia 12 kakoku karano hōkoku. 1993. *Views,* 10 March, 18–27.

Nikkanchūbei 4 kakoku yoron chōsa, 2000. *Asahi Shinbun,* 5 December.

Nikkanchūbei 4 kakoku yoron chōsa, 2001. *Asahi Shinbun,* 25 December.

Nippon seifuku bijo. 1995. *DENiM,* September, 82–89.

Nishi Tadashi. 1997. *Hōsō bigguban.* Tokyo: Nikkan Kōgyō Shinbunsha.

Nishino Teruhiko. 1996. Honrai no imi no "aidoru" ga dondon tōnoite iku. *Aura* 115: 19–24.

Noda Masaaki. 1990. Mō hitotsu no Nihonbunka ga sekai o kaeru. *Voice,* July, 56–57.

No kidding! S'pore youths are into J-pop. 1999. *New Straits Times,* 19 December.

Nomura Susumu. 1996. *Ajia teijū: 11kakoku 18nin no Nihonjin.* Tokyo: Mekon.

Nye, Joseph S. Jr. 1990. *Bound to lead: The changing nature of American power.* New York: Basic Books.

Odagiri Makoto. 1996. Nihonsei sofuto shinshutsu no jittai. *Hōsō Hihyō* 322: 14–19.

Ōe Kenzaburō. 1995. *Aimaina nihon no watashi.* Tokyo: Iwanami Shshinsho.

Ogawa Hiroshi. 1988. *Ongaku suru Shakai.* Tokyo: Chikuma Shobō.

Oguma Eiji. 1995. *Tan'itsu minzoku shinwa no kigen.* Tokyo: Shinyōsha.

Ogura Kazuo. 1993. A call for a new concept of Asia. *Japan Echo 20* (3): 37–44.

———. 1999. Atarashii Ajia no sōzō. *Voice,* March, 123–35.

Ōhata Kōichi. 1996. Animerika e no shōtai. *Yuriika,* August, 88–94.

Ohmae Kenichi. 1990. *The borderless world.* London: Collins.

Okada Toshio. 1995. Anime bunka wa chō kakkoii. *Aera,* 2 October, 43–44.

———. 1996. *Otakugaku nyūmon.* Tokyo: Ōta Shuppan.

———. 1997. *Tūdai otakugaku kōza.* Tokyo: Kōdansha.

Okakura Kazuko. 1904. *The ideal of the East with special reference to the art of Japan.* 2d ed. New York: E. P. Dutton.

Okamura Reimei. 1996. Media ō Mādokku no dejitaru na kuwadate. *Ushio,* September, 126–35.

Oliver, Nick, and Barry Wilkinson. 1992. *The Japanization of British industry: New developments in the 1990s.* Oxford: Blackwell.

Ong, Aihwa. 1996. Anthropology, China, and modernities: The geopolitics of cultural knowledge. In *The future of anthropological knowledge,* edited by H. L. Moore, 60–92. London: Routledge.

Ongaku sangyō wa Ajia mejā o mezasu. 1992. *Nikkei Entertainment,* 9 September, 4–19.

"Ongaku to owarai" de Chūgoku o nerae. 1994. *Asahi Shinbun,* 30 July.

Ono Kōsei. 1992. Sekai de shōhi sareru Nihon no terebi anime. *Chōsa Jōhō* 404: 16–20.

———. 1998. Nihon manga no shintō ga umidasu sekai. In *Nihon manga ga sekai de sugoi!,* edited by I. Ogawa, 76–91. Tokyo: Tachibana Shuppan.

Ōno, Shin'ichi. 1996. Asia in print. *Pacific Friend* 23 (12): 36–37.

O'Regan, Tom. 1991. From piracy to sovereignty: International video cassette recorders trends. *Continuum* 4 (2): 112–35.

———. 1992. Too popular by far: On Hollywood's international popularity. *Continuum* 5 (2): 302–51.

Osaki ni hōsō senshinkoku. 1997. *Asahi Shinbun,* 14 November.

Oshii Mamoru, Itō Kazunori, and Ueno Toshiya. 1996. Eiga to wa jitsu wa animēshon datta. *Yuriika,* August, 50–81.

Otaku no sekai kara mejā e. 1997. *Newsweek Japan,* 30 July, 42–49.

Ōtomo Katsuhiro. 1996. Anime. *Aera,* 8 April, 73.

Ōtsuka Eiji. 1994. Komikku sekai seiha. *Sapio,* 8 July, 10–11.

Oxford Dictionary of New Words. 1991. Compiled by S. Tulloch. Oxford: Oxford University Press.

Papastergiadis, Nikos. 1995. Rentless hybrids. *Third Text* 32 (autumn): 9–18.

Parry, Anita. 1987. Problems in current theories of colonial discourse. *Oxford Literary Review* 9 (1–2): 27–58.

———. 1994. Signs of our times: A discussion of Homi Bhabha's *The Location of Culture. Third Text* 28/29 (autumn/winter): 5–24.

Peattie, Mark. 1984. Japanese attitudes toward colonialism. In *The Japanese colonial empire,* edited by R. Myers and M. Peattie, 80–127. Princeton, N.J.: Princeton University Press.

Pia info-pack: Kowloon's Gate. 1997. *Asahi Shinbun,* 25 February, evening edition.

Pieterse, Jan Nederveen. 1995. Globalization as hybridization. In *Global modernities,* edited by M. Featherstone et al., 45–68. London: Sage.

Pieterse, Jan Nederveen, and Bhikhu Parekh. 1995. Shifting imaginaries: Decolonization, internal decolonization, postcoloniality. In *The decolonization of the imagination: Culture, knowledge, and power,* edited by J. N. Pieterse and B. Parekh, 1–19. London: Zed Books.

Pollack, David. 1986. *The fracture of meaning.* Princeton, N.J.: Princeton University Press.

Pop passions. 2001. *The Nikkei Weekly,* 21 May.

Poppu Eijia. 1990. Special issue of *WAVE* 27.

Poppu na Ajia no fan kurabu in Japan. 1998. *Pop Asia,* no. 20, 72–74.

Pratt, Mary Louise. 1992. *Imperial eyes: Travel writing and transculturation.* London: Routledge.

Pro-Japan vs. anti-Japan in Taiwan. 1997. *The Journalist,* 1–7 June.

Radway, Janice. 1984. *Reading the romance: Women, patriarchy, and popular literature.* Chapel Hill: University of North Carolina Press.

Redwood Research Service. 1996. *An index survey of cable TV in the second half of 1996.* Taipei: Redwood Research Service.

Ritzer, George. 1993. *The McDonaldization of society.* London: Sage.

Robertson, Jennifer. 1998a. It takes a village: Internationalization and nostalgia in postwar Japan. In *Mirror of modernity: Invented traditions of modern Japan,* edited by S. Vlastos, 110–29. Berkeley: University of California Press.

———. 1998b. *Takarazuka: Sexual politics and popular culture in modern Japan.* Berkeley: University of California Press.

Robertson, Roland. 1990. After nostalgia? Willful nostalgia and the phases of globalization. In *Theories of modernity and postmodernity,* edited by B. S. Turner, 45–60. London: Sage.

———. 1991. Japan and the USA: The interpenetration of national identities and the debate about Orientalism. In *Dominant ideologies,* edited by N. Abercrombie et al., 182–98. London: Unwin Hyman.

———. 1992. *Globalization: Social theory and global culture.* London: Sage.

———. 1995. Globalization: Time-space and homogeneity-heterogeneity. In *Global Modernities,* edited by M. Featherstone et al., 25–44. London: Sage.

Robins, Kevin. 1997. What in the world's going on? In *Production of culture/Cultures of production,* edited by P. du Gay, 11–47. London: Sage.

Robinson, Richard, and David S. G. Goodman, eds. 1996. *The new rich in Asia: Mobile phones, McDonalds, and middle-class revolution.* London: Routledge.

Rosaldo, Renato. 1989. Imperialist nostalgia. *Representation* 26: 107–22.

Rouse, Roger. 1995. Thinking through transnationalism: Notes on the cultural politics of class relations in the contemporary United States. *Public Culture* 7 (winter): 353–402.

Ryokō, shoku dake de naku eiga, ongaku made—Ima wakai josei no me ga Ajia ni mukidashita riyū. 1993. *Dime,* 16 September, 19.

Ryū Momosuke. 1996. Hōsōkai kiro ni tatsu. *Hōsō Hihyō,* September, 28–33.

Saeki Keishi. 1998. Ajia teki kachi wa sonzai suru ka? In *Ajiateki kachi to wa nanika,* edited by T. Aoki and K. Saeki, 21–41. Tokyo: TBS Buritanika.

Said, Edward. 1978. *Orientalism.* New York: Vintage.

———. 1994. *Culture and imperialism.* New York: Vintage.

Saitō Akihito. 1990a. Ajia no poppu. *Poppu Eijia. WAVE,* vol. 27: 22–28.

———. 1990b. Dick Lee. *Poppu Eijia. WAVE,* vol. 27: 9.

Saitō Eisuke. 1997. Komuro Tetsuya no ongaku sekai senryaku wa seikō suru ka? *Sekai,* June, 305–11.

Saitō Minako. 1997. Kaisha o yameta wakamonotachi ga nishi o mezashite iku riyū. *Hatoyo!,* March, 114–15.

Saitō Seiichirō. 1992. The pitfalls of the new Asianism. *Japan Echo* 19: 14–19 (Special Issue on Japan and Asia).

Sakai, Naoki. 1989. Modernity and its critique. *South Atlantic Quarterly* 87 (3): 475–504.

———. 1996. *Shizan sareru Nihongo, Nihonjin.* Tokyo: Shinyōsha.

Sakimonogai! Honkon, Taiwan biteki dan'yū zukan. 1996. *Crea,* January, 66–71.

Sakurai Tetsuo. 2000. Sokudo no nakano bunka. *Daikōkai* 35: 52–59.

Satellite TV is way off beam. 1994. *Asian Business Review,* May, 24–25.

Satellite TV sees gold in local content. 1996. *Asian Business Review,* October, 26–36.

Satō Hikaru. 1998. Bunmei no botsuraku no nakano Ajiateki kachi. In *Ajiateki kachi to wa nanika,* edited by T. Aoki and K. Saeki, 223–38. Tokyo: TBS Buritanika.

Sawaki Kōtarō. 1986a. *Shinya tokkyū,* vol. 1. Tokyo: Shinchōsha.

———. 1986b. *Shinya tokkyū,* vol. 2. Tokyo: Shinchōsha.

———. 1992. *Shinya tokkyū,* vol. 3. Tokyo: Shinchōsha.

Schiller, Herbert. 1969. *Mass communication and American empire.* New York: Beacon Press.

———. 1976. *Communication and cultural domination.* New York: M. E. Sharpe.

———. 1991. Not yet the post-imperialist era. *Critical Studies in Mass Communication* 8: 13–28.

Schodt, Fredelik L. 1983. *Manga! Manga!: The world of Japanese comics.* Tokyo: Kōdansha International.

———. 1996. *Dreamland Japan: Writings on modern manga.* Berkeley, Calif.: Stone Bridge Press.

Scott, Alan. 1997. Globalization: Social process or political rhetoric? Introduction to *The limits of globalization: Cases and arguments,* edited by A. Scott, 1–22. London: Routledge.

Sekai ga maneshita Nipponryū, Nippon wa erai! 1992. *DENiM,* September, 143–49.

Sekai tenkai senryaku Komuro Tetsuya shi ni kiku. 1997. *Nihon Keizai Shinbun,* 10 January.

Sekai yusaburu media no ōmono. 1996. *Nihon Keizai Shinbun,* 25 June.

Sekai-ichi no yūsen rasshu. 1995. *Naruhodo the Taiwan,* October, 66–69.

Sekikawa Natsuo. 1984. *Souru no renshū mondai.* Tokyo: Jōhō Sentā Shuppankyoku.

Sengo 50 nen Ajia 7 toshi yoron chōsa. 1995. *Asahi Shinbun,* 13 August.

Shima Keiji. 1994. Mohaya Ajia ha teokureda. *Hōsō Hihyō,* July, 28–33.

Shimizu, Shinichi. 1993. The implication of transborder television for national cultures and broadcasting: A Japanese perspective. *Media Asia* 20 (4): 187–93.

Shinohara Toshiyuki. 1994. Sekkyokuha NHK to shkōkyokuteki minpō. *Hōsō Hihyō* 303: 24–29.

Shinozaki Hiroshi. 1988. *Kasetto shoppu ni ikeba Ajia ga miete kuru*. Tokyo: Asahi Shinbunsha.

——. 1990a. Ajia o oou "Subaru," "Kitaguni no haru" bunkaken. *Poppu Eijia. WAVE,* no. 27: 97–112.

——. 1990b. *Boku wa Maddo Chainaman*. Tokyo: Iwanami Shoten.

Shirahata Yōzaburō. 1995. *Karaoke, Anime ga Sekai o Meguru*. Tokyo: PHP Kenkyūjo.

Shiraishi Kenji. 1996. Higashi Ajia no ongaku o shiru tame no bukkugaido. *Latina,* June, 26.

Shiraishi, Saya. 1997. Japan's soft power: *Doraemon* goes overseas. In *Network power: Japan and Asia,* edited by P. J. Katzenstein and T. Shiraishi, 234–70. Ithaca, N.Y.: Cornell University Press.

Shoesmith, Brian. 1994. Asia in their shadow: Satellites and Asia. *Southeast Asian Journal of Social Sciences* 22: 125–41.

Shohat, Ella, and Robert Stam. 1994. *Unthinking Eurocentrism: Multiculturalism and the media*. London: Routledge.

Siji, Alessandro. 1988. *East of "Dallas": The European challenge to American television*. London: British Film Institute.

Sinclair, John. 1992. The de-centering of cultural imperialism: Televisa-tion and Globo-ization in the Latin world. In *Continental shift: Globalization and culture,* edited by E. Jacka. Double Bay, New South Wales: Local Consumption Publications, 99–116.

——. 1997. The business of international broadcasting: Cultural bridges and barriers. *Asian Journal of Communication* 7 (1): 137–55.

Sinclair, John, Elizabeth Jacka, and Stuart Cunningham. 1996a. Peripheral vision. In *New patterns in global television: Peripheral vision,* edited by John Sinclair, Elizabeth Jacka, and Stuart Cunningham, 1–32. Oxford: Oxford University Press.

——, eds. 1996b. *New patterns in global television: Peripheral vision*. Oxford: Oxford University Press.

Singhal, Arvind, and Kant Udornpim. 1997. Cultural shareability, archetypes, and television soups: "Oshindorome" in Thailand. *Gazette* 59 (3): 171–88.

Sklair, Leslie. 1995. *Sociology of the global system*. 2d ed. London: Prentice Hall/Harvester Wheatsheaf.

Smart, Barry. 1993. Europe/America: Baudrillard's fatal comparison. In *Forget Baudrillard?,* edited by C. Rojek and B. S. Turner, 47–69. London: Routledge.

Smith, D. Anthony. 1990. Towards a global culture? In *Global culture: National-*

ism, globalization, and modernity, edited by M. Featherstone, 171–92. London: Sage.

Smith, Michael Peter. 2001. *Transnational urbanism: Locating globalization.* Malden, Mass.: Blackwell.

Smith, Michael Peter, and Luis Eduardo Guarnizo, eds. 1998. *Transnationalism from below.* New Brunswick, N.J.: Transaction Publishers.

Sofuto kyūbo! Ajia hōsōkyoku. 1995. *Nihon Keizai Shinbun,* 5 November.

Sonoda Shigeto. 1997. Wadaino hon o yomu: *Asian Japanese* 1 & 2. *Sekai,* October, 103.

Souru ga hamaru Tokyo fasshon. 2000. *Aera,* 5 June, 58–60.

Spark, Alasdair. 1996. Wrestling with America: Media, national images, and the global village. *Journal of Popular Culture* 29 (4): 83–97.

Sreberny-Mohammadi, Annabelle. 1991. The global and the local in international communications. In *Mass media and society,* edited by J. Curran and M. Gurevitch, 118–38. London: Edward Arnold.

STAR drops MTV to help it capture China. 1994. *The Australian,* 11 May.

Stewart, Susan. [1984] 1993. *On Longing: Narratives of the miniature, the gigantic, the souvenir, the collection.* Reprint, Durham, N.C.: Duke University Press.

Straubhaar, Joseph. 1991. Beyond media imperialism: Asymmetrical interdependence and cultural proximity. *Critical Studies in Mass Communication* 8 (1): 39–59.

Stronach, Bruce. 1989. Japanese television. In *Handbook of Japanese popular culture,* edited by R. Powers and H. Kato, 127–65. Westport, Conn.: Greenwood Press.

Swallowtail Butterfly. 1997. *Kinema Junpō,* no. 1202: 44–53.

Tachanneru no nami 6: Nihon bangumi būmu. 1996. *Asahi Shinbun,* 11 January, evening edition.

Tadashii Ajia no hamarikata. 1997. *Nikkei Entertainment,* December, 50–57.

Taiwan ga Nippon ni koi o shita. 1996. *Views,* February, 36–47.

Takahashi Kazuo. 1991. Hitoriaruki suru sekai no Oshin. In *Sekai wa Oshin o dō mitaka,* edited by NHK International, 25–32. Tokyo: NHK International.

——. 1994. Sekai no Oshin genshō. *Kokusai Kōryū* 64: 62–69.

Takenaka Heizō. 1995. Can Japan glue together Asia and the Pacific? *Japan Echo* 22 (4): 18–22.

Takeuchi Yoshimi. [1961] 1993. *Nihon to Ajia.* Reprint, Tokyo: Chikuma Shobō.

Tanaka, Stefan. 1993. *Japan's Orient: Rendering pasts into history.* Berkeley: University of California Press.

Taussig, Michael. 1993. *Mimesis and alterity: A particular history of the senses.* London: Routledge.

Thomas, Nicholas. 1994. *Colonialism's culture: Anthropology, travel, and government*. Princeton, N.J.: Princeton University Press.

Thome, Katarina, and Ian A. McAuley. 1992. *Crusaders of the rising sun: A study of Japanese management in Asia*. Singapore: Longman.

Thompson, John B. 1995. *The media and modernity: A social theory of the media*. London: Polity Press.

Thought of in Japan. 1994. *Far Eastern Economic Review*, 16 June.

Tobin, Joseph J. 1992a. Domesticating the West. Introduction to *Re-made in Japan: Everyday life and consumer taste in a changing society*, edited by J. Tobin, 1–41. New Haven, Conn.: Yale University Press.

———, ed. 1992b. *Re-made in Japan: Everyday life and consumer taste in a changing society*. New Haven, Conn.: Yale University Press.

Todorov, Tzvetan. 1984. *The conquest of America: The question of the other*. New York: Harper and Row.

Tokyo FM Shuppan, ed. 1995. *Ajian Poppusu Jiten*. Tokyo: Tokyo FM Shuppan.

Tomlinson, John. 1991. *Cultural imperialism: A critical introduction*. London: Pinter Publishers.

———. 1997. Cultural globalization and cultural imperialism. In *International communication and globalization: A critical introduction*, edited by A. Mohammadi, 170–90. London: Sage.

Toransu Eijian entāteinmento. 1993. *Across*, April, 62–69.

Torgovnick, Marianna. 1990. *Going primitive: Savage intellects, modern lives*. Chicago: University of Chicago Press.

Tracy, Michael. 1985. The poisoned chalice? International television and the idea of dominance. *Daedalus* 114 (4): 17–56.

Trinh T. Minh-ha. 1996. The undone interval: Trinh T. Minh-ha in conversation with Annamaria Morelli. In *The post-colonial question: Common skies, divided horizons*, edited by I. Chambers and L. Curti, 3–16. London: Routledge.

Tsuda Kōji. 1996. Kokkyō o koeru Nihon eizō bijinesu no genjō. *Tsukuru*, February, 52–59.

Tsunagime Honkon. 1997. *Asahi Shinbun*, 6 May, evening edition.

Tsunoyama Sakae. 1995. *Ajian Runessansu*. Tokyo: PHP Kenkyūsho.

Tsunoyama Sakae, and Kawakatsu Heita. 1995. Tōzai bunmei shisutemu to bussan fukugō. In *Fukoku Utokuron*, edited by H. Kawakatsu, 185–250. Tokyo: Kinokuniya Shoten.

Tsurumi Kazuko. 1972. *Kōkishin to Nihonjin*. Tokyo: Kōdansha.

Tsurumi Yoshiyuki. 1980. *Ajiajin to Nihonjin*. Toyko: Shōbunsha.

———. 1982. *Banana to Nihonjin*. Tokyo: Iwanami Sensho.

Tunstall, Jeremy. 1977. *The media are American: Anglo-American media in the world*. London: Constable.

———. 1995. Are the media still American? *Media Studies Journal* (fall): 7–16.

Turner, Bryan S. 1987. A note on nostalgia. *Theory, Culture, and Society* 4(1): 141–56.

Turner, Graeme. 1994. *Making it national: Nationalism and Australian popular culture*. Sydney: Allen and Unwin.

TV kaigai hōsō, mienu tenbō. 1994. *Asahi Shinbun,* 7 September, evening edition.

TV's new battles. 1994. *Asiaweek,* 19 October, 34–55.

Uchimoto Jun'ichi. 1995. Miwaku no Eijan gāru poppu. *Bart,* 9 October, 120.

Ueda Makoto. 1994. Datsu-kindai, datsuō-datsua, datsu-Nihon 1: Ajia? Ajia towa nanika. *Gendai Shiō* 22 (1): 34–54.

———. 1996. Datsu Ajiasattoken. *Kigōgaku Kenkyū* 16: 57–68.

———. 1997. Ajia to iu sabetsu. In *Kōza sabetsu no shakaigaku 3, Gendai sekai no Sabetsu Kōzō,* edited by A. Kurihara, 34–47. Tokyo: Kōbundō.

Ueno Toshiya. 1996a. Ragutaimu: Diasupora to "roji." *Gendai Shisō* 24 (3): 238–59.

———. 1996b. Japanoido ōtoman. *Yuriika,* August, 178–97.

Ueyama Shunpei. 1990. Juyō to sōzō no kiseki. In *Nihon bunmeishi no kōsō,* vol. 1, edited by U. Shunpei. Tokyo: Kadokawa Shoten.

Umesao Tadao. 1957. Bunmei no seitai shikan. *Chūō Kōron,* February.

Umesao Tadao, and Kawakatsu Heita. 1998. Nihon yo, tate ni tobe! *Bungei Shunjū,* August, 262–76.

Urry, John. 1990. *The tourist gaze: Leisure and travel in contemporary societies.* London: Sage.

Utatte odoreru aidoru shūdan Pafōmansu Dōru wa Ajia o sekken dekiruka? 1994. *Dime,* 20 October, 142–43.

Vogel, Ezra. 1979. *Japan as number one.* Cambridge, Mass.: Harvard University Press.

Wakamono wa hōrō mezasu. 1996. *Aera,* 18 November, 34–36.

Wallerstein, Immanuel. 1991. *Geopolitics and geoculture.* Cambridge: Cambridge University Press.

Wang, Georgette. 1996. Beyond media globalization: A look at cultural integrity from a policy perspective. Paper presented at the seminar on Telecommunications Policies in Western Europe, 29 August–1 September, Bruges, Belgium.

Warai no Yoshimoto, mezasu wa Chūgoku. 1995. *Asahi Shinbun,* 25 September, evening edition.

Wark, Mackenzie. 1991. From Fordism to Sonyism: Perverse reading of the new world order. *New Formations* 15: 43–54.

———. 1994. The video game as an emergent media form. *Media Information Australia* 71: 21–30.

Wasei poppusu wa Ajia o mezasu. 1994. *Forbes,* December, 92–95.

Washida Kiyokazu. 1996. Dōjisei to iu kankaku: Shanhai toshi no mōdo. *Kokusai Kōryō* 70: 40–45.

Watch out! Your children are becoming "Japanese." 1997. *The Journalist,* 13–19 April, 61–72.

Waters, Malcolm. 1995. *Globalization.* London: Routledge.

Watson, James L., ed. 1997. *Golden Arches East: McDonalds in East Asia.* Stanford, Calif.: Stanford University Press.

Wee, C. J. W.-L. 1996. Staging the new Asia: Singapore's Dick Lee, pop music, and a counter-modernity. *Public Culture* 8 (3): 489–510.

———. 1997. Buying Japan: Singapore, Japan, and an "East Asian" modernity. *Journal of Pacific Asia* 4: 21–46.

Weiner, Michael. 1994. *Race and migration in imperial Japan.* London: Routledge.

Welsch, Wolfgang. 1999. Transculturality: The puzzling form of cultures today. In *Spaces of culture: City, nation, world,* edited by M. Featherstone and S. Lash, 194–213. London: Sage.

Westney, Eleanor D. 1987. *Imitation and innovation: The transfer of western organizational patterns to Meiji Japan.* Cambridge, Mass.: Harvard University Press.

Wilk, Richard. 1995. Learning to be local in Belize: Global systems of common difference. In *Worlds apart: Modernity through the prism of the local,* edited by D. Miller, 110–33. London: Routledge.

Wilkinson, Endymion. 1991. *Japan versus the West: Image and reality.* Rev. ed., London: Penguin.

Williams, Raymond. 1990. *Television: Technology and cultural form.* London: Routledge.

Wolferen, Karel van. 1989. *The enigma of Japanese power.* New York: Knopf.

Yamaguchi Fuminori. 1979. *Honkon tabi no zatsugaku nōto.* Tokyo: Daiamondosha.

Yamamuro Shin'ichi. 1998. "Ta ni shite itsu" no chitsujo genri to Nihon no sentaku. In *Ajiateki kachi to wa nanika,* edited by T. Aoki and K. Saeki, 43–64. Tokyo: TBS Buritanika.

Yamashita Shinji. 1996. "Minami" e: Bari kankō no naka no Nihonjin. In *Iwanami Kōza Bunkajinruigaku,* vol. 7, *Idō no minzokushi,* edited by T. Aoki et al., 31–60. Tokyo: Iwanami Shoten.

Yamazaki Masakazu. 1995. Datsua-nyūyō no susume. *Ronza,* July, 10–20.

———. 1996. Asia, a civilization in the making. *Foreign Affairs* 75 (4): 106–18.

Yasui Nippon e Honkon no wakamono sattō. 1998. *Aera,* 7 September, 36–38.

Yoda, Tomiko. 2001. A roadmap to millennial Japan. *South Atlantic Quarterly* 99(4): 629–68.

Yoshihara Mai. 1994. *Singapōru Rojiura Hyakka.* Tokyo: Toraberu Jānaru.

Yoshimi Shunya. 1997. Amerikanaizēshon to bunka no seijigaku. In *Gen-*

daishakai no shakaigaku, edited by S. Inoue et al., 157–231. Tokyo: Iwanami Shoten.

———. 1999. "Made in Japan": The cultural politics of "home electrification" in postwar Japan. *Media, Culture, and Society* 21 (2): 149–71.

Yoshimoto, Mitsuhiro. 1989. The postmodern and mass images in Japan. *Public Culture* 1 (2): 8–25.

———. 1994. Images of empire: Tokyo Disneyland and Japanese cultural imperialism. In *Disney discourse: Producing the magic kingdom,* edited by E. Smoodin, 181–99. New York: Routledge.

Yoshino, Kosaku. 1992. *Cultural nationalism in contemporary Japan.* London: Routledge.

Yoshioka Shinobu. 1992. Te no todoki sōna Nihon. *Voice,* September, 91–95.

———. [1989] 1993. *Nihonjin gokko.* Reprint, Tokyo: Bungei Shunjū.

Young, Robert. 1990. *White mythologies: Writing history and the West.* London: Routledge.

———. 1994. *Colonial desire: Hybridity in theory, culture, and race.* London: Routledge.

Yuasa Takeo. 1994. 21 seiki ni okeru shobunmei no kankei. *Hikaku Bunmei,* October, 51–62.

Zakaria, Fareed. 1994. Culture is destiny: A conversation with Lee Kuan Yew. *Foreign Affairs* 73 (2): 109–26.

Index

Hannerz, Ulf, 6–7, 15–17, 40, 43, 45, 51–52, 83, 118, 202
Hara, Tomoko, 190, 191
Hara Yumiko, 94–95, 98, 139–41, 212 n.4
Hardware. *See* Consumer products
Harootunian, Harry D., 9, 10
Harvey, David, 36
Harvey, Paul A. S., 77
Hashizume Daizaburō, 170
Hatakeyama Kenji, 30, 94
Hattori Hiroshi, 139, 141
Hawkins, Richard, 119
HBO, 141
Hein, Laura, 14
Hendry, Joy, 150
Herman, Edward, 37
Higuchi Takafumi, 192
Hirano Ken'ichirō, 64
Hirst, Paul, 202
Hitachi, 103
Hobsbawm, Eric J., 51
Hollywood studios: Japanese companies, 23–24, 29–30, 37–38; VCRs and marketing potential, 25. *See also* Columbia; MCA
Honda, 103
Honda Shirō, 77–78, 82, 221 nn.14–15
Hong Kong, 19–21, 123–24; films, 21, 112; Japanese music, 115–18, 173; Japanese TV dramas, 123, 135; localization experiences, 90–91; music exports to Japan, 181–89, 228 n.9; pop idols, 112–13, 181–82, 185–86; return to China, 205–6; TV programming, 136–37. *See also* Fans, in Japan
Honkon Tsūshin (magazine), 124
Honkon Yamucha Kurabu, 183, 230 n.27
HoriPro Entertainment Group, 102, 104, 107–8

Hoskins, Colin, 26–27, 95
Hosokawa, Shuhei, 216 n.6, 227 n.7
Howes, David, 20, 35, 60, 215–16 n.2
Hsieh Yamai, 209
Huntington, Samuel P., 11–12, 131–32, 200, 214–15 nn.16–17
Hybridism, strategic, 53–56, 219 nn.5, 7; assimilation of cultures, 59–63; civilization theories, 65–66; extroversion in the late twentieth century, 63–66; introversion in postwar era, 56–59
Hybridity, 51–54, 218 nn.1–2, 219 nn.5–6; "banana" identity, 166; essays by Katō Shūichi, 57–58; racial/ethnic concerns, 55–56, 218 n.4
Hybridization, 43–44, 167–70, 218 n.2

Ibuka Masaru, 24
Ichikawa Takashi, 99, 104, 143, 170–73
The Ideal of the East with Special Reference to the Art of Japan (Okahura), 166
Idols, 207–8; female Asian, 181–89, 229 n.20; from Hong Kong, 186, 190–91; Japanese, 141–43, 225 n.16; local pop stars, 97–107, 113, 224 n.8
Igarashi Akio, 34–35, 73, 104
Imada Takatoshi, 13–14
Imamura Yōichi, 76–77
Imitation. *See* Mimicry
Immigration: to Japan from Asia, 179–81, 231 n.2
Imperialist history of Japan, 5, 8–11, 19, 75, 180, 212 n.7, 220 n.10; history revisionism, 208–9; Japanese popular culture in Taiwan, 121, 124–127, 140. *See also* Asianism in Japan; Nationalism in Japan; Protectionism, cultural; South Korea
Imports to Japan, of media products, 88, 181–89, 229 n.18

Asia, 89–92; limitations of, 107–12; marketing strategies, 92–97; Pokémon, 38; preferences for local programming, 90–91; spatial and cultural proximity, 48–50; of Western cultural imports, 85, 95–97. *See also* Glocalization/global localization

Los Angeles Times, 30

Love Letter (film), 207

Lull, James, 17, 40, 43, 133

Macluhan, Marshall, 36

The Mad Chinaman (CD), 164, 167, 168

Maekawa Ken'ichi, 160

Magic Stone, 115–17

Mahathir, Mohamad, 12, 66

Malaysia, 12, 13, 19

Malsch, Thomas, 23

Manabe Masami, 30

Manga Entertainment, 38

Maribeth, 101, 103–4, 224 n.8

Marketing strategies: format/concept trade, 97–98, 107, 224 nn.4–7; glocalization/global localization, 93–94; Japanese music, 114–18; localization, 33, 92–97, 115–18; media industry, 85–120, 201; tie ups, 104; toward the new middle class, 103–4; VCRs, 25

Marlboro, 103

Marume Kuraudo, 171

Maruyama Masao, 58

Massey, Doreen, 48

Matsushita, 23–24, 29, 37–38. *See also* Panasonic

Mattelart, Armand, 39

Mattelart, Michelle, 39

Maxwell, Richard, 92

MCA, 23–24, 29, 37–48

McAuley, Ian A., 23

McChesney, Robert, 37

McCormack, Gavan, 13, 111

McDonald's, 27–28, 46, 90, 224 n.3

McKinley, Graham E., 148, 226 n.8

McNeely, Connie, 92

The Media Are American (Tunstall), 40

Media exposure. *See* Promotion

Media industries: centralized decision making practices, 109–10; globalization, 3–4, 16, 29–32, 37–38, 212 n.4; marketing strategies in the 1990s, 85–120, 201. *See also* Glocalization/global localization; Music; TV dramas; TV exports

Mediamatic, 23

Meyerowitz, Joshua, 165

Mickey Mouse, 30, 103

Middle class, development of, 36, 78; in Asia, 67–68, 103–4; emulation of Western lifestyles, 106–7

Miki Kiyoshi, 214–17 n.17

Miller, Daniel, 45, 50, 60, 79, 92, 106, 134

Mimicry, 80–84, 125

Minami, Hiroshi, 55, 58

Mirus, Rolf, 26–27, 95

Miyazaki Hayao, 38, 217 n.8

Miyoshi, Masao, 3, 213–14 n.14

Mizukoshi Shin, 6, 7, 112, 173

Mobile privatization, 25–26

Modernity, 204–5, 220 n.9; association with Western culture, 15, 45, 151–54; and Dick Lee, 164–68; indigenized, 15–16, 41–42, 45–50; and Hong Kong popular culture, 182–186, 189–98; and Japanese popular culture, 77–79, 104–6, 117–18, 119–20, 130, 141–47, 150–51, 155; spatial aspects, 49–50

Mononokehime (animation film), 38, 217 n.8

Mooij, Marieke de, 89

Mōri Yoshitaka, 216 n.4

Morieda Takashi, 82, 113, 162, 227 n.2

Morissette, Alanis, 118

Koichi Iwabuchi is Assistant Professor of Media and
Cultural Studies at International Christian University
in Tokyo. For many years he was a reporter and
producer for Nippon Television Network
Corporation (NTV).

Library of Congress Cataloging-in-Publication Data
Iwabuchi, Koichi.
Recentering globalization : popular culture and
Japanese transnationalism / Koichi Iwabuchi.
p. cm.
Includes bibliographical references and index.
ISBN 0–8223–2985–9 (cloth : alk. paper) —
ISBN 0–8223–2891–7 (pbk.: alk. paper)
1. Popular culture—Japan—History—20th century.
2. Japan—Civilization—1945-   3. Popular culture—
Asia—History—20th century. 4. Asia—Civilization—
Japanese influences. I. Title.
DS822.5 .I9 2002
952.04—dc21   2002006329